28 462

799.2
GR   **20 great trophy**
                    hunts

DATE DUE

FEB 23			

20 GREAT
TROPHY HUNTS

20 GREAT TROPHY HUNTS

Personal Accounts of Hunting
North America's Top Big-Game Animals

Edited by JOHN O. CARTIER

David McKay Company, Inc.
NEW YORK

Acknowledgments

The idea for this book has been with me since I "ghosted" my first trophy-hunting story many years ago. The hunter involved knew nothing about writing, but the two of us, working together, came up with a great story for *Outdoor Life* magazine.

It occurred to me then that a book loaded with such stories could very well be one of the most exciting hunting books ever published. Though the book idea was mine, the excitement within these pages obviously originates with the hunters who lived the adventures and told me their stories. To them, I wish to acknowledge my thanks.

Of equal importance, I wish to show my appreciation to the publishers of *Outdoor Life* for their permission to use the material about the hunts. For many years, *Outdoor Life* has spared no expense or effort in finding and publishing the best stories of big-game trophy hunting in North America. The personal accounts in this book, all originally published in *Outdoor Life*, have been selected as the best stories of North American trophy hunts in recent years.

Copyright © 1980 by John O. Cartier

Library of Congress Cataloging in Publication Data
Main entry under title:

20 great trophy hunts.

1. Big game hunting–North America. I. Cartier,
John O.
SK40.T86   799.2'6'097   80-14802
ISBN 0-679-51379-5

1 2 3 4 5 6 7 8 9 10

MANUFACTURED IN THE UNITED STATES OF AMERICA

For my daughter Judy,
who was enthralled while proofreading
the stories in this book.

Contents

Foreword

By Ben East

This is a book that will interest any hunter, whether he or she has a big-game trophy listed in the record books or is content simply to take good heads for the den walls at home. It is also a book for the sportsman or sportswoman who enjoys hunting of any kind, who thrills to its action and excitement, and who revels in the outdoor world.

I know no outdoor writer better qualified to edit such a book than John O. Cartier. To explain and justify that statement, I must backtrack a bit.

Outdoor Life was the first of the outdoor magazines to recognize the need for a staff of roving field editors to cover every part of the country, and to put such a staff together. I joined the group at the beginning of 1946, with the Midwest as my beat.

Within a couple of years, I came to the realization that many of the best outdoor stories were not being written. I was approached time and again by men who had made exciting hunts, who had suffered severe ordeals in the outdoors, or who had experienced narrow escapes and high adventure.

These men were from all walks of life: doctors, priests, laborers, plumbers. But they were not writers. They had terrific stories to tell but lacked the ability to put them on paper. The things that had happened to them simply do not happen to a handful of professional journalists.

I started to sit down with these men, get their stories in a notebook, and put them in shape for publication. In short, I became an outdoor ghost writer. That was to be my specialty for the next 30 years, and it resulted in some of the most interesting and exciting copy I have written.

In 1965, *Outdoor Life* advanced me to senior field editor and hired John O. Cartier to cover the Midwest. Almost at once, Bill Rae—the brilliant editor-in-chief who then directed the policies and determined the content of the magazine—set John at ghost writing.

John is an enthusiastic trophy seeker who has unflagging interest in that type of hunting, so he took naturally to such assignments. He began to seek out hunters who'd made outstanding hunts and had taken exceptional trophies. He interviewed them at length and got their stories down on paper. Over the years, the result was a great deal of topnotch writing for *Outdoor Life.* Few top trophies have been taken in North America in the past 15 years that escaped John's investigation. He made it his business to get the stories of the best hunts.

Now comes this book, which is made up of the finest of the lot. If you have never understood the spell that trophy hunting casts, you will learn it between these covers.

Occasionally a hunter takes a great trophy by sheer luck. But generally a trophy hunt that ends in success is hard to come by. So are great stories about them.

The late Jack O'Connor, one of the most respected sportsmen and writers of his day, whose craft and persistence in hunting were fully matched by his skill as a storyteller, once said of wild-sheep hunting that he delighted in it for its challenges because it pitted him against a superb and wonderful game animal on the animal's home ground and on its own terms.

"It lets me prove," said Jack, "that I have enough air in my lungs and iron in my legs to do it." That is the essence of trophy hunting for any sportsman worthy of the name.

As for the trophy-hunting story, John O. Cartier knows all that is involved. He knows how rare they are and why more of them never get into print. Unless such a story captures the challenge, the drama, the excitement, and the satisfaction of the hunt, it is no story at all.

John says of his own book: "No writer can ghost such stories properly unless he has an extensive hunting background, knows how to interview, and knows how these special stories should be written."

John himself qualifies admirably on each of these counts. I feel entirely safe in predicting that when you finish this book, you will agree you have read the best hunting stories in print.—*Ben East*

20 GREAT
TROPHY HUNTS

What Makes a Trophy Hunt Great?

By John O. Cartier

This book has been 15 years in the making. It took that long to get stories exceptional enough to deserve a place within these pages. This is not primarily a book about how to hunt big-game animals. Though you will find a great many hunting tips, the focus of these personal accounts is on adventure, excitement, and what it means to take a big-game trophy that ranks high in the records.

The average big-game hunter values a trophy head according to what his experience tells him. For example, a Michigan hunter who takes a whitetail buck with an 8-point rack measuring 14 inches across may very well have downed the biggest buck he has ever seen. To this man, his buck is truly the trophy of a lifetime.

On the other hand, a south-Texas hunter who wants a bragging-size buck probably wouldn't consider downing a whitetail unless the animal wore a rack measuring at least 18 inches across and carrying 10 or more points. So when we talk about trophy hunting, it's important to realize that a head may be outstanding in one part of North America but hardly rate notice in another part. For instance, a big-game head might be a state record but could rank far down the list of North American records. The stories you will read in this book are about some of the best trophies taken anywhere in North America.

1

Size of the head, however is only one part of trophy hunting. Another way to assign value to a trophy head is to consider how much effort the hunter expended in getting it. A man who backpacks into high mountain ranges, lives on meager rations for days, sleeps in a tiny tent, and makes tortuous climbs where a mistake in footing could mean death, more than earns any animal he may get. Such a man might take a goat or a sheep that he would regard as his trophy of a lifetime, even though the head might measure far short of record-book size.

Perhaps the most common misconception about trophy hunting is that the spending of money will lead to success. The typical outdoorsman assumes that if a hunter has unlimited time and money, he can enjoy the best hunting on earth. The widespread belief is that such a man, because he can buy his way into the best game country, is most likely to take a trophy good enough to make the record books. This reasoning is not even half true.

The most important ingredient in trophy hunting is *desire,* not money.

Doug Burris, Jr., downed the world-record mule deer in Colorado's San Juan National Forest in 1972. While Doug and I were putting together his story, we talked about how important desire is to the hunter who wants to take a trophy. He told me about the determination he maintained before he scored on his astonishing buck.

"It rained every day for three straight days," Burris said. "I had good raingear, but when you hunt from dawn to dark in wet woods, you're going to get wet no matter what you wear. It was plain miserable hunting, but I'll tell you something . . . you won't get 'em unless you stay out there with 'em."

Consider the desire to excel that was the major ingredient in other personal accounts within these pages:

• Dr. Roy A. Schultz put in 62 days of hard climbing over a five-year period to finally take a sheep that ranks well up in the Boone and Crockett record book.

• Dwight E. Green hunted a specific giant whitetail buck for six years before he finally downed him.

• Tommy Cave was 11 years old when he broke his right leg while running a trapline. Bone infection set in and stopped normal growth. By the time everything cleared up, Cave's right leg was three inches shorter than his left. Nevertheless, Cave took his world-record black bear during a rugged hunt in mountain terrain.

• Ted Kelly hunted wet and chilled for six days before he finally got a chance for a shot at his grizzly. The bear scored only one digit less than the all-time best grizzly ever taken in North America.

The second most important ingredient in trophy hunting is *physical condition.*

If you can't hunt hard, the odds are usually against you. Bill Crouch, who also tells his story in this book, has this to say about mule-deer hunters: "The problem is that most deer hunters don't really hunt. They're out in the woods with a rifle, and they think they're hunting, but they don't really know what it takes to get close to bucks with trophy racks. The big bucks are way back in the roughest country. Most hunters never see it, because they're not in condition to hike back there."

During the decades that I've been hunting big game, I've paid special attention to what veteran guides and outfitters say about why many hunters fail. Without exception, the main reason mentioned was lack of physical ability. A typical comment goes like this: "Most of the hunters I get have no idea of what it takes to hunt hard. Many of my clients are so far out of shape they can't even begin to hunt hard enough to get fine trophies."

There is still another reason why money ranks far down the list of what it takes to make the record books. No matter what you do in this life, *luck* can be a very important factor in being in the right place at the right time. Bob Knutson had astounding luck. He shot the first caribou he ever saw. His bull turned out to be the second best woodland caribou taken since 1910. The reason Knutson's story rates high enough to be in this book is that his hunt had a great many exciting elements besides the taking of an outstanding trophy.

No story in these pages is about the taking of a great trophy solely by luck. A great trophy hunt must have many elements of interest and excitement; otherwise it can't be the basis of a top story.

I'll first mention in passing a few stories that didn't make it into these pages.

3

• A few years ago I tracked down a hunter who took an enormous nontypical whitetail buck in Clay County, Iowa. The head scored 282, a mere four digits below the best nontypical whitetail ever taken in North America. That whitetail was killed by Larry Raveling, a young man who had shot only one other deer.

I was sure I'd find great story potential. Imagine taking a near world-record whitetail in heavily populated Iowa. How could a buck get that big in corn country that harbors thousands of hunters? And how could a young hunter trying for only his second deer outwit a savvy buck that had managed to avoid scores of veteran hunters for many years?

It turned out that all Raveling needed was an enormous dose of good luck. Other hunters in his group told him to take a stand at the edge of a trail. Then the unfortunate buck tried to run across the trail right in front of Raveling but didn't make it. Though Raveling can be extremely proud that his buck ranks No. 2 in the Boone and Crockett record book, the story of his hunt involves little adventure or exertion.

• In 1965, John O. Band took a top-ranking whitetail near his ranch in Republic County, Kansas. When I asked Band about his hunt, he had this to say: "I finished chores one afternoon and decided I had enough daylight left for an hour or so of deer hunting. I picked up my rifle and walked over a hill. The big brute jumped up right in front of me, and I dropped him on the spot."

A good number of high-ranking trophies in the record books came easily, but you won't read about them here. A top story can't be built around an outstanding trophy alone.

Still, the taking of a head good enough to be listed in the record books is an incredible feat. The odds against any hunter's taking such a trophy are staggering. Let's look at some statistics.

During a recent Boone and Crockett Club big-game awards period—which covered three years—only three typical whitetail deer qualified for the record book, in which 392 heads are ranked. Because roughly 1.5 million whitetails are bagged annually in North America—or roughly 4.5 million during that three-year period—the odds that any one hunter would bag one of those three bucks were 1,500,000 to 1 against.

How impressive must a typical whitetail rack be in order to make the Boone and Crockett book? Well, the No. 1 head has a score of 206-5/8. One of the bottom-ranking entries in the book scores an even 170, the minimum required for a typical whitetail's entry into the book. The buck that scores 170 has main antler beams averaging 27 inches long. The *inside* spread of the antlers is 24-1/8 inches, and the rack has 14 points. Visualize those measurements for a moment and you'll realize how massive they are.

Don't be misled, however, into thinking that it's impossible to bag a real trophy buck today. And don't conclude that most of the record-book bucks were taken many years ago when hunters were scarcer than they are today.

Here's another shocker: Six of the 10 highest-ranking typical whitetails were taken during the past 15 years. In the nontypical category, the comparable figures are seven of 10.

The comparable figures for mule deer are seven of 10 in the typical category and three of 10 in the nontypical category.

In other words, more than half of the 40-top-rated whitetail and mule-deer trophies were taken in relatively recent history.

Are these two popular deer species some kind of flukes in this respect? Not at all. In the black-bear category, nine of the top 10 heads were taken during the past 15 years. And here are the comparable figures for other species: Grizzly, seven of 10; elk, four of 10; Canada moose, five of 10; Alaska-Yukon moose, six of 10; mountain caribou, four of 10; barren ground caribou, five of 10; pronghorn, five of 10; and Rocky Mountain goat, four of 10.

How about the four species of sheep? Here we have a very interesting situation. Earlier I pointed out that money is far less important than normally believed in trophy hunting. Now consider that the wild sheep inhabit the wildest and most remote areas of North America. It would seem that a wealthy sheep hunter has the best odds on downing a record-book trophy because he can pay the thousands of dollars it takes to hunt country that is never seen by the average hunter with average means. He hunts animals that live long enough to grow trophy heads.

Also—if you have the money—getting into sheep country is far easier than it used to be. The rough pack-trip hunts of the old days are mostly a thing of the past. Modern aircraft, modern camping equipment, and modern clothing and rifles make sheep hunts far more efficient than in years gone by. It would be easy to assume that most of the top-ranking sheep trophies were taken in relatively recent years.

They were not.

Not a single one of the top 10 Bighorn sheep was downed in the past 15 years.

Here are the figures for the other three species of sheep during the same period: desert, four of 10; Dall, three of 10; and Stone, four of 10.

All of these facts and figures lead me to the conclusion that today's serious big-game hunter is just as likely to take a record-book head as was his counterpart of many years ago. The likelihood that any hunter will take such a trophy, though, is extremely low. My own trophy-hunting experience is a case in point.

As I mentioned earlier, a typical whitetail buck must have a minimum score of 170 in order to make the Boone and Crockett record book. Ten years earlier, that magical minimum figure was 160. That fall I killed a typical whitetail in Saskatchewan that astounded me. When I approached the downed animal, I couldn't take my eyes off his enormous antlers. The beams were so thick and the tines so long they seemed unreal.

In my mind there was no doubt that my buck would make the record book. The only question was how close to the top he would rank. Months later, when my rack was scored after drying, I was dumbfounded to learn that it scored only 156. When I shot that buck, I honestly believed he was one of the best whitetail bucks that had ever walked North America. He certainly wore the best antlers I've seen on a live whitetail before or since.

Another incident shows how unlikely anybody is to take a record-book trophy. One of the best whitetail racks ever scored was found by a farmer on his own property. This man was an avid deer hunter who thought he knew just about every deer that lived on his place. When you realize that this man had never seen the elusive buck alive, and that the average whitetail's home range is about one square mile, you can begin to appreciate how difficult it can be to down a trophy whitetail.

Most big-game animals range far wider than whitetail deer, so the taking of any other record-book specimen can be even more difficult. So it is a very rare hunter indeed who takes a big-game trophy that ranks high in the record books. The hunter who takes a world record in any big-game category is the only one in all of North America who has accomplished that specific feat at that period in history. And the story of that hunt is the only story of its kind.

Six of the stories in this book tell about the taking of current or former world records. The rest of the stories are about the taking of trophies that rank well up in the record books. These are 20 of the most unusual hunting stories ever published because they are the personal accounts of the hunters who took the trophies. Many world-record heads were taken by hunters now deceased. Their eyewitness stories can never be published.

Consider the history behind the world-record whitetail deer. Sixty-five years and then some have passed since James Jordan shot a whitetail buck with an exceptionally large rack near Danbury, Wisconsin, along the Yellow River in 1914. Although no one who saw this rack could remember a larger one, nobody suspected it was a world record. The time was long before formal recordkeeping for native, North American big game was begun by the Boone and Crockett Club.

Shortly after killing his deer, Jordan accepted the offer of a part-time taxidermist to mount his trophy for $5. The taxidermist soon moved to Minnesota and took the rack and hide with him. Jordan did not see his trophy again for more than 50 years.

In 1964, Bernard A. Fashingbauer—in his capacity as an official measurer for the Boone and Crockett Club—measured the rack and found that it surpassed the score of the then world record. Later, a select panel of judges certified this trophy as the world record, with a score of 206-5/8. By the time the information was first published in the record book (1971 edition: *North American Big Game)* the trophy was the property of a Dr. Arnold. It was recorded with the remark, "Hunter unknown."

In 1964, a relative of Jordan's bought a huge deer rack at a public rummage sale in Sandstone, Minnesota. Jordan heard about the rack. And when he later viewed it, he knew it was the same deer he had shot many years ago. For more than a decade, however, Jordan would be frustrated in his quest for recognition in the record book as the hunter of that deer.

Jordan's claim to the trophy was convincing to many people who talked with him. Ron Schara, outdoor writer for the *Minneapolis Tribune,* featured Jordan's story on several occasions. The trophy owner (Dr. Arnold) wrote to the North American Big Game Awards Program (NABGAP) in late 1977, suggesting that Jordan's story be fully explored and that, if the records office was convinced, Jordan be designated as the hunter.

7

The NABGAP office then asked Fashingbauer to gather all evidence he could find on the trophy, in order that Jordan's claim could be fully considered by the Boone and Crockett Club's Records of North American Big Game Committee. Information gathered by Fashingbauer, and from other sources, was considered by the Records Committee at their December 1978 meeting. After review, the committee decided to list James Jordan as the hunter for the world-record whitetail deer (typical antlers), with a kill date and location of 1914 on the Yellow River near Danbury, Wisconsin.

The next edition of the record book, *North American Big Game,* will be corrected with this information when it comes out in 1983. The current edition of the record book was published in 1977. The usual interval between editions is six years.

Unfortunately, James Jordan died in October 1978, at age 86, before he could be informed of the decision. Isn't it ironic that Jordan couldn't be here to tell the story of his hunt in this book?

All through this chapter, I've been referring to big-game record books. There are two of these books that are limited to North American big game. One lists records of firearms hunters; the other focuses on records of bowhunters. (Incidentally, this book has several bowhunting stories.) Today, because of changes made during recent years regarding the keeping of records for trophies taken with firearms, there is a good deal of confusion about the official record book. Following is what all big-game hunters should know about the situation.

The first formal recognition of outstanding North American big-game trophies by the Boone and Crockett Club was in 1932. Only a few specimens were listed according to simple criteria of length and spread of horns, antlers, or skulls.

In 1947, the Club held its first "competition" for outstanding trophies, ranking them by a series of measurements. That approach was refined in 1950 into the current trophy-scoring system.

Since 1947, there have been 16 recognition programs (called competitions until the last few years). Recent programs have been held after the close of a three-year period of trophy entry. The 15th Awards Program of 1974 was the first to be jointly sponsored with the National Rifle Association of America, with whom the Boone and Crockett Club signed a formal agreement in 1973 to cosponsor all future awards programs.

This joint venture in big-game recordkeeping is known as the North American Big Game Awards Program. It is administered by the NRA Hunting Activities Department. The Boone and Crockett Club continues to serve as governor of the awards programs and records, while the NRA staff performs the everyday functions necessary to administer the program and keep the records.

The name Boone and Crockett has long been synonymous with trophy North American big game. The long-time recordkeeping for native big game is only one of the many conservation activities of the Boone and Crockett Club. The Club's prominent role in conservation activities and leadership during this century is well documented and second to none.

Basic procedures of the jointly sponsored program remain the same as in past years. Trophy entry is allowed during a three-year period, followed by a public display of invited trophies of each category, and an awards banquet and presentation of medals or certificates to the finest trophies entered.

Six editions of the record book, *North American Big Game,* were issued by the Boone and Crockett Club through 1971. The seventh edition, published in 1977, was the first jointly sponsored by the Boone and Crockett Club and the NRA. All accepted trophy score charts are entered into the record archives, and their data are accepted for publication in the next edition of the record book.

Over the years, the record books have become valuable handbooks for the trophy hunter, wildlife manager, and serious student of big-game populations. The 7th edition brings the total to well over 6,000 individual trophies in 31 categories. Also included are reproductions of the official score charts, photos of the top trophies of each category, and a dozen chapters on a variety of hunting-oriented subjects, including a history of the record keeping. The book is available from NRA Sales and Services as item ASB11660 for $25 per copy.

The correct title of the record-keeping program is "North American Big Game Awards Program," with the acronym of NABGAP. Thus, there is no Boone and Crockett record book nor a Boone and Crockett Awards Program, but rather a North American Big Game Awards Program and a NABGAP record book. For further information, write to: North American Big Game

Awards Program, c/o National Rifle Association of America, 1600 Rhode Island Avenue, N.W., Washington, D. C. 20036.

The office of the Boone and Crockett Club is at 424 North Washington St., Alexandria, VA 22314.

Although there now officially is no Boone and Crockett record book and no Boone and Crockett Awards Program, the words Boone and Crockett have been part of the vocabulary of trophy hunters since the 1930s. It will be a long time into the future before most big-game hunters realize the connection between B&C and NABGAP. To prevent confusion among readers of this book, I have retained the Boone and Crockett terminology originally used in the stories.

The Pope and Young Club is recognized throughout the world as the authority on North American big-game trophies taken by archers. Pope and Young is to bowhunters what Boone and Crockett is to firearms hunters. The Club collects and maintains official records of bowhunting trophies, and it has regularly scheduled displays and awards programs. It uses the same scoring system used by the Boone and Crockett Club.

The Pope and Young Club encourages archers to consider qualitative hunting through promoting their interest in outstanding examples of North American big-game animals. The Club believes that hunting in the future is almost certain to be based on quality rather than quantity.

The Club's official record book—published in 1975—is titled, *Bowhunting Big Game Records of North America*. It sells for $17.50. You can get details about the Club's activities by writing to: Pope and Young Club, Inc., Route 1, Box 147, Salmon, ID 83467.

As I have pointed out, your odds on taking a trophy outstanding enough to be listed in either record book are extremely slim. This is certainly not to say that you won't take an exceptionally fine head. Maybe you have already done so. Perhaps, like most big-game hunters, you have little knowledge about how a score is determined for antlers, horns, or a skull. It's possible that the big buck's rack in your den scores better than you think. How can you find out?

The first thing to know is that the Official Scoring System has worldwide recognition as the standard method of ranking all big-game trophies taken in North America. When any hunter uses it, he gets an exact index of the quality of his trophy. When you know how to score your trophy, you can accurately compare it with those taken by your friends. You can also find out exactly how it stands in relation to record-book entries.

All big-game trophies are scored by measuring specific parts of antlers, horns, or skulls. Individual measurements are recorded in inches and segments of inches. The grand total of all of the required measurements taken from any given trophy represents its final score. In order to standardize shrinkage, a trophy must dry in natural atmospheric conditions for a minimum of 60 days after the kill before it can be officially measured.

Bears are the easiest trophies to score. A bear's final score is determined by adding the greatest length of the skull (without lower jaw), and the greatest width of the skull.

Goats, sheep, and pronghorn are slightly more difficult. Several circumference measurements at various specific locations on each horn must be made, in addition to length and spread measurements. Eight measurements are made on each horn of a pronghorn, for a total of 16. A goat gets 14 individual measurements, as does a sheep.

Individual measurements can get into the dozens when antlered animals—deer, elk, caribou, and moose—are measured. It could take several hours to accurately measure one of these trophies if it has 20 or more antler points.

And there's a lot more to it than just totaling up a great many individual measurements. The ideal trophy has identical antlers or horns on each side of its head. When the individual measurements differ between the right antler (or horn) and the left, the differences must be subtracted from the total score. For example, perfectly matched antlers on an 8-point (Eastern count) whitetail buck could easily score higher than somewhat unmatched antlers on an 11-pointer. The idea behind all of this is that a trophy must be outstanding in all respects to rate a high total score.

The easiest way to learn the basic scoring system is to get scoring charts (there is a specific chart for each species of big game) from the North American Big Game Awards Program at the address just mentioned. These charts include how-to-score directions. Request the free charts for the species you want to score. If

11

you kill a trophy that appears exceptional, you should also request a list of official Boone and Crockett measurers in your area. No trophy makes the record book unless it's scored officially.

If you want in-depth detail on the entire scoring system, see the book *How to Measure and Score Big-Game Trophies* by Grancel Fitz, published by David McKay Company, Inc., New York.

Greatest Mule Deer of Them All

By Doug Burris, Jr.

(EDITOR'S NOTE: *The original version of this story appeared in the December 1975 issue of* Outdoor Life.)

I was walking the edge of a small canyon in Colorado's San Juan National Forest when a rifle roared half a mile or so ahead of me. Up until then I'd figured on still-hunting to a plateau covered with scattered oak brush 400 yards to the north. It was a logical spot to take a stand.

When the shot rang out, I decided I'd better get to my intended vantage point as fast as I could. I took off on a dead run and was almost to the plateau when I noticed movement in the oak brush and aspens on the other side of the canyon. I slammed to a stop and stared at the biggest deer I'd ever seen. His body was enormous, and his rack seemed large enough for an elk. He wasn't running flat out, but he was traveling fast enough to make me realize I'd better shoot soon if I expected to have any chance at him.

The range was about 250 yards. The buck was moving up the canyon and away from me when I found him in my Leupold 3-9X scope. I put the crosshairs on his back and touched off my Sako .264. The 125-grain Nosler bullet backed with 66.5 grains of 4831 powder put him down in his tracks.

13

I watched him for a while to make sure he wasn't going to get up; then I ran down a finger of the canyon and up the other side to the fallen buck. When I reached down and touched him and that huge 18-point rack, I just knew the antlers were something special. I was sure the deer would score high in the Boone and Crockett record book.

If someone had told me at that moment in 1969 that my buck wasn't good enough to make the minimum score for listing in the record book, I wouldn't have believed him. And if he had told me that three years later, within a half mile of this spot, I'd shoot a buck that would be recorded as the new world-record typical mule deer, I'd have considered him crazy. How was I to know what the future held?

I'm 37. My wife and I live in Sequin, Texas, with our 17-year-old son and two daughters aged 15 and eight. I earn our living as a construction superintendent. The outfit I work for builds shopping centers, high-rise office buildings, and similar units.

Except for 3-1/2 years spent in the U.S. Air Force, I've lived in Texas all my life. I began hunting when I was seven. My dad, who got me started, gave me the desire to be a good hunter.

I killed my first Texas whitetail when I was 13, and I've been nuts about deer hunting ever since. Though many of our deer are small—we call them "rabbits"—we do have some large whitetails in our south-Texas brush country. Some of those bucks will field-dress to 200 pounds or more, and they wear exceptional antlers. Many years of going after those deer gave me the trophy-hunting fever.

My long-time desire has been to make a hunt for Dall or Stone sheep in Alaska or British Columbia, but I've never had the money or time to make a guided trip. So I figured the next-best thing was to stay with deer and hunt the horns. By this I mean I always concentrate on trying for a trophy.

My interest in camping had a lot to do with making that first mule-deer hunt in Colorado in 1969. Between some of my hunting buddies and myself, we have four-wheel-drive vehicles and an assortment of camping gear. Charlie Fuller of Floresville and Jack Smith of San Antonio do a lot of hunting with me. Jack, who is my age, is a carpenter while Charlie, a few years younger, has a fertilizer-application operation. Both of these fellows like to hunt deer the way I do, and they like to camp. That's why, back in early 1969, we wanted to hunt the mountains where we could camp on public land and enjoy what we've come to call our "poor-boy hunts."

I did quite a bit of research on areas for trophy mule deer before we picked the San Juan National Forest. From what I'd read in *Outdoor Life* and other outdoor magazines, it seemed that many giant bucks were taken near the four-corners area, where Utah, Arizona, New Mexico, and Colorado join.

I had also bought a copy of the 1964 edition of the Boone and Crockett Club's book *Records of North American Big Game.* Study of the book's section on mule-deer trophies backed up my contention that southwestern Colorado would be a good place to go. There were better bets, such as the Jicarilla Apache Reservation in New Mexico, but we couldn't get permits. We consequently had to go into country where we could camp on our own in a public-hunting area. We decided to drive to Cortez, Colorado, and hunt somewhere northeast of there.

The three of us all got bucks that first year, and the one I mentioned earlier wore a rack that measured 41 inches across the outside spread. The reason it had such a tremendous spread is that each antler had "cheater" points sticking straight out from the outside curves of the main beams. Though the rack had a very unusual spread, it didn't have large tines. That's why the head didn't make the record book.

At the time I killed that deer, I didn't know much about official scoring systems for big-game trophies. But I did know that where there was one "Grandote" (a Mexican term we use meaning big) buck, there should be more. My buddies and I didn't need a better reason for heading back into the same area. We've never been sorry. Each fall, one or two of us down bucks with racks far better than average.

The second year, I got a buck with a 33-inch outside spread. The third year, I was lucky enough to come up with another good deer. Every season I've hunted up there, with the exception of one, I've taken bucks with outside antler spreads of 30 inches or better. Many hunters in the area kill bucks with antler spreads as narrow as 12 inches. I pass up a lot of deer when I'm going for the big ones.

15

Most of the boys in our group hunt that way. We all love the mountains, and we like to hunt hard from dawn to dark. We don't want to miss one minute of hunting on these trips, so none of us will take a small buck unless time is running out on our last day. We have so little time each year to devote to this mountain hunting that we want to make the most of each trip.

I don't want to imply that we're trophy crazy. Much of the fun and sport and fellowship we receive comes from planning and getting everything ready for our hunts. And for months after each trip, we enjoy talkfests. We make the most of camp life, too. I'm generally the cook because I enjoy it. We come into camp each evening, warm up by our wood stove in the cook tent, swap stories of what happened during the day, and take our time eating while we plan the next day's hunt. Then we sack out in time to get rested enough to do it all over again.

We go back into the Cortez area each year because it has proved itself with lots of deer and more than the average number of big bucks. The area is also very well suited to the type of general camping equipment we have. We're not equipped to backpack or pack in with horses.

Our cook tent, which also serves as a sort of community area, is a 14 x 16-foot wall tent. We also have 9 x 12-foot Coleman sleeping tents, as well as Coleman stoves, lanterns, and the usual assortment of general camping gear. Everybody contributes something. We found out during our first trip that it's best to take additional blankets, raingear, and other equipment.

All this equipment would be too much for some people, but we make our trips from Texas to Colorado in two 4WD's. The big unit is my three-quarter-ton Dodge Power Wagon equipped with a winch. We trailer a jeep behind the Dodge. We usually ride in the larger vehicle and pack much of our gear in the smaller unit and trailer that carries it. They hold a lot of extras that add to the joy of camping.

Our average cost per man totals about $155, and that includes Colorado's nonresident deer license, which sells for $50. [*Editor's note:* Colorado's 1979 nonresident deer license sold for $90.] A big chunk of the rest of each man's expenses goes for gas. We drive straight through from Texas to our hunting area. That's a trip of about 20 to 24 hours, depending on driving conditions. We also use the jeep each day to drop off the men in hunting areas, so we burn a lot of gas. Except for plenty of steaks, we take along normal groceries such as beans, potatoes, flour, canned goods, breakfast mixes, and lunch supplies.

We plan to arrive in our hunting area the Thursday before the Saturday opening of the deer season, which is always in late October. It takes a couple of days to set up camp, get organized, and do a little scouting. We figure on hunting three to five days. As far as the schedule is concerned, everything is more or less open. We have no hard and fast rules, because our primary objective is to have a good time.

I've had as few as two men go up there with me and as many as eight. Everything seems to go smoothest with about four. In 1972, the year I shot my biggest mule deer, there were four of us. Jack Smith went along, but Charlie Fuller couldn't get away. Robbie Roe and Bruce Winters were my other partners. I knew them through my job associations, and we'd done a lot of hunting together.

We drove up into Colorado and camped in the same spot I'd picked out four years earlier. By then I knew the territory pretty well. From my previous experience I'd selected five areas that seemed to hold the most deer and the biggest bucks. These places are all pretty well laced with relatively thick oak brush, some aspens, and a few pines. Thick oak brush is the key to success. If you've got tangles of that stuff—and lots of them—you're going to have deer. Mule-deer bucks just love these thickets.

The oak-brush areas most attractive to deer offer broken terrain in the form of canyons and fingers running off the canyons to mesas or plateaus. All five of my areas offered these combinations. I'd found that the best technique for hunting them is a combination of still-hunting and working from stands. I like to still-hunt the plateau and fingers of canyons coming off them. I've learned that deer work these fingers, get down into the very bottoms of them, then range back and forth through the canyons and up to the mesas and plateaus.

That's why the combination of hunting techniques works well. When I'm still-hunting, I'm apt to spot deer ahead or across canyons and draws. If I take a stand on a good vantage point, I may have deer working toward me. So I walk awhile, then sit awhile, and just keep going like that from dawn to dusk.

The problem is that deer may use one area today and vacate it tomorrow. So I pick an area and hunt it out. If it has deer, I stick with it. If it doesn't have deer, I move over to the next area. This isn't hard to do, because the San Juan mountain country is mostly rolling terrain with an altitude of only about 8,500 feet in the section we hunt.

Our first day's hunt began in typical fashion. We checked the wind direction before dawn, then decided which area each man would hunt. With that, we piled into the jeep and headed up a mountain two-track. I dropped Robbie off first, then Bruce. Jack got out of the vehicle a few miles farther on. Dawn wasn't much more than a dull gray promise in the eastern sky. The black void above us was spitting drizzle.

"Robbie and Bruce will walk back to camp whenever they feel like it," I said. "You want me to pick you up at any given time, or you want to hunt all day in the rain?"

"I'll meet you right here at dark," Jack answered.

I knew he'd say something like that. Jack likes to hunt as much as I do.

We all saw deer that day, but every buck was small. No one fired a shot. But on the second day of the hunt, I came very close to filling my tag.

It drizzled again most of that day. I just ambled about until 10 o'clock. Then I got real serious with my still-hunting. I don't know why, but the really big bucks in that area seem to move best from 10 in the morning until about 1 in the afternoon.

About noon, I spotted a deer in thick oak brush 200 yards ahead. We were both on a plateau. The animal was a big one, so I assumed it was a buck. I started moving in. Stalking conditions were quiet because everything was wet. The problem was that I couldn't close the distance very quickly in that thick brush, especially because my deer kept moving away from me as he browsed.

At one point I saw part of his rack, enough to know he wore heavy antlers in the trophy class. The excitement ended, though, when I tried to cut him off along the edge of the plateau. As I got close to where I thought he should be, he was gone. I waited awhile, but he didn't show. I'll never know if that buck detected me or if he just drifted off on a predetermined course. Some of the good ones get away.

When Jack and I got back to camp, two bucks were hanging on

our game pole. Robbie had nailed his 5-pointer (Western count) with a 7mm Remington Magnum equipped with a Leupold scope. Bruce's buck was also a 5-pointer, but a slightly better trophy because it wore heavier antlers. Bruce collected his venison with a Winchester Model 70, a 30-06 topped with a Leupold scope.

When we awoke the next morning, the drizzle was still with us. I suited up in my Browning raingear, filled my pockets with dried fruits and jerky, and realized it would be another long day before I could dry out again next to the wood stove in the cook tent. I dropped Jack off on the trail, then drove the jeep on up and parked near the country I'd hunted the day before.

A slight breeze was coming down off the mountain, so I decided to still-hunt into it and get farther back into rougher country. About 9 o'clock, I approached a 400-yard-wide canyon and began working up its edge. I was about three quarters of the way to the top when I spotted two bucks feeding in a clearing 1,000 yards up the canyon. I stopped and watched them for several minutes because I was a bit astonished that I could see their racks from such a great distance with the naked eye.

I zeroed in on those bucks with my Bausch & Lomb binoculars. Both were definitely in the trophy class. It was getting pretty late in our hunt, so I decided I'd better try cashing in on this opportunity. My first thought was to get on with the stalk and decide which trophy was better when I closed the distance to shooting range.

I'd eased on through the oak brush for about 200 yards when I busted out a doe. She pushed straight up ahead of me. I didn't think she'd spook the bucks, but I watched them for several minutes to make sure. They continued feeding up and away from me. I could keep them in sight at this point because they were still in the clearing.

I eased back into some cover and stalked ahead for about 45 minutes while the drizzle came on even stronger. During this time I didn't see the bucks, because they'd moved into a pocket of brush. I was pretty sure, though, they were still in their original area. There was a 75-yard-wide opening at the top of the canyon. I would have spotted them if they'd crossed that, and I would have seen or heard them if they'd run back toward me or along the bottom of the canyon.

Probably another 30 minutes passed before I decided I couldn't be more than 200 yards from the deer. Still, I couldn't see them. The oak brush ahead of me was up to 10 feet tall. Right then I busted out that doe again, or maybe it was a different doe. Anyhow, she exploded down the canyon and crashed up the other side directly toward the bucks. I figured they'd spook, so I took off on a dead run for an opening 20 yards ahead. If I hoped to do any good, I'd have to get a shot off in a hurry.

At the same time I broke into the opening, three deer ran into view across the canyon. Two of them were the bucks I'd been stalking. The third was a bigger buck, and he was lagging a bit behind. But even in the split second I had to shoot, I knew he was by far the best trophy.

My hand-loaded Nosler slug zipped 300 yards across the canyon, ripped into the buck's heart-lung area, and blew up. He stumbled, hit the ground, and lay still.

When I examined the antlers—six unbelievable massive tines on the right side and five on the left—I knew I'd just killed the finest trophy buck I'd ever seen. But I had no idea I'd taken the best typical mule deer of all time. What concerned me most at the moment was the enormous body of the deer.

Normally we can drive a vehicle close to our kill sites, drag a deer out to the 4WD, and haul it back to camp. But I was way back in rough country we couldn't approach with a vehicle, and I knew I couldn't drag that big brute very far by myself.

I decided the best thing to do was hike out to the jeep, drive back to camp, and get help. Since Robbie and Bruce had already killed their bucks, the odds were they'd be in camp. They were.

We went back to my buck, quartered it, and hauled the pieces out to the vehicle. When we returned to camp, Jack was waiting. He needed help with a heavy-antlered 5-pointer he'd killed with his 270 Weatherby Magnum. By the time we got that buck out, the day and the hunt were finished.

When I got home, I took my buck's head and cape to taxidermist Ed Schlier in San Antonio for mounting. He's an official measurer for the Boone and Crockett Club, so we rough-scored the antlers. Our preliminary figures indicated my buck would probably make the top 10 mule deer in the typical category. That news was exhilarating for me, but I didn't think much more about it. Then, several months later, my phone rang at 1 o'clock in the morning.

20

At first glance, all three of these outstanding mule-deer trophies seem like record-book candidates, but only one makes the grade. The buck in the middle is the world-record typical mule deer. Doug Burris, Jr., shown here with the impressive array, shot the monster buck on a public-hunting area in 1972. The buck on the left has an unbelievable outside spread of 41 inches—far wider than that of the world record—but its total score fell below the minimum required for the record book. The tines are too short to produce a high score. The buck on the right has a better rack than most hunters will ever see, but it also failed to make the record book. Burris took each of these bucks while hunting on his own, without a guide or outfitter.

"Doug," Ed blurted, "I think your buck may be the best ever taken. I scored the antlers this evening, and I couldn't believe it when I came up with a score of 226. That's nine better than the current world-record typical mule deer. I've been double-checking my figures for hours but they always come out the same. If they hold up with Boone and Crockett officials, you've got a new world record. This news is worth waking you up."

Indeed it was, but the realization of what I'd accomplished was just beginning.

The North American Big Game Awards Program—jointly sponsored by the Boone and Crockett Club and the National Rifle Association—requires any big-game trophy likely to win an award be rescored by a panel of judges. So I sent my mounted head off to the Program's headquarters in Washington, D.C.

In February of 1974, the Program's coordinator phoned me and invited me to attend the 15th North American Big Game Awards to be held on March 24, in Atlanta, Georgia. I figured that my buck had proved good enough to win some kind of an award, but I was just too busy to go to Atlanta.

That was my position until I received a couple more calls from other officials of the Program. They told me that if I missed the Awards, I would seriously regret it later. So I scraped together some cash and flew to Atlanta.

At the Awards Banquet I was presented with the 1st Award for the best typical mule deer taken during the last three-year competition period. I also received official recognition for taking a new world record.

In addition, I was presented with the Sagamore Hill Award, which is given only to hunters whose outstanding trophies are worthy of great distinction. This award is the highest given by the Boone and Crockett Club. Only one may be given during any Big Games Awards Period, and only 10 had been awarded during the club's history.

I was stunned. Somehow I couldn't quite believe that a farm boy from Texas could be so highly honored.

(EDITOR'S NOTE: *Burris's trophy still ranks as the all-time best typical mule deer ever taken in North America.*)

A Grizzly is For Keeps

By Ted Kelly

(EDITOR'S NOTE: *The original version of this story appeared in the May 1976 issue of* Outdoor Life.)

We had walked and jogged about seven miles through sleet and snow when we came to the river. Another couple of miles of hiking would put us into the area where my guide Don Martin had seen the enormous tracks of a grizzly a few days before. Don had figured we could wade the river in our hip boots, but as we approached it he saw that it was high and rushing with white water.

"A little sleet and snow can make these Alaskan rivers go wild," he said. "I didn't think the water would be so high. We can't cross after that bear today."

A wave of determination swept over me. My dream hunt in Alaska was now six days old and I had yet to fire a shot. It seemed as though I was ordained to get hit with every type of bad luck in the book. At this point it would have been easy to quit the hunt, go home to Minnesota, and admit total defeat. Instead, I decided there was no way I was going to give up.

"There has to be a way to get across this river," I said. "I'll swim it if I have to."

Don needed only a glance at me to realize I wasn't kidding. "Okay," he said. His tone indicated I didn't know what I was getting into. "If you're crazy enough to keep trying, I'm nuts enough to keep guiding you. But we're not going to swim these currents in 28°F temperature. There's no way we can keep hunting if we get our clothes soaked. Our only bet is to see if we can find a wider spot where the water is shallow."

We were standing in an area where the river ran between two hills showing scattered birch trees and conifers. It was only about 20 yards wide but probably up to eight feet deep in the middle. Our problem was to find more level land. After half an hour of walking, we finally came to a flat area where the river spread out to a width of about 60 yards.

Don broke a stout branch off a birch tree, waded into the water, and probed the bottom while checking for depth. At one spot he got fairly close to midstream before the water began lapping at the tops of his hip boots. As he splashed back toward shore, he said: "We'll never make it without going over our boots. The only thing we can do is strip naked, hold our clothes and rifles on our shoulders, and feel our way across."

If someone had made a movie of what happened during the next 10 minutes, I bet it would grab your attention. The sight of two grown men peeling off their clothes in a sleet and snow storm would certainly indicate that something far out of the ordinary was going on. And there would have to be some humor if you watched us putting our boots back on after stripping. A couple of guys pulling hip boots up to bare fannies wouldn't seem to make much sense, but Don said some of the rocks on the river's bottom were sharp and we had to protect our feet.

My guide led the way. I had to laugh to myself when the first icy water poured over Don's boot tops. At the precise moment he let out a whoop, I realized we were heading dead south. "Keep going," I said with a chuckle, "the water's always warmer on the south side."

Then the laugh was on me. I've had water go over my boots on other hunts, but deliberately letting it flow in while you're naked as a jaybird is something else. By the time the first frigid pint of water had topped my hippers and sloshed down to my toes, my grin was long gone.

The water depth reached chest level at one point, but we made it across the river with no further difficulties. We drained our

24

boots onto the snow-covered ground on the far bank, hurried back into our clothes, and took off with wet feet. We knew they wouldn't be dry until we got back to camp.

Two miles farther on we topped a knoll and looked down on a small lake bordered on its north, west, and south sides by mountains. On the east end of the lake was a relatively treeless flat stretching 100 yards from the water back to a large area of thick willows. Below us, 75 yards from the brushy tangles, some big rocks nestled on the side of the knoll.

"Those rocks are as far as we go," Don said. "If your bear is still in this area, he's likely to be somewhere in that brush. It's too thick to try going in there after him. He could be on us in one jump from anywhere in that jungle. We'll get down behind those rocks and wait. If we're lucky, he may get up and head toward the lake. It's a slim chance, but it's the only one we have."

I had been sitting for only a few minutes when I began to shake from the cold wind and dampness. Don was shivering too. The thought went through my mind that this whole situation was ridiculous. The way my luck had been running, the grizzly was probably 50 miles away in another mountain range. We wouldn't be able to put up with this freezing torture too long.

It seemed as if we'd waited an eternity when I suddenly glimpsed a movement out in the willows. At first I didn't know what it was that I saw; all I knew was that I had seen something in motion. I glanced at Don. He was unaware of the activity because he was watching the brush on our left. I didn't say a word, but just riveted my eyes back on the thickets in front of us.

I saw the movement again. This time my heart tried climbing into my throat. The grizzly was in plain view as suddenly as if he'd jumped out of a hole in the ground. I knew grizzlies were big, but this enormous hulk of animal only 75 yards away astounded me. My initial reaction was to throw up my rifle and shoot before the bear could be swallowed by brush. But I controlled my emotions, nudged my guide, and nodded toward the bear.

"He's a monster," Don whispered. "He's headed for the flat. Let him get out of the bush so you'll get a clear shot. You've got to nail him dead. If you wound him and he gets back into the bush, we're in bad trouble. Trying to follow a wounded bear that size could mean death for both of us."

It only took a moment or two for the bruin to clear the brush, but in that short time my adrenaline flowed so fast that my numb feet turned warm and my whole body tingled with excitement. The grizzly had walked 10 yards into the open now and was broadside to us. What the hell was Don waiting for?

"Okay," he said in a whisper trembling with tension. "Take him!"

This adventure had its beginning back in February of 1972 when I received a phone call from Ike Rygajlo. Ike and I live in the Minneapolis area and had met through a mutual friend who knew we both like to hunt. Ike is in his late 40s and has done well enough in the import/export business to afford considerable big-game hunting. He has made two trips to Alaska and has hunted moose, caribou, and polar bear with Jack Lee, a guide and outfitter based in Anchorage.

"Jack is coming to Minneapolis in a few days," Ike told me. "I'm planning to book another hunt with him. Would you like to go along?"

"Would I ever. I don't know if I can swing it from a financial standpoint, but count me in on talking with Jack."

I'm a 40-year-old manufacturer's representative. My wife Betty and I have a daughter 11 and a son 17. Kids are expensive while they're growing up, and I knew my wife wouldn't take kindly to my spending a lot of money to go hunting in Alaska, especially because some of the money would be hers. She has had her own job ever since we've been married.

I'd need all my ability as a salesman to sell her on the hunt, but I knew I'd never take on a selling job more enthusiastically.

Since boyhood I've considered the grizzly to be the top trophy in North America: It is smart, huge, unpredictable, and dangerous. I knew that Alaska was the best place to get one, that the scenery there is magnificent, and that a hunt in the rugged mountains would be a physical challenge of the type I really go for. If Jack Lee could promise me a reasonable chance at a grizzly, I knew I'd book the hunt even if my wife put up strong objections.

In addition to knowing that Alaska was the best place to get a grizzly, it was about the only place as far as I was concerned. I'd read enough about the declining grizzly populations in our west-

26

ern states to know that I wanted no part of shooting one anywhere south of northern Canada.

Hunting serves a definite purpose if the game taken is a harvestable surplus, but I'm not about to hunt any animal having difficulty holding its own. My reading about grizzlies informed me that many of the giant bears of interior Alaska live out their lifetimes without ever seeing a hunter, and that their numbers are in little danger of declining due to legal hunting pressure.

I was born and raised on a farm in central Missouri. A lot of quail, ducks, geese, deer and rabbits were around our place, and I developed the urge to hunt when I was young. I had a tough time getting involved because my father had little interest in hunting or fishing. I got started on my 14th birthday, when my folks gave me a Stevens single-shot 22 rifle.

I went out that same day and shot a rabbit. I brought home a lot of game in the few years that followed. Since I left Missouri I've hunted deer, elk, black bear, and pronghorn in the west; and I never miss the Minnesota hunting seasons.

When Ike and I met with Jack Lee, Jack told us stories of fantastic hunts, showed us photos of game and his camps, and pointed out that we might be able to hunt Dall sheep, moose, grizzly, and caribou during a 10-day hunt. What rang true with Lee is that he didn't promise anything. He said that a successful hunt would largely depend on good weather and my physical condition. In effect, he said he could put me into excellent game country if I could hunt hard and keep up with his guides.

That was enough for me. That evening I went home and told my wife that I wasn't getting any younger, that I had a good contact with a reliable outfitter, that the hunt would cost a lot more in the future, and that there was nothing in this world I would rather do than make a hunt for a grizzly.

I hurried through the costs of the trip. Jack's fee, covering everything except personal gear, was $250 per day per man for a standard 10-day hunt. My plane fare from Minneapolis to Anchorage would be $300 round trip. Jack said my hunting licenses would total about $200. Incidentals would raise the overall cost to a little more than $3,000, but I decided not to mention any lump-sum figures to my wife. [EDITOR'S NOTE: Comparable costs in 1980 were two to three times higher than those noted above.]

27

I guess I made a pretty good pitch because Betty didn't object as much as I expected. Within an hour I knew my hunt was definitely in gear.

The next day Ike and I signed Jack's contracts for a 10-day hunt. We each gave him checks of $1,500 to cover the standard deposits. Our hunt was to start September 5, 1972. I told Jack my priorities were grizzly No. 1, sheep No. 2, moose No. 3, and caribou No. 4.

I jogged daily from February to September to get myself into peak physical condition. I bought two new rifles: a Sako 7 mm magnum topped with a 4X-12X Redfield scope and a Browning 338 magnum equipped with a 3X-9X Redfield scope. I then spent hours shooting these rifles on a public-shooting range. My reason for so much shooting practice was that I didn't want to put my life on the line or miss the trophy of a lifetime simply because I wasn't totally familiar with what my rifles could do.

There was also purpose in my selection of rifles. I believe in matching my weapon to the type of game I'm going to hunt. I figured that the Sako 7 mm would be ideal for possible long-range shooting at sheep or caribou. I wanted the larger caliber rifle with more knockdown capacity for grizzly or moose.

Three weeks before our planned departure date, Ike got involved in unexpected business problems. When he told me he had to cancel his hunt, I phoned Jack Lee and asked him if I could come on alone. He told me there would be no problem. I flew to Anchorage via Northwest Orient Airlines on September 3.

Jack's son John met me at the airport. He took me to a sporting-goods store where I bought my hunting license and permits. Then he dropped me off at the Captain Cook Hotel and told me that Jack would get in touch with me that evening. I shopped around downtown Anchorage to pass the time. I had to chuckle when I looked at the label on a fur-trimmed coat in one store. The label read "Berman Buckskin, Minneapolis, Minnesota."

The first hint that my hunt might be turning sour came as the evening turned into late night. I lolled around my hotel room for hours waiting for Jack's call that never came.

I called Jack's office the next morning. John told me that his dad was still out in the bush with another party of hunters. It was 10:00 p.m. before Jack finally got in touch with me. He said bad weather in the mountains eliminated flying, and that such delays are common. He added that he'd pick me up in the morning and we'd fly out to his main camp in the Talkeetna Mountains and make a try for a grizzly.

I didn't sleep much that night. I kept thinking that by this time tomorrow my lifelong dream of scoring on a grizzly could be a reality. I really didn't get bears out of my mind until Jack and I were crossing the early-morning sky in his Cessna 185. Then the fantastic beauty of Alaska drew my total attention.

Cook Inlet, blue as the sky, was like a jewel inlaid in mountains. Green vegetation on mountain slopes contrasted with snow on higher peaks. In the distance, Mt. McKinley rose in spectacular grandeur. When Jack tipped his plane down toward a landing on a small lake near his main camp, I felt as though I'd like to fly across Alaska forever.

Main camp consisted of a spacious lodge and four cabins. After getting my gear unloaded in one of the cabins, I got acquainted with Jack's wife Jane, guides Don Martin, Dan Whatley and Ken Sorenson, and Ken's wife Hazel (who assisted Jane with the cooking). The weather had already turned for the worse by the time I began getting into my hunting gear. Don and I had planned to go by plane into a good grizzly area, but a wild wind was blowing and the clouds were so low that flying was out of the question.

When I awoke the next morning, the snarling wind was spitting sleet and snow. There wasn't much we could do except sit around camp and hope for a change in the weather. I had now been in Alaska three days and hadn't even seen a wild animal. Discouragement was becoming difficult to shrug off.

That afternoon Jack learned by radio that the weather was pretty good in the Wrangell Mountains where he wanted me to hunt sheep.

"We'll fly back to Anchorage, get one of my bigger aircraft, and head for sheep country," Jack said. "Dan will go with us and be your guide."

Everything continued to go bad. Weather forced us to spend the night in Anchorage. We flew into the Wrangells the next morning, but found the clouds so low that we couldn't land at the glacier campsite. We flew to Palmer, landed, had lunch, then tried again. This time we got through a hole in the clouds and landed on a

This small tent on a glacier was Kelly's home during three days of blizzards. He took the photo just before plane flew them out in a brief period of good weather.

narrow glacier with deep gorges on each side. I realized how concerned I'd been with the pinpoint landing when I noticed that I'd pulled my seat belt so tight it hurt.

We taxied up to a 6 x 8 foot canvas tent that was to be my home for the next few days. That afternoon we had time enough to climb a mountain and glass for sheep with Dan's 60X Bushnell spotting scope. We spotted a ram with a full-curl horn on one side. The tip of the other horn was broken off. The sheep was so far away I could hardly see him with my naked eyes. It didn't make any difference. Mountain gorges made him inaccessible.

We still had spotting light left when it began to sleet and snow. Dan said we'd better get down off the mountain fast or we'd be sliding down if the temperature dipped below freezing. It was snowing hard by the time we reached our tent.

Then came more trouble. As Dan lit our little three-burner stove, the whole unit burst into flames. I dived out of the tent. Dan was right behind me with an armload of fire. We doused the stove with snow and the fire went out. Dan found a loose fitting, tightened it, and got the burners operating properly.

"Man," he said, "I knew I had to get that fire out of the tent. We'd be in tough shape if we'd lost our shelter, especially if this blizzard continues."

It continued for two days. The most exciting thing we did during that time was knock snow off the tent so it wouldn't collapse. It was a miserable experience. The temperature held around 20°F, the wind blew continuously, and the snow swirled around our tent. We huddled inside because there was nothing to do outside. At over 8,000 feet up on the glacier, there was no vegetation, no trees, nothing interesting to look at, just snow, ice, and rocks.

The weather cleared a bit by dawn on the third day. I was a pretty sad individual but I cheered up when I heard a plane circling through the cloud cover. One of Jack's pilots finally put his aircraft down on the glacier. He asked me if I wanted to stay longer or go back to Anchorage. I started packing in a hurry. I'd had enough of winter tent life on a glacier.

Back in Jack's office I learned there was a chance of flying back to the main camp if the cloud cover would break up just a little more. By now I guess my luck was beginning to change for the better. We sat around for only an hour, then Jack told me to load my gear into the 185. He said we'd make a try at flying.

It was a rough flight, but I didn't care because at least I was going out again. We made it to the main camp in time to have a late lunch with Don Martin. What he had to say really charged me up.

"I was out a couple of days ago with one of our moose hunters," he began. "We were hunting an area about nine miles from here when we came upon the entrails of a moose killed during an earlier hunt. The guts were pretty well torn up and there were huge grizzly tracks all over the place. There's a good chance the bear may have cleaned up the rest of the mess by now and be long gone, but there's at least a slim possibility he may still be hanging around."

Martin went on to say that we'd be faced with a long and hard hike over rough terrain, that we'd have to go out of our way to come in on the bear's area with the wind in our face and, even if we didn't find the grizzly, it would still be well after dark before we got back to camp. Was I game to try?

Was I ever. I was just about shaking with anticipation.

Five hours later my moment of truth was at hand when the enormous bear walked out on the flat I described at the beginning of this story. As I raised my rifle, he stopped and looked directly at me.

He appeared so huge when I put my scope on him that it shook me up for a moment. I took a deep breath, laid the scope's crosshairs on his chest area, and touched off a Herter's 200-grain softpoint bullet. If I live to 100, I'll never forget the results of that shot.

I could see water spray off the bear as if he'd exploded when my slug hit him. He went down flat, but bounced right back up and charged us. My second shot knocked him down again, but he was back on his feet so fast that I couldn't believe it. He went down again on my third shot. When I nailed him with my fourth slug, he finally stumbled into a little ditch and went wild. He began slamming the ground with his front paws, and he had enough strength left to send roots and mud flying 30 feet into the air. It was an awesome sight, which ended as suddenly as it had started.

Kelly shows his grizzly in spot where it finally fell into a ditch. He was barely able to lift the grizzly's heavy head into view for this photo.

As I was reloading, Don told me not to shoot anymore. "I think he's had it, but we'll stay here and watch for a while before going down there."

By the time we finished skinning the grizzly, the sky was clear but it was almost dark. Don said the hide and skull together weighed about 150 pounds, and that my grizzly had to be one of the biggest bears ever taken. I was so thrilled that I forgot about the river until we reached it in darkness. Its water didn't seem nearly as cold as we waded it naked for the second time.

Don's guess that my bear was a truly exceptional trophy was borne out by the Boone and Crockett Club. At the club's Fifteenth North American Big Game Awards program held in Atlanta, Georgia, on March 24, 1974, I was given an award for the second-best grizzly taken in North America during the club's latest awards period covering the years 1971, 1972, and 1973. My bear's skull measurements totalled 26-2/16, only 1/16 less than the first-award grizzly taken in 1971 by Robert Lawrence Tuma in the Tatla Lake area of British Columbia. I was astonished to learn that my bear had an official score of only one digit less than the all-time world-record grizzly.

I had the giant's hide made into a rug, which is now the focal point of my den.

(EDITOR'S NOTE: *Kelly's trophy now ranks No. 14 out of 235 grizzlies listed in the current Boone and Crockett record book.*)

Top of The World

By Lowell L. Eddy, M.D.

(EDITOR'S NOTE: *The original version of this story appeared in the December 1971 issue of* Outdoor Life.)

The bull moose upset our plans. Our goals for the day had been to get possible bow shots at mountain caribou or goats. It was early morning, but the four of us had already climbed to a 6,000-foot elevation on the side of a mountain in northwestern British Columbia.

We were glassing surrounding slopes when I spotted the moose feeding slowly through an opening in timber about 2,000 feet below us. We decided to hurry back down the mountain and try to intercept him. But when we got to where the bull should have been, he was gone.

Bill Love, one of our two guides, climbed 50 feet up a huge fir tree and scanned the area with his 7 x 35 Bausch & Lomb binoculars. He suddenly stiffened, then backed down the tree in a hurry.

"I spotted a bigger bull," he said, "and it's a real good one. He's bedded half a mile away. Wind's wrong to stalk straight in from here, but if we detour around we've got a good chance to get him."

We had an unusual advantage that helped in the roundabout two-mile stalk. The moose was bedded near two deformed spruce trees that served as homing points. The trees were tall and irregularly limbed, and they had dead crowns that differed from sur-

35

rounding timber. We made a very slow approach through rolling evergreens and soft marsh. But when we reached our destination, there was no sign of the bull. Bill figured the animal had moved but was still close to us.

"Hold tight," he whispered, "I'll climb another tree."

He cautiously started up a tall spruce, then excitedly pointed to a spot on my left. I nocked an arrow, pulled it to half draw, and sneaked ahead.

I'd moved only a few yards when I saw the antlers of the bull. I couldn't believe my eyes. The huge rack seemed to be lying on the ground only 25 yards away. I figured I had the animal dead to rights. There was every chance that I'd have a clear shot when he stood up. Then the seemingly impossible happened.

The antlers appeared to float away at ground level. I never even saw the bull's body. His rack just went forward into the brush and disappeared. It was an eerie feeling, but I soon figured out what happened. When I approached the area, I found that the moose had been standing in a hollow, not lying down as I'd suspected. He had simply walked away, leaving me dumbfounded.

That was only one of many exciting incidents during a 10-day hunt that has to be recorded as the most satisfying of my life.

Two partners made the trip with me. Dr. Buzz Mosiman, an orthopedic surgeon, Dr. Jim Mathwig, an anesthesiologist, and I work together at the Ballard General Hospital in Seattle, Washington. We've been hunting partners for several years. Buzz and I are archers, and Jim is a confirmed rifleman.

I'm 56 years old and do general surgery at the hospital. I was raised in a small logging town in Oregon, where I had the usual interests of hunting squirrels and rabbits with a 22 rifle. My interest in bowhunting developed when I was 16. That's when I became acquainted with L. L. Dailey, a famous archer of that era. Dailey fired up my interest in bowhunting, and it hasn't dimmed in 40 years.

I've had many unsuccessful hunts—from a meat-in-the-pot standpoint—but every one of them has been enjoyable. I've had my share of good luck too. My bow kills include a cougar and a mule deer that are listed in the Pope and Young Club record book. I've also taken bear and bull moose.

Buzz, Jim, and I had previously hunted in Canada's Tweeds-

36

muir Park area for moose, in Idaho for elk, and in Washington for deer. Both of my partners are seasoned outdoorsmen. Jim is so taken up with the wilderness that he goes to Alaska every year to serve as a physician for a fishing cannery and camp. Buzz has killed record-book polar and brown bears, in addition to taking other big-game animals with rifles. Except for rare firearms elk hunts with his sons, he has remained true to the bow for 10 years.

Our hunt took place during the last part of August and the first part of September. We were interested in mountain caribou, moose, and goat. Preliminary plans centered on finding a hunting region harboring trophy animals. Jim and Buzz laid the groundwork since they had hunted grizzlies and moose near the Kispioux River in northwest British Columbia with guides Bill Love and Jack Lee.

After an exchange of several letters, Bill and Jack suggested the Duti Lake area, 180 miles north of the town of Smithers. After we arrived at Smithers, we flew by Omenica Charter Air Service direct to the lake.

I was more than impressed when I met Jack and Bill. They're full-time guides and outfitters and are descendants of pioneer families of the Kispioux River Valley. At the time of our hunt Jack was 60 years old, but still in prime physical condition. Bill was 47. They live near the river in the New Hazleton area.

Our crew was rounded out with Jack's wife Fran, and Alan Curtis, a local camp helper. Fran often goes along on Jack's hunts to cook and help spot game. Camp consisted of a plywood cookhouse and two large wall tents for sleeping quarters. The plywood cabin contained a small wood stove that served heating and cooking requirements. The prefabricated cabin had been flown in and set before our arrival.

Our guides had also brought in a prefabricated plywood boat that was assembled and ready to go. There were no horses involved in our hunt, as plans called for traveling the two-mile-long lake with the 20-foot outboard-powered boat. We would beach the boat at various places depending on each day's hunt plans. The high mountains across the lake were the best bets for caribou and goats. The top moose country was the Duti River valley and willow swamps stretching away from the far end of the lake.

The first day of the hunt proved uneventful as we spent much of our time getting organized. The second day, though, was loaded with excitement.

We decided to try for moose in the valley, which is about two and one-half miles wide. It's a beautiful spot, with mountains rising steeply from the drainage floor to 6,500-foot peaks. The valley itself is swampy and marshy with thick patches of brush, willows, and occasional clumps of spruce. Several ponds are scattered about, and stunted evergreens cover the hillsides up to timberline 1,500 feet above the Duti River.

Buzz, Jack, and I started up the valley shortly after dawn on a clear Indian-summer day. It wasn't long before we jumped a giant bull moose that crashed away through the thickets as if he were trying to tear the valley apart. We got a good look at his antlers and they were huge.

"That bull would rank well up in the Pope and Young records," Jack said. "But there's no way we can get him now. He's really spooked, and he'll go for miles."

About an hour later Jack spotted a good bull feeding near a small pond 600 yards south of us.

Buzz and Jack took off on a circular stalking route since there was open marsh between our position and the moose. They headed west into evergreen cover at the mountain edge. Their plan was to circle downwind from the bull, then try to sneak into bow range through thin willow clumps. It was an ambitious plan since the last 200 yards of their stalk would have to be made through mud, water, and thin cover that wouldn't come close to hiding them.

I headed down the valley floor in an opposite circular route. My intention was to get on the other side of the bull. I figured I might get a shot if he spooked and ran by me.

I ended up across the pond—crosswind to the moose—and about 200 yards from where he was now bedded. I couldn't have chosen a better grandstand seat if I'd tried. The animal was undisturbed and facing toward my area.

When I spotted Buzz and Jack emerging from the last of the evergreen cover, my nervous system hit high gear. I expected to see the bull bolt each time my partners took a step. Yard by yard they closed in with a superb demonstration of stalking skill. One hundred yards, 75 yards, then about 50.

Suddenly the bull got to his feet. I watched Buzz draw his arrow and release it. Then the moose did an astonishing thing. He didn't run, but simply turned slowly and walked into the pond.

Buzz quickly fired another arrow at the standing target. His aim was true and the big bull died on his feet and collapsed into the shallow water. I ran over to congratulate Buzz, who was the most delighted hunter I've ever seen.

"That big brute never knew we were there," he said with a grin. "When we finally made it within easy range, Jack grunted at the bull. He jumped up, but he was quartering away and my first arrow entered too far back of his ribs for a quick kill. The second shaft drove into his lungs and did the job. I'm sure he saw us after my first shot, but I'll bet he thought we were wolves. That's probably why he headed for the pond as a natural escape."

The next week proved to be the most frustrating of my bow-hunting career. The game of wits began at camp when we located several goats with the help of a 30X Bausch & Lomb spotting scope. They were high on the mountain across the lake.

During our first trip up there, Bill and I made an exploratory wide sweep to look for the general area the goats used. It was a different world in those peaks. Though it was Indian summer in the valley, it was almost winter far above timberline. Patches of snow, rocky slopes, and high winds made for tough hunting.

In the afternoon, we found the band of goats about a mile away. They were 100 yards below the top of a high ridge. When I studied them with my 8 x 32 Leitz Trinovids, I couldn't take my eyes off an exceptionally big billy. He was so much larger than the other animals that there was no question he was an outstanding trophy.

While Bill studied the terrain for the best stalking route, I watched as the old billy bedded down. I became more and more convinced that he would rank near the top of any record book. Even at the extreme distance, I could see his long and thick-black horns silhouetted against the light-colored rocks. I decided I'd go to almost any hardship to score on that goat.

"We're going to have to back down this ridge and circle way around to keep out of sight," Bill said. "The best bet is to get behind and above him, then try to work down. He won't expect danger from a higher elevation, but it looks as if that cliff behind

Dr. Eddy takes a break in area of his many unsuccessful attempts to outsmart a record-class mountain goat.

the band may be almost straight up and down. All we can do is try."

The stalk started out fine, but the last several hundred yards licked us. We had to detour down through an area laced with large boulders. A strong wind swirled and seemed to be blowing from several different directions. When we were finally able to check the area where we had last seen the goats, we saw that they were gone.

We walked down and studied the area and learned a few things. The trophy billy was obviously a cunning critter when he chose that particular terrain as a bedding area. The ridge was backed with vertical cliffs laced with honeycombed holes in the rocks. It was an impossible approach route. The front side of the mountain was a wide bowl that gave the goats an open view. There was no way a stalker could work up that bowl without being seen.

But we did discover a trail that the goats used for crossing over to a southern-exposure grassy side ridge. At one place a large chimney of rock bordered the trail. Other well-used goat trails were in the area, in addition to fresh beds, droppings, and other sign.

The next day, we hunted unsuccessfully on another part of the mountain so we wouldn't disturb the big billy too much. The following morning Bill and I left camp long before dawn. It was a three-hour hike up to goat heaven, and we wanted to be there before the animals moved to their feeding area. We piled rocks for blinds near the tall chimney and hid ourselves with camouflaged ponchos and nets. We spent hours practically freezing on the hillside and wondering why the goats didn't show.

Just as we were ready to give up, we spotted the big goat coming down a trail 150 yards away. If he stayed on course, he would walk about 30 yards below me. He wasn't alerted, the wind was in my favor, and I was sure that my shot of a lifetime was moments away. I'll never know why, but the animal suddenly sensed danger. He walked off the trail and passed about 90 yards away. There was no chance for a stalk, so I risked a shot. My arrow flew over his back. He immediately spooked and ran down the mountain.

The next day Buzz accompanied Bill and me when we climbed the difficult route up the ridge. We spent eight hours in blinds and failed to see a single goat.

41

When not hunting, members of the party often caught trout from Duti Lake for camp fish fries.

We planned a different strategy for our third try. Jim and Bill waited for me to circle around the goats, then worked straight up the open bowl of the slope. Their plan was to expose themselves in hopes of driving the band over the ridge where I waited in ambush. It didn't work. The goats watched my partners approaching and then circled around into steep cliffs.

Jim went after them and killed a fine billy with his 375 Magnum Model 70 Winchester. The report of his rifle spooked a larger goat my way. I ran as fast as I could over loose shale to an interception point. When I got there, he was on a cliff just below me. I could hear the goat moving below, but I couldn't see him because of an overhang. At one time I'm sure we were within 20 feet of each other since I could hear him breathing. I couldn't be positive the goat was the animal I wanted, but I'd bet on it.

Bill and I kept hunting the trophy goat for several more days. Once my partner hid in the valley while I climbed around the goats to a good vantage point on a narrow ridge. When the big billy appeared, Bill alerted me with prearranged hand signals. I couldn't see the animal, but Bill directed me to a position behind the goat. Then my companion walked slowly up the slope in hopes the target would top out near me.

The wise old monarch sensed something wrong and angled across the slope. I tried to stalk him on the sharp ridge that kept getting narrower and narrower. Finally I had to crawl on my hands and knees for safety's sake. The wind was whipping hard, and I finally came to my senses and retreated from the dangerous place.

On the last day we hunted the goat, we got within 150 yards of him and then ran out of stalking cover. By then even Bill was frustrated. "Here," he said, "take my rifle and knock him down. That billy's horns are good enough to rank near the top of Boone and Crockett records."

I refused. He had outwitted us fair and square and deserved to be met again on his own grounds with a bow. But there wasn't much sense in spending more time trying to take him on this trip. He was too alerted, our hunting time was running out, and my original objective was to score on a fine mountain caribou.

It would have been perfectly legal for me to kill the goat with Bill's 375 Magnum Winchester. We were hunting during regular rifle seasons. Though I chose to use archery tackle, my license covered the use of firearms or bows. The moose and caribou seasons opened August 15; goats became legal August 1.

Jim was the only hunter to use a rifle on our trip. Our guides carried rifles for possible backup use or grizzly trouble. I hunted with a Bear Kodiak Special 64-inch, 55-pound left-handed bow. I also had a Takedown Groves 60-inch, 55-pound bow. Buzz had two Bear Super Kodiak 60-inch, 55-pound bows. We both used Olympic fiberglass arrows tipped with Bear razorhead broadheads. I also used Kwick Kill razor blades glued to my broadheads with Plybond.

The guide costs for our 10-day hunt were $600 per hunter. We also had to pay $125 each for our flights in and out of Smithers. [*Editor's note:* Guide fees in 1980 were about triple this cost.] A trip such as ours is expensive, but the high cost gets you into some of the best big-game country in North America. During our hunt Jim Mathwig bagged fine specimens of bull moose, caribou, and goat with his rifle. Buzz dropped the big bull moose I described earlier. At one point during the hunt I stalked within 20 yards of a wide-racked moose but couldn't get an arrow away because the bull was almost hidden by thick willows. On the last day of our trip I had my only good opportunity.

The weather was rotten at dawn when Bill and I left camp. Drizzle and hail continued all morning while we worked down the Duti valley. At noon we hunkered over a small fire coaxed from damp wood. Lunch consisted of soggy sandwiches, but while we were eating our spirits got a tremendous shot in the arm. We were glassing the fog-shrouded slopes above timberline when we spotted three caribou bulls.

The animals appeared as mirages as clouds of fog alternately covered and exposed them. They were half a mile above us, just past timberline. The largest bull seemed to dwarf his companions, and his record-class rack was by far the best we'd seen. He swaggered down from a snowbank, then bedded in open grassland.

"Bad news again," Bill said. "There's no way we can stalk upwind because of that steep cliff to his north. There's another cliff below the bull, and there's no way we can get around him. Our only bet is to wait and hope he moves into another area."

As time passed it became obvious the animals had settled for

The mountain caribou Dr. Eddy shot with bow and arrow has a total score of 374-1/8.

the day. We had no choice except to move on and hope to find other game. Thirty minutes later we spotted another caribou bull. This one was near some scrub evergreens at timberline 600 yards above us. He was only an average bull, but as we studied him in our glasses we made a startling discovery. Just below the standing caribou were the antlers of a bedded bull extending above a lush field of summer flowers. It hardly seemed possible, but this animal was a better trophy than the one we had just passed up. And he was bedded in a spot we could approach.

Bill is usually calm, but his excitement built in a hurry as he studied the bull's antlers. I noted distinct nervous tension in his voice when he lowered his binoculars and said, "Lowell, that's one giant of a caribou. I'm sure he'll top Pope and Young records. If the fog doesn't wreck our stalk, I think you can get a shot at him."

My heart was banging my ribs as we climbed up through timber, angled across matted evergreens that had been crushed by winter snows, and sneaked into acres of grasslands and flowers. Bill left me there and pointed to where he thought the bulls were lying.

"You'll have to belly in from here," he whispered.

It took me about an hour to crawl 125 yards through the flowers. They were in full bloom, and some stood about two feet tall. The wind was whipping, the hail was heavy, and the temperature had dropped so much that my hands were becoming numb. Plenty of thoughts went racing through my mind. Had I gone past the animals? Had they heard or otherwise sensed me? Had they spooked when we were making the initial stalk? Was my luck turning sour again?

Those thoughts evaporated in a flash when the younger bull stood up suddenly only 20 yards away. The animal was in a hollow, which was why I hadn't spotted him sooner. He was obviously alarmed, but I didn't pay much attention to him. I wanted grandpa. Then I noted the giant bull's antlers about 35 yards away. He was still bedded. I debated whether to whistle or grunt to get him up. I decided to try for him while he was still lying down.

I raised to one knee, drew an arrow as calmly as I could, aimed just behind the bull's shoulder, and released the shaft. I almost

Posing with some of the trophies at camp are, from left: Bill Love,
Dr. Eddy, Dr. Jim Mathwig, Dr. Buzz Mosiman, and Jack Lee.

died when I watched it zip over the hair on his back. Both bulls were in high gear immediately. They galloped to a knoll 100 yards away, stopped, and looked back.

I was so disgusted that I just slumped into the flowers. In moments Bill crawled to my side. Both bulls still stood on the knoll. The big one was throwing his antlers from side to side, and he was pawing the ground like a jersey steer. He didn't appear alarmed, just mad at something he didn't understand.

I knew that caribou are extremely curious about moving objects, so I whispered to Bill to wave his hat above the flowers. As soon as the young bull saw the hat, he spooked and ran; but curiosity got the best of the king of the mountain. He slowly walked toward us, then stopped broadside to our position. He was 75 yards away, a long but possible shot.

I eased back up on one knee, aimed slightly high to compensate for the wind, then watched the broadhead fly over his back. I'd allowed too much for wind deflection. I immediately sent another arrow on its way. This one felt right when it left the bow. It sliced into the bull's left chest and lodged into his right shoulder area. The giant animal dropped his head, stood for a moment, then walked a few feet and laid down. In minutes he struggled to his feet, wobbled into some brush at timberline, then toppled over on his back. He was dead when we reached him.

Bill slapped me on the back and exclaimed, "I'm sure my guess was correct. I keep up on Pope and Young records, and I've no doubt that you just shot the new world-record mountain caribou."

Two months later Glen St. Charles officially scored the antlers for the Pope and Young Club. The right main beam measures 43-6/8 inches and the left measures 47-1/8 inches. There are 16 points on each antler, the inside spread of the rack is 35 inches, and the total score is 374-1/8. That's a score of 85-7/8 better than the second-ranked mountain caribou, which was taken by Peter Halbig in another area of northern British Columbia. Peter's story of his hunt is also in this book.

(EDITOR'S NOTE: *Eddy's trophy now ranks No. 2 in its category in the Pope and Young Club record book. The No. 1 mountain caribou was taken near Firesteel Lake, Canada, in 1970 by Melvin K. Wolf. It scored 390-1/8.)*

48

Making of a Grand Slam

By Dr. Roy A. Schultz

(EDITOR'S NOTE: *The original version of this story appeared in the March 1972 issue of* Outdoor Life.)

Three desert-bighorn rams stood in the Mexican mountain basin 1,200 yards below us. Browsing among saguaro cactus, they were unaware of us even though we had been glassing from a high ridge for half an hour.

Just before we discovered them, I was wondering how much longer I could keep climbing the torturous terrain in 95°F. heat. Now I took another look at the largest ram's horns through my 7X35 Leitz binoculars. A renewed strength surged through me. I vowed there was no way I'd give up the stalk until that great ram was mine.

We had spotted the sheep from a ridge of about 5,000 feet elevation. The basin they were in was surrounded by higher mountain peaks of the Sierra San Borja range in central Baja California, Mexico. It's a rough place laced with knife-sharp ridges, huge boulders, vast piles of rock, deep canyons, and stretches of soft sand. The only vegetation consists of cactus and desert growth. Everything that grows in this hot and dry climate seems to scratch, stick, or sting.

It was the eighth day of my hunt when Pippy and Johnny, my

While glassing a slope near main camp, Dr. Recio spots a 3/4-curl ram.

two Mexican guides, suddenly discovered the sheep far below us. At first we saw just the white rump patch of the smallest ram. Then, with my Bushnell 20X spotting scope, Johnny had made out the two larger animals as they moved from behind a group of high cactus. They were all respectable rams in their own right, but the largest sheep dwarfed his companions.

"Mucho grande borrego," Johnny exclaimed with great excitement. "Treinta-siete, treinta ocho."

I knew those statements meant "Much large ram with 37- or 38-inch horns." My own glassing of the sheep convinced me that the largest ram wore the most massive horns I'd ever seen. I had waited six years for this moment.

Johnny remained on the high ridge so he could keep the rams in sight. His job was to give Pippy and me hand signals while we made the stalk.

It was a tough descent down through boulders and rocks, and it ended when I glanced up to see Johnny motioning frantically for us to get down. We dropped to the canyon floor immediately. In moments we spotted the big ram walking out on a ridge 500 yards above us. The range was too long to risk a shot, and we had no choice except to crawl into a side gully and climb back up the mountain to plan a new stalking route.

By the time we got back to Johnny's position, the ram had gone.

"Other direction," he said while motioning to an opposite ridge. "Beeg borrego that side."

After I got my breath back, we peeked over the ridge and relocated the sheep. The big ram was butting a barrel cactus with his heavy horns. He was far below us, but apparently content to stay more or less where he was. Pippy surveyed the situation and decided we would have to skirt around steep cliffs to reach the ram's position. I was mentally determining that the hike would be at least two miles when Pippy said, "We march."

I'm 38. I live in Avoca, Iowa, where I practice veterinary medicine, mostly on large animals. I was born and raised on a farm in southwestern Iowa, and that's where I learned to hunt with my father.

My first big-game hunt with a high-powered rifle was in 1961, a year after I graduated from veterinary college and started a practice at Avoca. My neighbor, John Scheffler, interested me in be-

Guides Johnny (foreground) and Pippy study band of sheep on slope of a far mountain.

coming a member of the NRA. Soon after, I bought a 30-06 model 1903A3 Springfield. That fall, John and I hunted on the ranch of my wife's cousin in Wyoming. I was lucky enough to down a real trophy mule deer on that hunt, and I've been trophy conscious ever since.

John and I hunted deer and pronghorn on the ranch for the next two years. After that, I wanted to try for other big game. In 1964, I hunted in Ontario and killed a bull moose. The next year, I made my first pack trip with horses. I went after elk in Wyoming's Shoshone National Forest. I never saw a bull large enough to make a trophy, but I did see some bighorn sheep. That's when the sheep-hunting fever hit me hard.

I climbed my first sheep mountain in the Yukon during the fall of 1967. The day I killed my sheep—a Dall—the weather was as rough as it comes. It was raining in the morning when my guide and I rode our horses as far as they could go up a mountain. Then we started climbing on foot. Halfway to the peak, we were stopped by fog so thick that we couldn't see anything. It finally cleared, but then we ran into hail and snow three quarters of the way to the top.

We kept going, even up on a cliff that we had to climb by finding hand holds in rock crevices. When we crested out, we spotted a basin holding 18 sheep. There were three good heads in the group. We had worked up a sweat climbing the mountain, but after stalking within 300 yards of the Dalls we were so cold in the bitter temperature that we couldn't hold our binoculars steady. My guide finally picked out the best ram and told me to nail him. I was shaking a little, from both the cold and the excitement, so I rested my 300 Weatherby on a rock. My first bullet went over the sheep's back, but the second one dropped him. A fine ram, but not good enough to make the Boone and Crockett record book.

I had gone to the Yukon because I'd twice been unsuccessful in my attempt at drawing a permit to hunt Rocky Mountain bighorns in Wyoming. In 1968 I decided to try for my bighorn in the Canadian Rockies of Alberta. Those mountains make up the most beautiful sheep terrain on earth. They're also the most demanding to hunt. You must climb at a very high altitude over severely steep terrain.

Each day for 14 days I climbed mountains at the head of the

Cline River until my legs grew weak and my lungs ached. You do that because you know that each beautiful mountain basin you climb to may be the long-awaited one that harbors sheep. If you reach enough basins, you'll eventually spot a full-curl ram. I didn't find one on the Cline River trip, though. I went home skunked.

The next fall, I hunted Alberta's Brazeau River area with guide Harry McKenzie. We climbed mountains for 12 days before we spotted a legal ram. Then we hit paydirt when we found six fine rams together in a high basin. They were bedded, but located in such a position that it was impossible to stalk them. It was very windy and freezing cold, but we decided to stay on the high ridge, watch the animals, and hope to intercept them when they moved out to feed before dark.

We shivered for hours, but our vigil paid off. Late in the afternoon the sheep got up, stretched, and walked our way. We didn't even have to change our position. The rams came over the ridge single file, with the best trophy leading. When my Weatherby roared he went down kicking, rolled over and over in the snow, and finally stopped just short of a 500-foot dropoff.

You could say that it took me 26 days of the toughest kind of hunting to score on that bighorn, but I certainly wouldn't put it that way. I'd say my two hunts represented 26 days of extremely enjoyable physical exertion, and of meeting the challenge of mountains in addition to matching wits with ever-watchful sheep.

Sheep hunters are a breed in themselves. I don't think they ever get sheep hunting out of their blood. I've had several outfitters tell me that most hunters have little idea of what the game is all about until they try to climb their first sheep mountain. Many hunters make it about halfway to their first peak and then decide that a man must be out of his mind to climb the dangerous cliffs. They never again go on a sheep hunt.

But the true sheep hunter is enthralled with his first climb. When it's over, he will be planning ahead and dreaming about how and when he can get on his next sheep mountain. In my case I get a tremendous thrill while climbing in the unsurpassed beauty of high places. Nothing quite matches the challenge of climbing up among the clouds where the air is clean and everything is high, wild, and free. You just have to be the type of guy who climbs until his lungs ache and his legs go rubbery, rests a spell, then climbs again and enjoys every minute of it.

Soon after I started sheep hunting, I began thinking seriously of achieving a Grand Slam, the distinction that goes to a big-game hunter when he completes the taking of a ram in each of the four species of North American wild sheep. When I scored on the bighorn, I was two down and two to go.

For two years I had planned to hunt Stone sheep in the Muskwa-Prophet Bench area of British Columbia, but I couldn't get reservations with outfitter Garry Vince until the fall of 1970. My guide on the hunt was Bill Napoleon, a Treaty Indian. He sure knew how to climb mountains and find sheep. We looked over 35 legal rams during five days before I decided on one I was sure would make the Boone and Crockett record book. We stalked within 100 yards of that ram. He never knew what hit him when my 180-grain Nosler handloaded slug broke his spine. The official score of the horns was just four points short of making the record book.

I had long been aware that the ultimate challenge in achieving my Grand Slam would be to score on a desert bighorn. A North American trophy hunter has less chance of getting a desert ram than he has of getting any of the three other species. Among the several reasons, the most important is that desert bighorns are so scarce.

Game managers tell us that though measures were instituted early in this century for the desert sheep's protection, heavy poaching nevertheless cut his numbers drastically. Still, the experts point out that taking the older sheep (only full-curl adult rams are legal targets) has no effect at all on herd survival and alleviates unbalanced sex ratios. Such rams would eventually die of old age if not killed by trophy hunters.

A few southwestern states, plus the country of Mexico, hold special hunts to crop off the older rams. In the United States, desert sheep can be hunted by nonresidents in only Arizona and Nevada.

It's extremely difficult for a nonresident of the hunting areas to draw a permit because they're very limited. I had tried unsuccessfully two times to get a desert-bighorn license in Arizona. I knew my odds on drawing one of the 25 permits to hunt desert rams in Baja California, Mexico, were almost zero, but still I tried.

I got my license application by writing to the Direccion General, Depto. De Conservacion Y Propagacion, De La Fauna Silvestre, Mexico, D. F. I filled out the application and returned it with a certified check for $500, the license fee.

My first reaction to the news that I was a successful applicant was one of doubt that I should make the hunt. The first part of the Mexican split-season was scheduled for the first 10 days of March, 1971. That was only four months after I'd come off my last sheep hunt. My finances and free time weren't in shape for another extended trip, but I decided I'd be crazy to turn down the opportunity.

Then came the problems of setting up a hunt in Mexico. I first contacted Lloyd Zeman, a Des Moines, Iowa, friend who had taken a Mexican desert ram in 1970. He suggested that I get in touch with John Blackwell, another of my sheep-hunting friends who is a securities broker in Midland, Texas. I knew that he had completed his Grand Slam with a desert ram. John solved a lot of problems for me in a hurry.

"Your best bet is to get in touch with Dr. Edmundo Recio," he said. "Dr. Recio is a dentist in Saltillo, Coah, Mexico, but he's also an outfitter for sheep hunters during his vacations. I've hunted with him and he's the best. He speaks very little English, but he's a personal friend of mine. I'll call him and make the initial contact for you."

Later, a letter from Dr. Recio set our meeting spot as the tiny fishing village of Bahia de Los Angeles. It's located on the western shore of the Gulf of California about halfway between Tijuana and La Paz.

Step No. 3 in setting up my hunt was to get a tourist card to visit Mexico and arrange for a gun permit. The free tourist cards are easy to get if you send your birth certificate to any Mexican government tourist department or Mexican Consulate office. Getting a gun permit can be more difficult.

You begin by getting a letter from your local police department or sheriff's office stating that you have no criminal record, that you are a responsible citizen, and that you are not a threat to national security. Then you send the letter, complete with four photographs (two-by-two-inch front view) and a description of

56

your rifle (make, model, type, caliber, and serial number) to a Mexican Consulate office. Also enclose a check for $16, the cost of the gun permit. Keep in mind that you will have to present your letter of good conduct, tourist card, and gun permit to military authorities at the Mexican Port of Entry before they will issue another permit enabling you to carry your firearm.

As a matter of interest, I should mention that Mexican authorities at the Chicago Consulate Office (where I applied for my permits) said my 300 Weatherby was a military caliber and that I couldn't take it across the border. So I substituted my Model 70 Winchester 270.

All of the red tape connected with a Mexican hunt (made tougher by the language barrier) is something you have to put up with. But I contend that the most important preparation for any sheep hunt is to get yourself into the top physical condition that's required for climbing mountains.

I have an advantage over many hunters because of my work. I'm accustomed to wrestling with steers every day to restrain them for treatment. I also use the physical-fitness program featured by the Outdoor Life Book Club. In addition, I always run a couple of miles a day for several weeks before my hunts to get my legs in shape. I got some mighty strange looks from my neighbors when they saw me running up and down snow-covered Iowa streets in February.

My trip began when I boarded a commercial plane and headed for Hermosillo, Mexico. There, at an air-taxi service, I met two other men who were to hunt with Dr. Recio. One, Danny Galbreath, is the owner of the Pittsburgh Pirates. He was accompanied by J. D. (Des) Woods, a rice farmer from Katy, Texas. The three of us flew on a small plane to Bahia de Los Angeles.

Our outfitter was waiting at the airport with two Jeep trucks. We piled our gear into the vehicles and drove south for 40 miles into the mountains. Most of the drive followed two tracks in the sand, and I was amazed to discover that this route was the famous Baja Road. We saw no traffic signs, and we passed only two ranches.

We finally left the road and drove up a canyon to Dr. Recio's main camp. The entire camp consisted of one tent, three trees, and a water hole dug into the sand of a dry creekbottom. I left

Danny and Des at this point. (I learned later that they both scored on fine rams.) They were to go up into the mountains to a fly (spike) camp with our outfitter, while I was to go to another fly camp with my guides Pippy and Johnny. Both guides are 43-year-old Mexicans who can neither read nor write. Pippy (Jose Romero Gonzalez) is a turtle fisherman during the off-season, while Johnny (Juan Angel Martinez Romero) is a ranch hand.

We left the main camp and drove about 15 miles to a ranch house and corral in another canyon. There we loaded our gear on three mules that Dr. Recio had arranged for—I was told that horses can't survive in that mountain country—and rode them 10 miles up the canyon. Eventually we had to dismount and lead our mules up the treacherous side of a canyon wall to a plateau. It was quite a climb through loose rocks and cactus. I'd take three steps forward and then slide back two. The near-100°F. heat didn't help either. Even so, I was glad to be out of the homemade wooden saddle that had jolted every bone in my body.

Our fly camp wasn't much, just a flat spot cleared in the cactus where we laid our bedrolls. We didn't have a tent, and our supplies consisted of two five-gallon cans of water and a pack box of food.

We hunted out of that base for two days until Pippy decided we weren't seeing enough sheep. We moved our camp higher up the canyon, and relocated near a dry creekbed.

Each day we would hunt out in a different direction. We didn't use the mules. Instead, we climbed on foot, and were always climbing by 6:30 in the morning. We'd climb and glass the rocky ridges and basins until late afternoon, and then we'd descend to our camp. I'd guess we walked and climbed an average of 10 miles each beautiful day. The weather was unbelievably clear and hot during the days. The nights were cool.

I could have killed a legal ram several times during the first seven days of the hunt. We saw sheep on six of those days, and eight of the 35 or 40 animals were adult rams. Once we spotted three fine rams that bedded down out of sight before we could study them in the spotting scope. We made a perfect three-hour stalk to within 150 yards of the largest ram. I passed him up when I estimated that his horns wouldn't measure more than 33 inches. I was determined to hold out for a record-book trophy.

On the eighth morning of the hunt, we started up another of the area's many side canyons. We found sheep tracks in the sand on several ridges. Once, Pippy laid his doubled fist inside one especially enormous track and said, "Much beeg sheep."

Another time we found big tracks where a sheep had brushed against a bush. The animal had knocked loose some leaves that had then fallen to the ground. The leaves hadn't wilted yet when we spotted them in the intense heat . . . a sure sign the tracks were very fresh.

We worked our way up a ridge, stopping frequently to glass the surrounding terrain. It was shortly after noon when my guides spotted the three rams I mentioned at the beginning of this story. It took Pippy and me about two hours to make the unsuccessful stalk I described. Now we started our second descent on a new route.

We made a wide skirt around the ridge, picked our way through cactus, worked across a black-shale slide, slipped and skidded down between huge boulders, and then crossed a bed of beautiful quartz pigmented with red and green minerals. Eventually we were down in a basin that was blooming with spring desert flowers. We paused once to rest in the shade of a giant saguaro cactus. We saw where a sheep with the same idea had previously pawed out a bed in the sand.

We glassed back up the mountain, and Johnny signaled everything was going fine. Then we walked back into the scorching desert sunshine and climbed a rocky ridge. We knew the trophy ram should be in a basin on the other side. As we topped out, I noticed an oddly-shaped two-pronged cactus below us. I was looking for that landmark. The rams had been browsing next to it when I'd last seen it from the high ridge. Now there were no sheep to be seen. We glassed Johnny again. This time he signaled that the ram was right below us.

I was getting jumpy now. I knew we must be very close to the sheep, so I set my Redfield variable scope at 2X to gain a sighting picture with a wide field of view. Suddenly, a clattering of shale sounded from behind boulders 150 yards below us. The rams were obviously off and running, but for several horrible seconds they didn't show. Then they burst into view, running like wildfire up a draw to my left. The big ram was leading, and he was bolting

After eight days of climbing mountains, Dr. Schultz scored on his fine desert ram. With a total score of 173-3/8, the trophy made the Boone and Crockett record book.

for a twisting canyon that would put him out of my sight in a hurry. I had time for two shots at the most.

I knew my first bullet went low when it blew a small creosote bush off the ground under the ram's belly. When the rifle recoiled the second time, I heard a resounding "phunk" as the 130-grain handloaded slug smashed into flesh and bone. The big ram went down dead with a broken neck, and he rolled over and over down the canyon wall for 50 yards.

My Grand Slam was achieved. I learned later that I was the 220th hunter in the world to accomplish such a feat. It took me 62 days of hard climbing over a five-year period to finally take a sheep that ranks well up in the Boone and Crockett record book.

Mike Cupell, an official Boone and Crockett Club measurer from Phoenix, Arizona, measured my trophy on May 22, 1971. He came up with a total score of 173-3/8. It would have been higher except that the horns were well broomed. The right horn measured 36-7/8 inches, the left 37-3/8.

I knew that the ram was a giant while I was shooting at him, but I didn't realize how massive the horns were until I ran up to the dead animal. They seemed far too heavy for his slender neck. After Johnny arrived, we caped out the head, boned the meat, and started the six-mile hike back to camp. It had taken most of the afternoon to stalk the ram, so we had to descend much of the mountain in moonlight.

It was a long trip, but Pippy and Johnny soon had coffee boiling and sheep ribs roasting over a mesquite fire. I glanced at the ram's horns as they were highlighted by the flickering campfire. I was the happiest man alive.

Trophy for Two

By Harry E. Troxell III

(EDITOR'S NOTE: *The original version of this story appeared in the January 1972 issue of* Outdoor Life.)

The most important thing going for a bowhunter is the ability to get so close to a game animal that you can almost smell it. The cardinal rule is to use stalking techniques continuously. I ignored that rule on September 12, 1970, and missed a chance at a giant bull elk.

I had everything in my favor. Wrinkled gray clouds were hanging over the eastern slope of the Rockies west of Fort Collins, Colorado. Early-morning dew made the ground moist, a condition that's perfect for noiseless walking. A light breeze was on my face as I eased into a mountain drainage covered with lodgepole pines, aspen, and grassy meadows. It was familiar territory. I'd seen plenty of elk in the same area during past years.

For a couple of hours I sneaked around deadfalls and studied the forest ahead with my 7x35X Bausch & Lomb binoculars. I couldn't find any fresh sign, and soon became convinced that no game had used the basin for weeks. As a last resort, I tried bugling with my homemade elk call. There was no answer. I concluded that my best bet was to walk over a ridge and head down into another basin.

I came to a game trail as I started up the thick lodgepole slope. At one time it had been used heavily, but now it was barren of tracks. Moments later I approached a large bunch of blueberry bushes nestling in timber above me. I considered glassing that underbrush, decided it was a waste of time, then walked briskly ahead.

Suddenly I saw something moving in the midst of the undergrowth. Then my eyes zeroed in on the enormous antlers of a royal bull elk. The animal was lying down less than 50 yards away. The movement came when he turned his head to investigate the first slight sound of my approach.

Then things happened so fast I didn't have time to nock an arrow. As soon as the bull saw me, he exploded from the bushes and bolted up the ridge as if there wasn't a twig in front of him. He didn't dodge or run around anything, he just barreled over and through anything that was in his way. Dead tree branches snapped like pistol shots as his rack ripped between pines.

I was especially disgusted with my blunder because I'm a trophy hunter. That statement isn't unusual until I qualify it. When I jumped the bull I was only 22 years old, I had been hunting with archery tackle for nine years, and I had yet to score on any big-game animal.

I'm single and was born and raised in Fort Collins. Most kids growing up in this area develop outdoor interests at an early age. I enjoyed all types of sports, whatever was in season. I had the usual interests in hunting with firearms during my early school years, but I also had a desire to play football. By the time I entered Poudre High School, I had to choose between football and hunting since both are fall sports. I decided to stick with athletics. There would be plenty of time for rifle hunting after my high-school and college years.

Then, because Colorado archery seasons normally open in mid-August, I began trying to score on a deer or elk with a bow. That way I could spend a week or so in the mountains before reporting for football. My first four years of bowhunting were dismal failures. I often hunted two or three days in a row without even seeing a big-game animal.

About that time, a mutual friend introduced me to Ben Alexander. Ben is now 28, married, and the father of two small children. He works for a water-filter plant in Poudre Canyon, 20 miles west of Fort Collins. He grew up in the same area, and has a great

63

fund of mountain lore. When I first met him, he was 22 and had an earnest interest in bowhunting. He invited me to hunt with him, and I accepted eagerly.

That was the beginning of a very close friendship that has grown stronger through the years. The thing that intrigued me most about Ben was his dedication to the possibility of taking a real trophy with an arrow.

Ben readily admitted that he was crazy to try beating the odds, but he figured he had a chance if he tried long enough and hard enough. He'd killed several fine mule-deer bucks with a rifle, so that challenge was gone. He was also convinced that the object of hunting should be enjoyment, not the prospect of harvesting meat.

Ben figured that if he drove an arrow into an average deer or elk, his hunting season would be over for the species he killed. He reasoned that holding out for a big-racked animal offered a chance for success until the season ended. Most of all, he wanted the challenge of going after the very best on even terms.

I wasn't as trophy conscious as Ben during the first two years that we hunted together, but I soon picked up his way of thinking. That's one reason why neither of us—until the 1970 season—had made a bowkill.

Though Ben and I were unsuccessful for so many years, it wasn't because we failed to get shooting opportunities. We're picky about long-range shots. We don't like to draw an arrow unless we're within 40 yards of an animal. Many times both of us missed possible chances because we tried to get closer to fine trophies.

We messed up some good shots too. Once my partner stalked to within 15 yards of a 5-point elk. The bull heard the arrow rubbing against the bow while Ben was drawing. At the instant of release, the elk whirled and bolted. The broadhead missed by a split second.

The best shots I've had have been at timber mule deer. One time I got within 30 yards of a big 4-pointer. He was standing uphill from me near an aspen grove. I misjudged the steepness of the slope and overshot.

Another time I stalked a 5-pointer that was feeding along a sagebrush ridge. I closed the distance to 25 yards and was preparing to shoot when I spooked a doe I hadn't seen. By the time she made one jump, the buck was in high gear. Once I had an easy shot at a similar buck, but my arrow smashed into an aspen between me and the target.

My hunting hopes for 1970 were jolted when I was drafted into the Army on February 3. At the time I was working on a master's degree in computer science at the University of Arizona. While I was in basic training at Fort Lewis, Washington, I was sure there would be no hunting for me that fall. Then, by a stroke of luck, I was assigned to the Division Data Center at Fort Carson, Colorado. My outlook brightened even more when I learned that I could take a 20-day leave in September.

The 1970 Colorado archery season for deer and elk ran from August 15 through September 20, so I scheduled my leave to begin September 1. When that date arrived I hurried home, bought my hunting licenses, and packed my gear.

Ben and I usually hunt two general areas about an hour's drive west of Fort Collins. One area is good for both mule deer and elk, and the other harbors more elk but fewer deer. While discussing the situation with Ben, I decided to head for the better deer area and hunt it during the first half of my leave. Ben couldn't get off work and join me for about two weeks, and I knew that he was primarily interested in hunting elk in the second area.

"I'll drive my camping trailer in there on September 11th," he said, "but I can't start hunting until the 13th. You base at the trailer and scout for a couple of days before I join you."

We discussed more details, and then I headed out on my own. I drove my car as far as I could up an old logging road. A large 9,500-foot-high watershed covered with lodgepole pines, aspens, Douglas fir, and grassy meadows stretched for miles to the north. My plan for each day was to be out at dawn, hunt until dark, then return to my car and camp there nights.

I was still looking for my first shot of the season after a week of hunting. I wasn't discouraged, because the weather had been perfect and I'd seen 21 deer and eight elk. Not one of the animals wore antlers, but I had a lot of fun making practice stalks. I sneaked to within 15 feet of a deer, and I managed to get within 60 feet of an elk.

On September 8, I drove to Ben's home to make sure his hunt-

65

ing plans were still on schedule. Then I put in three more days of uneventful hunting. Late that last evening I loaded my gear into my car and drove 15 miles to the area where my partner had said he'd park his trailer. The comfortable unit was a welcome sight. Ben made it himself out of aluminum siding. It has an 8-by-17-foot base and is eight feet high. It's equipped with two sleeping couches, a table, a gas stove, lantern, and refrigerator.

The next morning I began scouting our elk-hunting territory, which is a bowl-shaped drainage eight miles long by four miles wide. Ben and I always found elk somewhere in this drainage when we hunted it. More often than not we'd find a herd in the particular basin I mentioned at the beginning of this story. That's why I headed for that spot first. As I pointed out earlier, I couldn't believe the lack of fresh sign. I shouldn't have gotten careless, but after blowing my chance on the royal bull I resolved to hunt the area as cautiously as possible.

For the next few hours I reverted to my normal hunting techniques. I'd stalk ahead about 10 yards, then glass the terrain around me. In heavy timber it's almost impossible to spot game before it sees you unless you do more glassing than sneaking. The almost constant use of binoculars is tiring on the eyes, but it's essential for a bowhunter to use an extraordinary amount of patience.

I continued my careful sneaking and glassing for several hours. Then I had to move on a bit faster since my primary purpose was scouting. It was late afternoon by the time I reached the southeast end of the drainage five miles from the trailer.

That's when I began spotting fresh elk tracks and droppings in a large stand of lodgepole pine and Douglas fir. The farther I progressed, the more I noticed that elk activity seemed to be everywhere. Numerous trees bore recent rub marks of antlers. One of those rub jobs astounded me. The pine was rubbed bare of bark from ground level to about 11 feet high. This rub was much higher than any I'd ever seen. The bull that made it had to be a giant.

I was so absorbed with my discoveries that I didn't pay much attention to a building storm. But as soon as rain began belting down, I headed out in a hurry. Then the temperature plummeted and the rain changed to sleet driven by a high wind. It was long after dark when I reached the trailer. I was soaked through, and my clothes were half frozen.

The next day I hunted unsuccessfully near the trailer since I didn't want to disturb the herd before my partner's arrival. Ben arrived in the evening and listened to my news with ever-increasing smiles.

"They're way back in the corner of the bowl," I explained. "That's too far away to hunt full days from the trailer. Our best bet is to pack into the area and stay near the herd."

The next morning we loaded our backpacks with camping equipment that many hunters might view with surprise. Our gear is selected on the theory that the quickest way to spook game from an area is to advertise your presence with scent or noise associated with humans. Consequently, we cold camp. In other words, we never use fires for cooking or warmth. We pack in food such as canned lunch meats, fruit, and other ready-to-eat items that don't require heating.

Cold camping may be uncomfortable, but it eliminates the sounds of chopping wood and many other normal camping activities. A bowman usually must get within 50 yards of his quarry, and that's almost impossible if your clothes carry odors of smoke or cooked food. It's especially improbable if game is already alerted to human activity. Though we could have driven close to our destination with Ben's four-wheel-drive vehicle, we didn't even consider it because of the noise.

During our hike to the corner of the drainage, a wet snow storm reduced visibility to almost zero. We were almost to the camping site I'd selected when we heard an elk go crashing from a grove of pines ahead of us.

"There we go, Ben," I exclaimed. "I told you they were in here."

An hour later we had my two-man nylon pup tent stretched between trees near the edge of pines that bordered a small meadow. A meandering creek flowed behind our campsite. We were in an ideal spot.

It was early evening by the time we'd finished eating and organizing our archery gear. We use Black Widow bows manufactured by the Wilson Brothers Company in Springfield, Missouri. Mine has a 53-pound pull. Ben prefers a 48-pound pull. We use

With homemade elk call, Harry Troxell sends out a challenging bugle in the aspens.

Bear quivers and make our own arrows from Easton XX75 aluminum shafts. We fit them with Bear magnum razorhead tips.

All of our caution paid off. We found action almost immediately after we began hunting. We were less than a quarter mile from the tent when I blew my first bugle. The high-pitched notes had barely died when an answering challenge came from across the basin. Again I bugled, and again the challenge was returned, closer this time.

After several more exchanges of bugles, we knew the bull was closing in fast. Soon we could hear his gurgling grunts in timber along the opposite edge of a 200-yard-wide meadow in front of us.

Then the bull became cautious. For an hour he continued answering my bugling invitations to fight, but he wouldn't yield his position. Daylight was fading, and it was now too late to make a stalk.

Ben and I separated and bugled from various spots along the edge of the timber. The bull began moving back and forth opposite our locations, but he still wouldn't show himself. Darkness eventually put an end to the game of wits.

As we walked back toward the tent, I gave one last whistle on my call as a sort of salute to the excitement. We were astonished when the bull answered from directly across the meadow. He was listening to our movements and following a parallel route.

Several times during the night we were awakened by ringing bugles in nearby timber. It was almost impossible to sleep when we knew a bull elk was so close to us.

We were up before dawn. Stars glittered in the sky, frost covered our archery tackle, and our camouflage clothes were frozen stiff. It was barely light enough to see when we were studying the tracks the bull had made in snow the night before. Ben is normally a quiet guy, but now he could hardly contain his excitement.

"I've never seen elk tracks that huge," he said. "If we get that animal, we're going to have a real good bull."

We hunted hard all day without success. We heard a few distant bugles but didn't get close to any game. A warm sun melted remaining patches of snow, but by late afternoon a cloudy, cold dampness settled into the valley. We returned to the tent, prepared some food, and were adjusting our elk calls when we heard

69

a faint bugle on the near ridge of the basin. We didn't pay much attention until 10 minutes later, when the bellowing whistle sounded again. This time it was so close that we scrambled for our bows.

The bull was grunting up a storm now. We heard brush snapping and guessed his position as not far into the pines and fir on the other side of the 50-yard-wide meadow in front of our tent. Our best bet seemed to get across the opening and into the timber before the elk reached the meadow. We could have made it easily by running, but we knew the bull would hear us if we made the slightest sound. We sneaked as fast as we could go for 25 yards; then Ben slammed to a halt. I stopped beside him.

"Look," he stammered in a harsh whisper, "I see his legs below the branches! He's coming straight at us!"

Then I saw the bull's legs as they moved into a dense clump of pines directly in front of us. We nocked arrows, positioned our bows in front of our bodies so we could shoot with as little motion as possible, then froze. The short-grass glade offered no cover to hide in, and we had no choice except to stand motionless.

I don't recall seeing the bull emerge from the pines. It seemed as if he jumped into the meadow. He was just there, standing broadside 30 yards away, completely in the clear. His great rack was held high and his body seemed swelled with overbearing pride. His arrogance so absorbed him that he didn't even notice us.

We drew our bowstrings at the same instant. My arrow flew first, Ben's zipped away a split second later. The bull heard the twangs of the strings and snapped his head toward us. His body seemed to shrink in fear and his eyes bulged with disbelief when he spotted us. As he lunged to his left, I saw a light-colored arrow that had driven through his back. The shaft was plainly visible on each side of the animal. I knew it was Ben's arrow since mine was camouflaged.

The bull was gone almost as quickly as he had appeared, but it sounded as if he were crashing out of control through the trees. Then the commotion ceased. We figured he was down, but we waited 45 minutes before following the blood-sprinkled trail. We wanted him to stiffen if he was only wounded. We found the dead bull just 90 yards from where our arrows had sliced into his body.

The two hunters pose with their trophy. Harry's on the left, Ben on the right.

When we field-dressed him, we discovered that either arrow would have killed the animal. Mine had broken a rib and slashed a gaping cut through the liver. It had produced so much internal bleeding that it put the elk down after his short run. Ben's broadhead had smashed a hole through the bull's backbone just above the spinal cord. If the arrow had been an inch lower, it would have dropped the trophy in his tracks. The wound would have killed the elk in a short time.

These facts led to the question of which one of us should legally claim the bull. That decision was necessary since state law requires that an animal be tagged immediately after the kill. If our friendship wasn't what it is, there might have been some difficulty since we were well aware that our bull's massive antlers were bound to win some recognition.

We finally decided I should tag the elk since my liver shot was a little better placed and caused quick death. Still, I'm convinced that Ben held his draw a bit too long in order to give me the first shot. He's the type of guy who would do a thing like that and never admit it.

A thick fog had blanketed the basin by the time we finished our field-dressing chores, so we decided to stay another night in camp. The next morning we marked a route from the bull to an old logging road by hanging small, blaze-orange trailmarkers from branches of trees.

Then we hiked back to the trailer and drove Ben's vehicle to his parents' home. His dad Herb, who is a lifelong firearms hunter, was enthralled with our story.

"Well," he said with a grin, "I didn't think you fellows would ever get a bull with those sticks. If your elk is as big as you say, I can't wait to see him."

Herb, Ben's wife Marion, and my brother Jim all went with us in Herb's jeep to help with loading the animal. The vehicle is rigged with a winch and pulley arrangement that made short work of the job.

After a 60-day drying period, we had the antlers scored for the Pope and Young Club by Marvin Clyncke of Boulder, Colorado. The main beams measured 47-7/8 inches and 49-3/8 inches. There are 8 points on the right antler, 7 on the left, and the tip-to-tip measurement is 45-1/8 inches. The total official score is 367-3/8.

That score is good for the No. 2 ranking in the Yellowstone elk category of Pope and Young Club records of North American big game. The world record has a total score of 376-6/8. It was taken by Jack Sheppard in Idaho. That means Ben and I scored on the best trophy elk ever taken in Colorado with archery tackle. It has been entered in Pope and Young Club records under both of our names.

Though such a joint entry is highly unusual, it does have a precedent. In 1957, hunting partners Dr. James Rumbaugh and John Ruyan fired their rifles simultaneously and dropped a typical whitetail buck in Ohio. Their trophy won first award in its category in the 1958-59 Boone and Crockett Club big-game period. The names of both those men are jointly listed in the record book as well.

(EDITOR'S NOTE: *The enormous bull elk taken by Troxell and Alexander still retains its No. 2 ranking.*)

Tactics for a Giant Mule Deer

By Bill Crouch

(EDITOR'S NOTE: *The original version of this story appeared in the April 1978 issue of* Outdoor Life.)

In July 1977 at the Denver Museum of Natural History, I received the Boone and Crockett Club award for the second-best typical mule-deer buck taken in North America during the previous three years. Getting the award was the highlight of my life, but something I saw in the museum also gave me an enormous sense of satisfaction.

The museum has many glassed-in wildlife displays, which are remarkably true to life. Each one features several specimens of mounted animals arranged in lifelike settings. The displays are complete with appropriate trees, bushes, grasses, rocks, and other natural features. The entire background of each display is a curved wall that is painted with scenic details complementing the foreground setting. When you look at one of these displays, you're looking at what appears to be many square miles of natural wilderness habitat.

The mule-deer display really caught my eye. In the foreground are several deer, including an average 10-point (Eastern count) buck. Far in the background is a tiny painting of an enormous trophy buck. You have to look carefully for several minutes before you can find him. He seems to be far in the distance—across several canyons, draws, and valleys. I'd bet that not one deer hunter in 10 would even notice that buck in the display. And not one hunter in 100 ever sees the biggest bucks in the wild.

My award-winning buck is not the first big brute I've taken. It's the only one of more than 40 bucks I've killed that made the record book, but I've downed other giants with massive racks. I've seen bucks that were as good as my award winner or better. When you hunt my way, you're almost bound to get your chance at a top trophy sooner or later.

My method of hunting is about as inexpensive as you can go. I can't afford to hire guides or rent horses. The key to my system is to mix a lot of hunting knowledge with a maximum amount of hunting effort. That display in Denver really tells it all. The big bucks are always way back in the roughest country that most hunters never see.

There are no gimmicks to my system. I do my trophy hunting on one million acres of public land. The thing is that most mule-deer hunters don't really hunt. They're out in the woods with a rifle, and they think they're hunting. But they don't really know what it takes to get close to bucks with trophy racks.

I'm 34. I was raised on a farm in East Texas. Hunting and fishing were a way of life in my family, so I was in on the action when I was a small boy. I killed my first buck when I was nine.

My grandfather decided I was old enough to help get some meat, so he fixed me up with a single-shot 12-gauge loaded with No. 00 buckshot. We didn't have much trouble finding a small 4-point whitetail. When Granddad told me to shoot, I touched off. Talk about getting kicked. That single-barrel gun just about spun me around. But my aim was true, and the little buck went down in his tracks. I probably told the story 100 times to the kids I knew.

Through the years I killed lots of Texas whitetails, and also made weekend hunts in Oklahoma, Arkansas, and Louisiana. I got my share of deer, but I never saw a real trophy buck until 1965.

One of my brothers-in-law had been hunting deer in Colorado for several years. He finally came home with an 11-point monster boasting an antler spread of 29 inches. I couldn't believe my eyes when I saw that muley. I didn't realize deer could get so big. Right

75

then I developed an enormous desire to hunt mule deer in the West, but I didn't get there for years.

I make my living as a painting contractor. By a stroke of luck, I teamed up with another painter on a job in 1970. Wayne Webb and his dad hunted mule deer in Colorado three different times, but they hadn't been back there in a couple of years. I talked up a storm about making a hunt, and I guess my enthusiasm really wore off on Wayne. We talked with his dad and pretty soon we were making specific plans.

This situation was made to order for me. Man's fear of going alone into wilderness he has never seen and knows nothing about had kept me from going to Colorado for five years. Now I had a chance to go with guys who had experience. All our talk about hunting conditions, weather problems, and huge deer was like a dream to me. I cataloged all the information in my mind. I had learned years before that the more you know about deer and hunting conditions in a specific area, the more successful you're going to be. This first hunt would be just a preliminary training session for me. I already had it in my mind that I'd go back every year until I scored on the buck of a lifetime.

I was lucky on that first hunt. I dropped a 7-point, 175-pounder with a 24-inch spread. It was the largest deer I had ever taken. But I saw bucks taken by other hunters that were far bigger. I wondered how those guys got those bucks. It had to be that they knew a lot more about how to find big-buck country than I did. Studying the subject became a passion with me. I read every book and magazine article about deer hunting that I could find.

The next year I got my own group together. Three of us went back into the same area I had hunted the previous fall. We didn't do well, though I finally killed a forkhorn. We saw a lot of deer but no bucks of the type I was after. In 1972 we tried a new area, but stayed with it for only two days before moving on. By this time I knew what I was looking for.

By now we were in the Montrose, Colorado, region. We weren't just moving about aimlessly; we were looking for what I call good trophy country. In looking for what I wanted, I was following a principle that many deer hunters ignore. I think most hunters find a chunk of woodland that looks like it should be loaded with deer, then hunt it with little regard to reading the signs that tell whether or not it is good hunting country.

A large chunk of deer range is something like a big lake. About 50 percent of the lake will contain no fish, even though all of the water may look like good fish habitat. The other half of the lake's water will contain fish, but only 10 percent or less of that water will contain big fish. Deer occupy their habitat in the same manner.

In a way, deer are just like people. Most people live in a town or city that offers the work necessary to support their needs. Such human-population centers aren't just anywhere. Towns and cities develop in the precise geographical locations that offer the most benefits to their citizens. Concentrations of mule deer are similar. They live in the part of the range that best suits their needs for food, water, shelter, and safety. Big bucks will utilize only a small part of range that all seems to be good deer country. The trophy-hunter's job is to find big-buck country before he ever gets down to serious hunting.

Most of the so-called experts who write deer-hunting stories in outdoor magazines claim that pre-season scouting is the only way to locate good deer country. This sounds great, but it isn't at all practical for most of us. How am I going to scout in Colorado when I live 1,000 miles away in Texas? Any nonresident deer hunter has the same problem. I knew when I first went to Colorado that I'd have to hunt in the state for years before I really knew the hunting country. That's the only way I could scout. I hunted 40 square miles of the Rockies before I wound up in the area where I downed my award-winning buck. The nonresident—unless he hires a guide—must do his scouting while he's hunting. There are some shortcuts, however.

One highly important thing is to make local contacts. The best way to make good contacts is to spend your money with the locals who know the hunting picture. I made it a point to buy my gas at the same gas station, groceries in the same little store, and hunting supplies and licenses in the same sporting-goods store.

Walk into these places once and you're just another stranger. Walk into them several times—and leave some of your money for things you need anyway—and you become a friend. Once the locals get to know you, and accept you as a serious sportsman, they'll readily share their knowledge and offer advice. They'll also tell you about big bucks because it's human nature to tell stories about trophy deer. Practically any hunter who sees a huge buck, or hears about one, will tell the story to friends every chance he gets.

The real key to getting a trophy mule deer is to hunt those very small parts of the overall range that big bucks utilize. This strategy takes an enormous amount of physical effort.

The only way a trophy buck gets his huge rack is by living long enough to develop it. This usually takes at least four or five years. By the time a buck gets that old, he has had plenty of narrow escapes from hunters.

Such a buck knows that trouble is coming each fall, when the woods become alive with a sudden invasion of cars, trucks, and campers. When a smart deer sees camps being set up, hears chainsaws cutting campfire wood, and sees many humans in the forest, he knows a new hunting season is about to begin. He heads into the most remote and roughest country he can find.

Big mule-deer bucks always get into country that's too rugged for the average hunter. They're relatively safe there, and they know it. The guy who hunts no more than a mile or two from backcountry roads or jeep trails is never going to see these monster bucks. The only way you'll get into trophy-buck country is to go into the very bowels of the roughest and most roadless terrain in the mountains. When you get down into one of these canyons, hunt it a while, and then start out, you'll know you've got one enormous climbing job on your hands. By the time you reach the top, you'll feel like throwing your rifle away. But guys like me always go back for more punishment because the big bucks are always the hardest to get.

The way to hunt this type of country is to camp as far away from the towns as you can get. The campsite I use now is nearly 50 miles from Montrose, the closest community. From there I walk into my hunting area, which is about eight miles away. I found the area on the third day of my 1972 hunt.

Before daylight that morning, three of us drove a jeep trail that wound back into some good hunting country. After we parked the Jeep, I headed out on foot, going back into an area that 4WD's can't reach. I finally got back into some deep canyons and valleys that were loaded with all kinds of deer sign. Once you find an area that's loaded with fresh tracks, fresh droppings, and well-used game trails, you know you're in an area of deer concentration. I

78

worked on down into the bottom of a valley, still-hunting and taking stands along the way.

Suddenly I spotted a deer herd that contained 40 to 50 animals. Later I watched a herd of elk that included a magnificent 10-point bull. I didn't get a shot that day, but there was no doubt that I had found one of those very small parts of overall range that are best suited to the needs of a lot of deer. I got into camp long after dark that night. I figured I had walked 18 to 20 miles over some of the roughest country in Colorado.

The next morning I was back in that valley before daylight. I heard deer running off in the dark. I found a good vantage point that allowed me to look out over much of the floor of the valley, and then I took a stand. Within the next hour I watched several deer move down a small draw about 500 yards away. I didn't spot any big bucks, but it was obvious that this draw leading to the valley's floor was a major travel route. I moved closer.

Shortly two does and a forkhorn came down the draw. One of the does kept looking back. I figured there might be a big buck following her, so I scoped every inch of the thickest cover. Suddenly I saw the flash of a deer's ear. As I stared at the precise area, I began to see parts of the deer's body, including a very big rack of antlers. That buck was just standing there in a patch of spruce. He must have known something was wrong even though the other deer had no inkling of my presence.

I put the crosshairs on his lung area, touched off, and put the 10-pointer down instantly. When I inspected him, I guessed his weight at 275 pounds. Now the work started. I was four miles down in a canyon and seven miles from camp. I quartered that big brute and packed him out of the canyon. Then I walked to camp to get help.

I should back up here and tell you my ideas about camping in this country. An efficient camp is vital to efficient hunting. If you make a mistake with camping gear when you're 1,000 miles from home, your hunt is ruined even if you're a millionaire. If you haven't got the proper equipment, you just can't run back to the closest motel when you're 50 miles from town. You have to think of everything before you take off on trips like mine.

We use two (sometimes three) tents. The two main tents measure 12 x 14 feet and 10 x 10 feet. I also have a 9 x 9-foot tent that we occasionally use for storage. Our main cooking stove is a three-burner butane unit with an oven. I also take two Coleman stoves. We use one to dry clothes and keep water and food from freezing. The other is a spare. The big tent is where we eat and sleep. Everything is dry in there at all times. You must be dry and comfortable at night or you can't hunt efficiently the next day.

Your selection of clothes is very important. Weather in the Rockies during hunting season can vary from 75°F. to 10° below zero. You have to take clothes for all conditions. Your other items must match weather conditions too. Snow chains for your vehicles may become a necessity. An extra battery is good insurance, and so is a set of booster cables. We take everything that might be needed. Even our medicine box is carefully planned. A month or so before we leave home, we take all of our camping gear out of storage and check every item.

We have collected our equipment over a period of years. Now that that expense is out of the way, our trips are pretty inexpensive. We usually take $200 each and bring money back. The major expense is $90 for a nonresident Colorado deer license. A few years ago it was only $50. I refer to my annual fall hunt as my "working man's vacation."

Some of my usual hunting companions couldn't make the trip in 1973, so my stepson Gary Sligar and I headed back to Colorado's Uncompahgre National Forest on our own. Gary was 16 that year. He hadn't been West before, but he had learned a lot about deer hunting during our many years of hunting in Texas. There was no question about where we would hunt. We'd hike back into the valley where I'd seen all the deer and shot the 10-pointer in '72.

This valley is about 400 yards wide and 1,000 yards long. It narrows as it goes up the mountains at about 8,500 feet elevation. One side is heavily forested with a mixture of pine, juniper, spruce, and aspen. Scattered aspens dot the valley's floor and its western side. Just over the top of the western side is a large expanse of jungle-like spruce thickets mixed with cedar and pine.

The first morning, Gary and I came in from the east side of the valley. We took stands for a couple of hours, saw no deer, and then began still-hunting toward the western slope. When we started up the slope, we spooked three big bucks. They went over the top so fast we couldn't get a shot. Gary took off running up the hill in hopes of seeing the bucks on the far side. He was puffing when he came back. "They ran into those greens and disappeared," he said.

The "greens" Gary referred to were the spruce thickets. I could have kicked myself. This area of thick spruce trees had to be a bedding area. If we had come in from the west side of the valley, we would have intercepted the deer moving toward their bedding ground. As it was, we pushed them right into it.

We came in from the west the next morning, but we were a little too late. We'd had to hike several miles farther to reach our new approach area and the deer were already in the greens—all except one monster buck that we jumped. I had just enough time to snap off two quick shots before he bolted over the ridge. Both missed. I ran to the edge and looked down into the valley, hoping the buck would cross it. He was too smart for that. We found out later, from studying his tracks, that he went over the side and then doubled back into the greens.

That buck wore the most massive antlers I had ever seen. Gary killed an 8-pointer and I got a 10-pointer before our hunt was over but their racks weren't nearly as impressive. Those antlers haunted my dreams for the whole year before our 1974 hunt.

Three friends made that trip with Gary and me. They were John Medford, a painting contractor; H. R. Medford, a painter I employ; and Don Pugh, an air-conditioner repairman. We camped in the same spot I had been using for several years. Some of the fellows did a little scouting the afternoon before opening day. Gary and I stayed in camp because I think scouting is the worst thing you can do when you know where you're going to hunt. It makes no sense to disturb a place if you know deer are there.

We all hit our sacks that night at about 10:00 p.m., but everybody was so excited about opening day that we didn't get much sleep. By 1:00 a.m. John was out of his sleeping bag and digging around in our grocery box. Then we all got up. After two pots of coffee, nobody could think about sleeping. We cooked up a batch of bacon and eggs and toast, polished it off, and then just stayed up.

Gary and I had just about finished our long hike to the valley

81

when daylight began breaking. We saw four does near the edge, but no deer in the valley. That didn't bother me because I figured the animals weren't moving toward the greens yet. We went down over the edge of the valley to the place where I wanted to take stands. I put Gary behind a large aspen tree near the top of the slope, and then walked 40 feet farther down to another big aspen. I had a good view of the valley's floor. My plan was to intercept deer on their way to the greens. Between Gary and myself was a cattle trail that angled up the slope. National Forest land is leased to ranchers during spring, summer, and fall, so it's not unusual to see these trails far back in remote wilderness.

Within moments, two does came out of the draw at the far end of the valley. They walked toward us on an angle and passed within 100 yards. Then three more deer came out of the draw. I saw antlers as soon as I saw them. It registered on me right away that two of the animals were huge bucks with massive antlers. The muleys were more than 300 yards away, but even at that distance the antlers were more visible than the bodies. When you see a sight like that—when all your eyes can focus on are enormous racks—you know you're looking at outstanding trophies.

I alerted Gary that he should get down and get ready to shoot. The two bucks and the doe had no suspicion of our presence. I figured that the deer would keep coming in our general direction for 100 yards or so, then turn broadside up the slope. They didn't. When they got to the cattle trail, they turned up it and walked straight at us.

The bigger buck began angling off to my side when he was about 80 yards away. I eased up my Sako 243, found his chest in my 3x-9x Leupold scope, and sent a 100-grain slug on its way. The buck went to his knees, but then regained his footing and bolted straight ahead. He had no idea where the shot had come from. I fired again at almost point-blank range. The huge buck hunched up when my second bullet hit him in the lung area, but he still didn't go down. He raced past me no more than 20 feet away. By this time I was well aware that Gary's 270 Winchester was roaring too.

I whirled around and fired again. This bullet put the giant muley down for keeps. At the same time I saw my buck going down, Gary's ran into view. But that muley was dead on his feet too. He caved in and hit the ground within 10 feet of my trophy.

I choked up. There's no greater thrill than scoring on the best buck of your life, unless you're there when your son gets his best buck. It was almost impossible to believe that a father-and-son team could drop two enormous bucks at the same time and in the same place.

It wasn't difficult to figure out what had happened. When I fired my first shot, all three deer had bolted straight at us. Mine ran past me while the other buck and the doe swerved around Gary. When they got past us, they closed ranks. But by then, the two bucks were mortally wounded. It was just by chance that they fell together.

Gary was almost beside himself while we ran the 30 yards to the fallen deer. The first thing he did was count points. All Texans count the points on both sides of a buck's rack. "Mine's got 13," he said. "Your's only has 12."

I got out my tape measure and found that the outside spread of my buck's antlers was 37-1/4 inches. Circumference at the base of each antler was 7-1/4 inches. Gary's buck had a 33-inch spread. I guessed the live weight of each deer at about 300 pounds. While we were field-dressing our animals, I knew it would be an enormous job to pack all that meat out. I decided it would be best to hike back to camp and get help.

When we arrived in our camping area, we found Bob King at his nearby campsite. Bob is a police officer in Montrose, and he's also a trophy hunter. He always takes part of his vacation during deer season. He has plenty of time to hunt, and he's always more than willing to help other hunters. When he heard about our bucks, he was just as eager to see them as he was to help us get them out. He asked if we could get to the animals in his Jeep.

"No way," I said. "We might get within 1,000 yards or so, but that would be it."

Bob shortened that 1,000 yards a bit with some of the most incredible driving I've ever seen. Many times he had to back up and go forward again to get through the aspens. He went down one slope that was so steep I jumped out of the vehicle because I thought it would surely turn over. Eventually, even Bob decided he could go no farther. When he got his first glance at my buck, he said he was absolutely certain it would make the record book.

Bill Crouch is on the left with his typical mule deer. On the right is Crouch's stepson, Gary Sliger, with buck that has an inside spread of 33 inches.

Up until then, I hadn't even thought about the record book. I'd heard about the Boone and Crockett Club, but I had some strange idea that it was exclusively some kind of a setup for millionaires. Now I know that anybody can make the club's record book—which is now published jointly by the Boone and Crockett Club and the National Rifle Association. But the catch is that you must score on a big-game trophy outstanding enough to meet or surpass the minimum requirements for listing.

The 1977 edition of the record book lists 288 entries in the category of typical mule deer. These 288 bucks are the best typical mule deer ever taken in North America. Mine, with an official score of 209-3/8, ranks No. 14.

Best Pronghorn in 100 Years

By Edwin L. Wetzler

(EDITOR'S NOTE: *The original version of this story appeared in the September 1978 issue of* Outdoor Life.)

I'd been stalking the buck for more than 15 minutes, and the tension had mounted during every second. I was crawling along a tiny draw in Yavapai County, Arizona. The pronghorn (popularly called antelope) was unaware of me, so I decided to rest my aching elbows and knees, get my breath, and try to slow my pounding heart. I was just too excited. I kept telling myself that if only I didn't blow the stalk, the buck was mine.

A half-hour before, I'd spotted the buck lying in a small depression about 500 yards away. I looked him over with my binoculars, then decided his horns had to measure a very respectable 16 inches. I sneaked back down the hill, walked around it to the closest approach point to the buck, and then bellied down in the dirt. A crawl job of about 250 yards would put me in fine shooting range.

I knew that if I botched the stalk, I'd have nobody but myself to blame. I was positive I wouldn't be bothered by other hunters because I was several miles inside the K-4 Ranch. The ranch was fenced, all the gates were locked, and vehicles were prohibited.

Other hunters could get walk-in permission as I had done, but I was sure no strangers were within miles.

After I got my nervous tension under control, I began worming ahead again. The pads on my elbows and knees cushioned my contact with the ground. I made another 100 yards with no problems. I was so absorbed in my mission that I didn't hear the Jeep until its engine gunned near the top of a rise 150 yards to my right.

Startled, I whirled to see the vehicle crest the rise. Then I jerked around to my left and saw the buck running full speed for the protection of a draw. Though the range was nearly 300 yards, I took a quick shot with my 300 savage. The 150-grain soft-nosed bullet erupted a tiny cloud of dust in line with, but below, the buck's shoulder. I'd aimed too low. Before I could line up a second shot, the pronghorn was gone.

For a moment my mouth hung open with amazement. Then I got mad, very mad. All my efforts had been ruined by those jokers in the Jeep. I wondered how they'd gotten through the gates. Then frustration hit me. I got to my feet, dusted off my clothes, and decided that this was just one more incident in a hunt that had been full of frustrations since its beginning.

Though I couldn't know it at the time, that Jeep turned out to be an enormous blessing. If it hadn't arrived on the scene, I almost certainly would have scored on that buck. If I had downed him, I wouldn't have been able to hunt the next day—a day destined to become the most memorable of my life. On that day, September 21, 1975, I killed the best trophy pronghorn taken since 1878.

I'm 36, and I work as a utility mechanic in Chandler, Arizona. I've been hunting ever since I was 12. My dad and I always go deer hunting in Camp Wood, Arizona, but I've made lots of other trips for bear, elk, javelina, pronghorn, and small game.

I guess the desire to take a trophy animal of any kind eventually comes to every experienced hunter. In any case I became absorbed with the idea of scoring on a truly outstanding pronghorn. I rate the taking of a prime antelope as the ultimate challenge in big-game hunting.

There is no other animal like the American pronghorn. He is the sole surviving species of a group that ranged the West two million years ago. He has no close relatives and is found nowhere else in the world. To top things off, there is no big-game animal that stacks the odds so highly against the hunter. The antelope lives in unbroken miles of almost barren plains that stretch away to the horizon. This vast, empty landscape offers practically no cover for the hunter.

I am always in awe of the pronghorn's physical capabilities. He can run with blinding speed, his marvelous eyes afford a field of vision that covers nearly 360 degrees, his sense of smell is at least as good as that of a deer, and his enormous lungs enable him to run for miles with almost no effort.

If you're in the right place at the right time, you can luck into most other big-game animals. You may be able to call a trophy elk or moose into easy shooting range. You may have a deer or bear walk past you while you're concealed in thick cover. But you cannot call a pronghorn, and you cannot hide in thick cover on open prairies!

The one thing that doesn't favor the pronghorn is the fact that he can be very visible. The same lack of cover that enables antelope to spot hunters at a great distance also allows the hunter to spot his quarry. Once you find a buck, he's yours if you can stalk within good shooting range. Though this is often an impossibility, there are some things in your favor.

First is the fact that the prairie is not as flat and devoid of cover as it may appear. There are always rolling hills, rises, cuts, draws, coulees, and ditches that you can use for stalking cover. You often will run out of such cover before getting within shooting range, but you can sometimes try another route when this happens. You have to live with the belief that you can sneak up on any pronghorn alive if you take the best advantage of all available cover.

You need dedication to develop this mental approach. I've hunted pronghorn for many years, and I've forgotten how many bucks made a fool of me because of my stalking mistakes. I'd often get disgusted, but I'd always tell myself, "There will be more bucks later. Each one will teach you something new, so keep trying."

The most important key to a successful stalk is to know that MOVEMENT is an instant danger signal to antelope. Once a buck spots movement of any kind at any distance, he'll focus on it until he can see if it represents danger. The lesson to be learned here is that you'll seldom get a smart buck if you hunt by vehicle. You must walk into prime hunting range because you have to spot your buck before he spots you.

The best way to spot a buck is to walk to a place that offers a good view of a large lay of land. Approach that place from a direction which will keep you concealed from any pronghorn that may be in the area you intend to check. This is usually accomplished by walking in draws or behind hills and rises. Belly up to the crest you intend to look over, visually examine the terrain as it comes into view, then go to work with a good pair of binoculars.

Now is when MOVEMENT begins to work for you. Antelope wander loosely when they're not hunted, but they tend to gather in herds after hunting season opens. Some animals in a herd may be bedded, but some are almost always moving—and moving animals can be seen at great distance with good optics. Most trophy bucks are usually solitary animals, but they're often near a herd nonetheless.

Expect a big buck to try melting into the landscape. Carefully glass every clump of bunchgrass and every part of the terrain that a buck could utilize to hide himself. Work with your glasses for an hour or more before giving up. It's far better to stay in one spot with a good view than it is to hike all over the landscape. A pronghorn's eyes are far better than yours, so the less you move the better. Unless you're stationary, it's almost a sure bet that a buck will see you before you see him. Again, it's impossible to successfully stalk a buck that is aware of your presence.

The key thing I learned during my early years of pronghorn hunting is that the upright stalker is rarely successful. If you don't stalk on your belly, you're going to be seen. You have to worm along on your elbows and knees. In my opinion, the most important equipment a pronghorn hunter can own is knee and elbow protection. You can't crawl very far on the prairies without knee and elbow pads. Expect to get dirty, dusty, and cramped.

Pronghorn stalking calls for an enormous amount of patience, too. Most of the stalks I botched resulted from being in too much of a hurry. The inexperienced stalker always feels that his buck is going to move away before he gets within shooting range. He consequently rushes the job. Actually, if your quarry is not alerted to danger, there is no reason for him to spook. Be as quiet as possible, and make a very slow stalk.

When the time came to apply for my 1975 Arizona antelope permit, there was no question as to where I wanted to hunt. I'd hunted on the K-4 Ranch twice before, and had killed fine bucks both times. I knew the area harbored plenty of pronghorn, and I knew the lay of the land too. This is an enormous advantage. The hunter who knows where antelope are most likely to be also knows those precise places where he can glass for bucks without being seen.

Jim Embree would make the hunt with me if we were both lucky enough to draw permits. This would be his first big-game hunt. We grew up together, went to school together, and have been lifelong friends. Jim, who's 35, didn't develop an interest in hunting during his early years because his parents and relatives didn't hunt. His interest in the outdoors began when he started courting his wife, a woman who thoroughly enjoys fishing, camping, and other outdoor activities. I think he always had the hunting bug in him, but he just never had the opportunity until he began hunting small game with me several years ago.

My childhood activities were loaded with hunting adventures. My dad, Art, developed a tremendous interest in hunting before I was born. He has hunted all legal game in Arizona except mountain lion, bear, and buffalo. His trophies include desert sheep, elk, mule deer, whitetail deer, javelina, turkey, and pronghorn. He has drawn permits to hunt pronghorn five times, and has taken five bucks. A lot of the hunting skills I have were developed with help from dad. He would be the third member of our hunt if he were lucky enough to draw another permit.

The three of us mailed our applications for permits in early June. The drawing date came and passed. Dad received word that he was unsuccessful in the drawing, but Jim and I heard nothing. Frustration began to mount day by day. Finally we decided that it was almost impossible that neither of us had a single word from the Arizona Game and Fish Department.

We called the department to find out what had happened to our applications. None of the officials we talked with could find any record that we had ever applied. Our long-planned hunt appeared to be down the drain.

About three weeks before the pronghorn season was scheduled

90

to open, Jim and I received letters from the Department. The letters explained that our permit applications—along with 10 others—had been misfiled. Since the error was not ours, the Department had decided to award permits to all 12 of us.

Two weekends before opening day, Jim and I drove to our hunting area in the Big Chino Valley north of Prescott. We intended to drive onto the ranch and scout, but when we got there we found that all the gates were locked. This surprised me because the ranch had always been open to vehicles when I'd hunted there before. I wanted to find out what had happened, so we drove to ranch headquarters and talked with owner-manager Johnny Khiekeffer.

"Well, I've had it with irresponsible hunters," Johnny told me. "I tell these guys not to drive off my established roads, but some of 'em don't pay any attention. Tire tracks in this country are bad news. They turn into deep ruts when it rains hard, and such ruts tend to ruin the range.

"Litter turned me off too," he continued. "I'd let most hunters camp back in the ranch, but some of 'em left their litter scattered all over. And I have to pick that stuff up. But the final straw was too many open gates. I told every hunter who ever came on this place to close each gate he opened. Well, some of those guys don't seem to hear very well. It takes too much of my time to round up cattle that get into the wrong areas. So, this ranch is now closed to hunters in vehicles. But you can walk in and hunt any place."

Later I told Jim that Khiekeffer was just one more landowner who has had too much trouble with slob hunters. "It's beyond me why some guys won't respect the rights of others," I said. "The guys who abuse their hunting privilege are causing more and more problems for all legitimate hunters. Still, the message just doesn't seem to get across."

The K-4 Ranch is about 12 miles wide. It mostly consists of open prairie covered with grass that's eight to 12 inches high. There are a few rolling ridges, some small and large washes, and some rolling hills showing a few stands of cedar.

The land goes into pine forests as it rises into mountains. We accomplished our scouting by walking over hills and glassing the terrain. We spotted several herds of antelope, and everything looked promising for opening day.

We were back in the hunting area a day before the season

91

opened to do more scouting and set up camp. I almost always camp on my hunts because I think it adds a great deal to each adventure. If I couldn't sit outside at night in open places and watch the stars and listen to the sounds of the outdoors, I'd figure I was missing a lot. Motels are for less adventuresome hunters.

Since there are few trees in the area, and since we couldn't drive onto the K-4, we had to find a shady campsite that would be suitable for hanging game. We eventually got permission to camp on the Wine Glass Ranch, which is the next ranch south of the K-4. There are very few pronghorn on this ranch, but we found a fine place to base Jim's pickup camper.

Dad drove up on Friday evening. Though he couldn't hunt, he had offered to help Jim with his first try for a pronghorn. That night, we mapped out our hunting plans for the next morning while grilling steaks and sitting around our campfire. We spread our sleeping bags under the stars and turned in early.

The next morning at dawn, I dropped Jim and dad at a locked gate on the K-4, then drove on to another area. I walked several miles into the ranch and glassed valleys and hillsides. I spotted several small herds, but couldn't pick out a single buck. About noon I walked out to the vehicle and headed back to meet my companions for lunch.

I waited at the gate for more than an hour, but they didn't show up. I figured they might have a buck down, so I decided to walk on into the ranch and look for them. I covered less than a mile when I came to a small hill. I climbed it, then glassed the prairie beyond me. I spotted the two men far out in the flat, walking toward me.

As they closed the distance, I saw that Jim had made a kill. Through my 7X50 Hurricane binoculars I could see that both men had dried blood on their hands and forearms. There is very little water in this area. When you field-dress a buck, you don't wash until you get back to your vehicle or camp.

Jim was so flushed with success that he couldn't talk about anything except his buck. Dad just wore a knowing grin. He began telling me what had happened.

"We were hunting slowly," he said. "We did a lot of glassing without spotting any bucks. Then we heard a couple of shots way off in the distance. I figured another hunter had some antelope moving, so we dashed up a small hill to see if anything was coming our way. Right away we saw a buck running on an angle toward the other end of the hill.

"I told Jim to run back down the hill and hurry over to try intercepting the animal. As soon as Jim took off, the buck changed his route. Now he was moving straight toward the place where Jim would top the other end of the hill. They almost ran into each other. They weren't 50 yards apart when Jim spotted the buck coming right at him. He was so surprised that he didn't even take time to aim. He just threw up his 30-06 and fired. He missed, of course, and the animal blitzed around the hill and disappeared.

"We figured he was gone for good," dad continued. "Then we spotted him about a mile out on the prairie. He slowed to a walk and then stopped. I guess he decided he had run far enough. We glassed him for a while, and he acted as if he were going to stay where he was. I worked out the best stalking route, then we took off. I think Jim better tell the rest of the story because I still can't figure out what was going through his head."

"Just too much excitement all at once," Jim chipped in. "When that buck almost ran over me, and I missed him, it really shook me up. I was positive I'd never get another chance. All during our stalk I figured that pronghorn would be long gone.

"We finally arrived at the bottom of a small rise. Art whispered that the buck should be on the other side, and that I should crawl up to the top and peek over. When I peeked through the grass, I saw an antelope about 100 yards below me. It was looking away from me, but I swear I couldn't see any horns. I was dead sure that the animal was a doe. Buck fever can do strange things to a man.

"When Art realized that I wasn't going to shoot, he crawled up to take a look. Right away he whispered, 'Jim, that buck won't stand there forever. Nail him!' I thought he was wrong. I just looked at him and said that the animal was a doe. Art insisted that I shoot, so I found the animal's shoulder through my Weaver scope and touched off."

"When that 150-grain slug hit the buck, he went down in his tracks," dad continued. "We ran down the rise and measured the horns at just less than 15 inches. We field-dressed the animal, then dragged him for a mile before we realized we were way late for our appointment with you. We hung the carcass in the shade behind a cedar tree. It's about three miles from here."

After a lunch of sandwiches, candy bars, and jerky, Jim and I headed back into the ranch to get his buck. There wasn't a cloud in the sky, and it was very hot. We wanted to get the carcass back to camp, skin it, and cool it.

We'd walked about two miles when we stopped to glass a small herd in the distance. We maneuvered behind some rises and stalked close enough to get a better look. My binoculars picked up two small bucks, but I wasn't interested in either one. Then, through force of habit, I glassed the complete area around us. My heart skipped a beat when I zeroed in on a nice buck lying in a small depression about 500 yards away. I began the stalk I described earlier that ended when the Jeep ruined my efforts.

Jim and I continued on to where his pronghorn was hanging. It was evening by the time we finished dragging the carcass to the locked gate. Back at camp, we skinned and washed it and hung it in a tree to cool. Fall nights on the prairie get quite cold when the sky is clear, and there was no question that the meat would be stiff and chilled by morning. We had just enough strength left to grill steaks, bake potatoes, toast some garlic bread, and wash it all down with a couple of beers. There was very little time to celebrate Jim's good luck before we fell into our sleeping bags.

We were up long before dawn. We polished off a breakfast of leftover steak and eggs, packed some lunch, filled our canteens, and got ready to drive back to the K-4. Dad headed for home, but Jim wanted to walk with me even though his hunting was over.

We were well into the ranch before daylight. My plan was to get into a deep wash before it got light enough for the pronghorn to see us. Once in the wash—it was about 10-feet deep—we could walk along while occasionally crawling to the top to peek out over various sections of prairie. We went through our crawling acts several times before I spotted an antelope about a mile away.

As soon as I got my binoculars on the animal, I knew I was looking at a buck of a lifetime. You usually have to study horns to determine if they're trophy size, but these horns were so long that they seemed to dominate the whole animal. This buck was by far the best I'd ever seen.

The pronghorn was walking in a direction that paralleled our wash, so we just kept even with him for more than a mile. Then he turned away from us and walked over a small hill. We broke out of the wash and dashed for the hill. We slowed down at its base, crawled to its top, and peeked over. A wave of disappointment swept over me when I surveyed the area. The buck was nowhere on the prairie below us. We quickly glassed the whole terrain and couldn't find any sign of life. It seemed as if the buck had evaporated.

I learned long ago that antelope can be very difficult to spot if they're bedded, so I went to work with my binoculars and began glassing the entire area again. This time I discovered a small herd lying down about 500 yards away. The enormous buck wasn't among these animals, so I decided to stalk around the hill. The pronghorn almost had to be just out of sight.

The odds are all against you with this kind of stalk. If you don't know exactly where your quarry is, it's a sure bet that he'll see you before you see him. That's exactly what happened. I hadn't gone more than 150 yards when the buck broke out of a small wash to my left. He was in a dead run by the time I saw him, and he was heading straight away. There was absolutely no question that he was the same buck; those enormous horns simply dominated the scene.

Even though the range was already 250 yards, I had been mentally prepared for a quick shot at a running target. My first slug slammed home into his upper rib cage with enough force to turn him broadside to me. I thought it slowed him down, but he was still running so fast that my second bullet hit the ground behind him. I took a longer lead, fired again, and broke a front leg. He just kept running. The fourth slug took him high in the back leg. This one put him down.

As he hit the ground, I realized that I was shaking. From the instant I'd spotted him, I'd been overwhelmed with the thought that he was getting away. It seemed that my bullets didn't have enough power to knock him off his feet. The feeling that I was losing my trophy was so great that my nervous system just flew out of balance. I stared at the fallen pronghorn for several moments before I knew it was all over. It wasn't until after we had him field-dressed that I calmed down enough to light my pipe.

The thought that I had a record-book pronghorn didn't occur to

The horns on Edwin Wetzler's trophy are massive in all respects, but their length is the most incredible feature of all.

Jim Embree (left) got a very fine pronghorn during the hunt. Notice the extremely long prongs on Wetzler's huge buck.

me until we had the buck hung back in camp. Some other hunters came by, and one of them told me that my trophy should rank well up in the Boone and Crockett Club record book. That statement really fired me up.

Months later my horns were scored by a Boone and Crockett measurer. Early in 1977, I received an invitation to the Sixteenth North American Big Game Awards Program in Denver on July 9. This program honors the takers of outstanding big-game trophies. When I received that invitation, I knew my pronghorn was something special.

I learned during the program that my trophy had a total score of 93. The world-record pronghorn, the only one that has ever scored higher than mine, has a total score of 101-6/8. It was taken in Antelope Valley, Arizona, in 1878. The third-ranking pronghorn also was downed in Arizona. It was killed by Wilson Potter in 1899, and it scored 91-4/8.

My trophy has horns that are 18-2/8 and 18-3/8 inches long. The corresponding measurements for the world-record pronghorn are an even 19-4/8 inches. The name of the hunter who took that animal is unknown, but I often wonder if he was as startled as I was when he first spotted his trophy. I'd bet a lot that he also wondered how an antelope could grow such massive horns.

A Phantom to Remember

By Jeffrey A. Brunk

(EDITOR'S NOTE: *The original version of this story appeared in the November 1971 issue of* Outdoor Life.)

The three does exploded from a brush-covered draw. They bolted across an opening and then melted into a small patch of timber 200 yards ahead of me. I heard those whitetails almost as clearly as I saw them because the farm country in northeastern Missouri was coated with heavy frost. It was bitter cold, and the blanket of white crackled as the deer raced away.

Dawn was half an hour gone on that November morning back in 1968. I wasn't interested in the does, but I wondered why they ran into small thickets when bigger woodlands were close by. Walking was so noisy that there wasn't much sense in trying to be quiet. I got within 150 yards of the thickets, and then the three deer took off again.

This time they ran across an open bean field and headed for a larger woods a quarter mile to my right. I was watching them run when a sudden crashing of brush erupted in the trees where the does had been. It took me a split second to whirl around, but the buck was already running full speed along the route the other deer had taken.

I choked up as soon as I spotted him. There was no doubt that I

99

was experiencing my second encounter with the Phantom. The buck was an enormous whitetail in body size, but it was his rack that took my breath away. The antlers were huge, seemingly outsize, but their color was what produced my eerie feeling. The massive tines were almost pure white. They seemed ghostly against the frost-covered hills.

I almost stumbled as I shouldered my Springfield single-shot 20-gauge. I took a careful lead ahead of the streaking buck and fired.

The slug exploded in frost behind the deer. I broke the action, fumble-fingered another shell into the gun, held a little higher, moved the barrel farther ahead of the target, and slapped the trigger again. A second cloud of frost erupted off the frozen ground. That one was just under the buck's belly. Then the Phantom ran over a knoll in the bean field and momentarily disappeared.

He was still in the open when he came into view again, but he was too far away for another try with the shotgun. My breath went out with a helpless gasp as I watched the old monarch run across the field and disappear into timber.

For minutes I fought the despair of extreme disappointment. Finally my mood changed to anger. I got about as mad as a 16-year-old boy can get. I wasn't mad at myself; I was mad at my dad. If he hadn't insisted that I hunt deer with a shotgun, I might have killed that buck.

"Sure," I told myself, "if I'd had a rifle I could have kept shooting."

I ran all the way home, stampeded into the house, and blurted out my story to my folks. Without being disrespectful, I made it very clear that shotgun slugs are useless for shooting at long-range bucks.

"Somehow," I emphasized, "I'm going to have a new rifle come next deer season."

I'm 19 now, and I attend Northeast Missouri State College where I'm majoring in animal science. I plan to get a B.S. degree and then go on to some university and get a master's degree in wildlife management. Those plans reflect my great interest in farming and hunting.

My folks own 245 acres of fine farmland four miles north of

Revere, Missouri. Dad rents an additional 45 acres. Our hog herd consists of registered Hampshires, and we grow a lot of corn to feed them. We raise up to 1,000 head of fat hogs each year.

The terrain around our farm is ideal deer country. Oak, hickory, and other hardwoods make up most of the woodlands, although we also have a lot of cedar. The underbrush is so thick in places that a man can hardly fight his way through it.

Our timber areas aren't as vast as the forests of northern states. Most of them vary from less than an acre up to 100 acres or more. The trees border pastures and corn and bean fields. The woodlands are hilly and harbor numerous ditches and draws running into croplands.

Our whitetails don't have any wintering problems. They have an unlimited food supply, and the thick woodlands offer perfect cover. The mineral content of our soil also helps to produce big-racked bucks, especially north of the Missouri River. This bright picture is a relatively modern development.

Back in 1936 Missouri's statewide deer population was estimated at no more than 2,000 whitetails spread over 28 counties. Thirty years later, in 1966, Show-me hunters harvested 28,423 deer. The whitetail population explosion is the direct result of fine game management by our state conservation department. Some of our northern counties have shown amazing herd growth. Our farm is in Clark County, where the deer kill jumped from 56 in 1960 to 239 in 1968. Biologists say Missouri's whitetail herd is still growing.

I was lucky that my deer-hunting career was getting under way at the same time the herd became well established. But I was bitten by the hunting bug even before then. Dad has been a hunter and trapper all of his life. I used to follow him on small-game hunts until my ninth Christmas, when he gave me the 20-gauge and I branched out on my own.

During the next few years I supplied the makings of many quail, rabbit, waterfowl, and pheasant dinners. When game seasons weren't open, I went after varmints. I carried my shotgun afield every chance I had. But dad wouldn't give me permission to hunt deer until I turned 14 in 1966.

I couldn't wait for the fall firearms season, so I bought a 50-pound Ben Pearson fiberglass bow. I bowhunted without success

101

from the first of October until the gun season opened. I was after deer just about every minute I wasn't in school, doing chores, sleeping, or eating. I found many well-traveled runways, feeding grounds, and bedding areas. I saw plenty of deer, but I wasn't clever enough to get within deadly arrow range.

I hunted with dad the first day of the firearms season, but neither of us got a shot. The next day dad had to work, so I was on my own. I hunted all morning without even seeing a deer, then walked home for lunch. After that I helped with chores until mid-afternoon, when I decided to still-hunt some nearby timber.

An hour or so later I jumped a big deer that was bedded under some cedars. The first thing that caught my eye when the whitetail bolted was the huge rack of antlers. The buck lined straight away across a small clearing. He was about 30 yards out when I aimed at his neck and touched off the 20-gauge. The slug went true and the buck pitched face down as if he'd been clubbed by an invisible hammer. He was dead when he hit the ground.

I didn't realize what a fine trophy I'd taken until dad and I got the buck home. The field-dressed carcass weighed 215 pounds and the 12-point rack was massive.

"Jeff," dad said, beaming, "your first buck is probably the biggest you'll ever shoot. I don't think I've ever seen a bigger deer. You're a lucky hunter."

At the time I figured dad was right. That was before the Phantom came into my life.

In Missouri it's legal for anyone of any age to take one deer with a gun, and another with archery gear, so I was able to keep hunting until the end of December. I scored on a button buck, but most of the time I was developing my hunting methods.

I soon found out that when deer are moving—early and late in the day—it's best to take a stand. If they're traveling to feeding and bedding areas, they'll walk within easy range if you're in the right place. I learned to pick spots where two runways meet or cross, as you double your chances of seeing deer in such places.

It surprised me that I saw more deer while I was still-hunting. When I was first learning still-hunting techniques, I'd just get glimpses of white flags flashing through the timber. But as time went on, I figured out how to get closer to the animals.

My theory is that a deer hunter is almost bound to find action

102

if he has an intimate knowledge of his hunting area. If you know where given herds feed, travel, and bed down, half of your still-hunting problems are licked. In other words, you're not still-hunting in hit or miss fashion; instead, you're concentrating on sneaking into specific areas over totally familiar terrain. Knowing your hunting territory means you can take precise advantage of wind conditions and cover areas. A skilled still-hunter sees plenty of deer because he knows where the animals are going to be at all times during the day—not just early morning and late afternoon. This principle doesn't hold true in vast forests, but it works great in the scattered timber of farm country.

The secret to success with my system is being in the woods so much that I'm practically living with the deer as they move about. During the off-season after I scored on the 12-pointer, I was afield often enough to discover some amazing facts. I learned that I could recognize individual bucks, and that I could come close to predicting what time of day they would move through a given area. I knew how many deer were in certain timber stands and what travel routes they used when hungry, tired, or spooked.

There was only one thing that stumped me during those scouting sessions. I kept running across an enormous set of deer tracks that were widely spread with unusual flares made by the hoofs. I often checked the tracks of big bucks after I jumped them, but I couldn't match any fresh tracks with the huge, mysterious imprints.

The puzzle was solved two days before the 1967 firearms deer season opened. I had just finished a day of quail hunting with three friends. It was dusk when we came out of some timber and headed for a road. Suddenly, we spotted three deer standing near the edge of a field 300 yards away. At first I thought I was looking at a doe and two fawns. Then I realized that I was staring at two adult does and a giant buck.

The more I studied the buck, the more I wondered if my eyes were playing tricks with me. The first thing that startled me was the sight of his almost-white antlers. For a moment I thought I might be looking at dead tree limbs. Then the buck moved slightly and the tremendously long white tines of his rack came into focus.

I hardly had time to realize that he was far larger than any buck

103

I'd ever seen. Then he seemed to evaporate. I did catch one glimpse of him while he was running, and that sight will be burned on my mind forever. The Phantom looked more like an elk than a deer. He ran with a very majestic gait, head held high and barely moving at all. Then he was gone. It was almost as if the buck had been a mirage.

I rushed across the field and looked at his enormous tracks. They were the same widely spread and unusually flared imprints that I'd seen before. A queasy feeling came over me when I realized how cunning that whitetail had to be. It was hard to believe that I hadn't spotted him a single time during my months of dedicated scouting. That's when I named him the Phantom.

The Phantom eluded me completely during that fall's gun and bow seasons. I followed his tracks several times and they helped me determine his home area. There wasn't much question that he stayed in an area of a few square miles just east of our farm.

I didn't say much to anybody about that buck during the hunting season, but later I decided it was a good idea to find out if any of the neighbors knew about him. I drew blanks with everybody.

"You sure you saw a buck that big?" asked one farmer. "And you claim his antlers are almost white? Seems like such a buck couldn't help but be noticed in farm country."

When the 1968 summer came along, I spent days following the Phantom's tracks. They told me quite a story. I discovered that he never traveled on specific trails, and that he never came out into feeding areas on routes used by other deer. He seemed to wander aimlessly through his territory, but there must have been a scheme to his travels. I decided that I'd never get that buck by taking stands along trails because he never used them. My only chance would be to still-hunt.

During the gun season that fall, I had the chance at the Phantom that I described in the beginning of this story. Some of my message to dad about the problems of hunting deer with shotguns rubbed off because he let me use his Winchester Model 94 30-30 while he was at work. One morning while still-hunting, I jumped a nice 10-pointer and dropped him dead with a shoulder shot. Then I switched to bowhunting for the rest of the year. I never saw the Phantom again.

My explosion about guns had a far more reaching effect than I had expected. When I graduated from high school the next spring, my folks presented me with a new Browning semi-automatic, Grade II 30-06 rifle.

I fitted my rifle with a 4.5X Weaver scope containing Duplex crosshairs. I wanted a low-power scope since its wide field of view would be excellent for the snap-shooting opportunities presented in still-hunting.

When the November 15-23 gun season opened, dad and I were joined by my uncle, Larry Brunk, a dentist from Burlington, Iowa, and my cousin, Greg, a college student from Burlington. Dad scored in a hurry when he dropped a six-pointer the first morning.

I saw one doe that day, and no deer at all the next day until late afternoon, when Greg and I decided to still-hunt some woodlands east of the farm.

Dusk was turning into evening when we spotted a deer running through a cornfield in front of us. The animal stopped near the edge of some trees 75 yards away, but it was almost dark and we couldn't tell if it was a buck or doe. Then the deer moved its head slightly and we could see he had a rack. Greg's rifle roared and the 7-pointer went down dead with a broken spine.

That fall I was attending junior college in Keokuk, Iowa, about 20 miles from our farm. I was living at home, but I didn't have much time to hunt except on weekends. My Uncle Larry came up on the Wednesday following opening day and killed a large 10-pointer. Now I was the only one in the foursome that hadn't scored.

The next Saturday I still-hunted from dawn to dark and jumped two does for my efforts. I went to bed early that night because Sunday would be my last full day of hunting during the gun season. I had a new plan that might work.

I'd discovered that the Phantom had a habit of bedding down in tiny timber patches on ridges close to big woodlands. He was especially careful to do this when hunters were in the woods. I suppose he reasoned that he could see in all directions from tiny cover areas, and that he could drop down into big, adjacent woodlands when trouble developed. I planned to still-hunt every likely piece of small brush in his area.

Dawn came on chilly with a slight overcast and a light breeze. I began to follow my schedule of still-hunting ridges. My plan involved walking silently to likely spots, stopping and looking, then moving on. Three hours of effort went for naught.

About mid-morning I walked down a ridge, crossed a creek, and started up a grassy hill leading to another ridge covered with scattered clumps of cedar and scrub oak. I was moving slowly and the grass allowed silent travel. As I look back on the situation, I'm sure the Phantom never even suspected I was on that hill. I'm convinced he simply decided on his own to move.

I was halfway up the hill when I saw a slight movement in a cedar clump 100 yards above me. Then, as if by magic, a huge, white set of antlers appeared above the cedars. I didn't see any other part of the deer except that ghostly white rack seemingly hung from the sky.

The antlers started to move as if they were floating in air. The buck was walking very slowly, so I lined my scope on an opening in the cedars and waited. I was half scared to death that he would hear my heart banging my ribs.

Suddenly his body was clear of the trees. The enormous brown shape offered a perfect broadside target. The crosshairs settled on his shoulder and my rifle roared.

I was positive the Phantom would collapse. I knew the 180-grain slug went true to its mark, but the buck bolted as if he hadn't been scratched. He wheeled toward some thick oaks and ran like lightning. I recovered fast enough to get in one snap shot before he disappeared in the timber.

It was deathly quiet now, as if the whole episode had never happened. I ran to the spot where he had been standing. There wasn't a trace of hair or blood.

I followed the familiar, wide-splayed tracks until I came to the paved highway leading north out of Revere. When I crossed the road, I got another shock because I couldn't find his trail. It dawned on me that the smart old whitetail had run the pavement to hide his hoof prints.

The thought made me sick to my stomach. I still hadn't found any blood or hair. The buck apparently was alert and not hurting at all. I wondered if I could possibly have missed that standing, wide-open target. "No way," I told myself. "That deer has to be hit."

I reasoned that if he were wounded, he would run the road

106

Here's The Phantom not long after Jeffrey Brunk shot him. The young hunter looks as though he can still hardly believe what happened.

downhill, then turn off into a brushy draw leading to big timber. There were several of these draws that cut a bean field. I checked the largest one first, found no sign of him, then I walked to the next draw. I didn't get very far into it when sudden crashing of brush erupted 50 yards ahead of me. I couldn't spot the Phantom, but it sounded as if he were going to run across the bean field. I smashed frantically ahead in hope I could get a shot at him in the open. I was too late, but I kept on running until I was across the field and into another draw.

Minutes later I jumped him again, not more than 40 feet ahead of me. I got a good view of the white rack and huge body, but the thick brush swallowed him so quickly that I didn't have time to shoot. When I picked up his tracks, I was elated. I found a few drops of blood where he'd been standing in a tangled thicket. Phantom or not, at least he had blood.

My only choice now was to stay on his trail. About two hours later I jumped him out of a creekbottom while I was walking down a hill. He busted out at full speed 100 yards away, but he was relatively in the clear. I thought I had him dead to rights, but he didn't react at all to my three shots. It seemed as if the bullets went right through a ghost.

About 15 minutes later I spotted him slinking through thick brush 200 yards ahead. I barely had time for one snap shot. I kept stalking and soon spotted him 75 yards away in some cedars. He was moving slowly and for the first time I realized that he must be badly wounded. I followed him in my scope until he moved into a tiny clearing, then I carefully squeezed the trigger. This time the Phantom crashed to the ground.

I ran up to the dead deer and stared at the white antlers. The 13-point rack was enormous, even bigger than I had expected it to be. As I field-dressed the buck, I discovered that he was far from a ghost. One bullet had pretty well blown up a shoulder blade. Other slugs had disintegrated the tip of his heart and had blown one lung to pieces.

It took me 20 minutes to run home, but it required three hours for dad, Uncle Larry, Greg, and myself to drag the monster buck out to a road. We loaded him in our pickup truck and then drove to a deer-checking station operated by the conservation department.

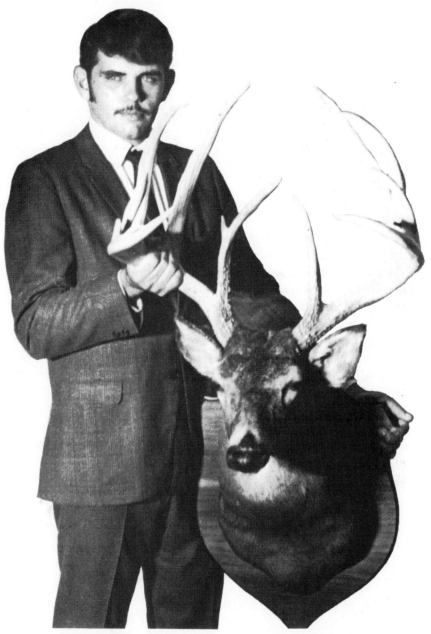

Brunk poses with The Phantom's mounted head. Notice the rack's whiteness and its extremely long tines.

Later we hung him in a locker plant that has an eight-foot ceiling. We hauled him up by his hind legs with pulleys until his back hoofs touched the ceiling. His head and rack were still lying on the floor.

After I got the Phantom's head mounted, I took it to Jerry Barton, our Clark County game warden. Jerry was so sure I'd taken a new state-record whitetail that he contacted Dean Murphy, Superintendent of Game Management for the Missouri Department of Conservation. In the summer of 1970, I received a letter from Dean.

"If Jerry's figures are correct, you may have more than a new state-record whitetail," Dean wrote. "I'm an official scorer for the Boone and Crockett Club, and I'd sure like to measure those antlers. I'll check them when I get up in your area."

On September 16, Dean measured the antlers and came up with a preliminary total score of 197-2/8. That's 13-6/8 better than the score of the former Missouri-record typical whitetail taken by Marvin Lentz of Sumner.

My biggest surprise was yet to come. On May 5, 1971, the Phantom won the Boone and Crockett Club's first award as the highest-scoring typical whitetail killed in North America during the club's 14th big-game awards period covering the years 1968-1970. The club's scoring committee officially established my trophy's final score at 199-4/8. That's just 7-1/8 below the score of the world-record typical whitetail, and it places my buck No. 4 on the club's overall records.

The news just about floored me. I never dreamed it was possible for a farm boy in Missouri to kill such a trophy just a few miles from home.

(EDITOR'S NOTE: *Brunk's enormous buck now ranks as the seventh-best typical whitetail ever taken in North America.*)

Stay for the Ending

By Peter L. Halbig

(EDITOR'S NOTE: *The original version of this story appeared in the February 1971 issue of* Outdoor Life.)

A bad beginning makes for a bad ending, they say. I think that applies to hunting too. If a hunt begins with poor omens, you're almost sure to be in trouble. That's the situation I was in during late August of 1968. My plans for a big-game hunt in northern British Columbia were coming apart at the seams.

The organizing had been under way for many months. Four of us had planned to meet guide Gene Boring at his ranch near Milepost 143 on the Alaska Highway. Then we would travel by pack string far up into the mountains where Gene had spotted some giant caribou bulls. I'd hunted with Gene before, and in my book he's the best guide I've ever been out with. I was going to hunt with bow and arrow, and I had no qualms about Gene's ability to get me close to game.

Things didn't start turning sour until a couple of weeks before I was scheduled to leave my home in Ocean Falls, British Columbia. Two partners cancelled the trip because of unexpected business problems. Then my third companion became unemployed. He quickly lost interest in the hunt.

I decided not to call off the trip even though I'd have to pay some of the expenses we'd planned on sharing. (Of course I knew I would have to pay only my own personal fee.) There was no way

111

I could contact Gene in a hurry. He doesn't have a telephone, and his ranch is 100 miles from the nearest town. As if those problems weren't enough, I had to contend with a postal strike. We had ordered our dehydrated food from Toronto, and it looked as if delivery couldn't be made.

I'm 49 and a physical therapist. I work as a first-aid attendant for a pulp and paper plant. I was born and raised in eastern Canada but moved to British Columbia 17 years ago because I think it harbors the greatest hunting country on earth. Consider that I don't have to travel very far to hunt mountain sheep, elk, grizzly bear, two species of deer, moose, caribou, mountain goat, and black bear. The local fishing is great—as my wife Chris can attest—and so is the small-game and waterfowl hunting.

Though I use a shotgun for wingshooting, I've given little attention to firearms for big-game hunting. I've killed enough game to make me far more intrigued with the thrills of a hunt than the idea of getting meat. I like the challenge of matching wits with wild animals on their own terms, and that's the name of the game for the bowhunter. To stalk within arrow-killing range of any big-game animal is a tough job. It's the stalk that produces the excitement, and that excitement lasts much longer for the bowman than for the rifleman because you must get so much closer to your target. You can be successful too. I've been lucky enough to bag 89 big-game animals with archery gear.

Veteran bowhunters know that shooting skill comes from constant practice. I shoot my hunting arrows year-round at various target arrangements. Archery must be learned properly and practiced almost continually if you expect to discover the tremendous enjoyment of the game.

Anyway, the bad omens of the 1968 trip continued almost until my scheduled departure date. Then the dehydrated food arrived just in time. I packed my gear, flew to Vancouver (there are no roads to the outside from Ocean Falls), picked up my car, and headed for Gene's ranch in late August. Though most big-game seasons in the zone I was to hunt had been open for a couple of weeks—and would remain open for about three months—I had several reasons for planning an early-September hunt. The flies would be almost gone in the mountains, the weather would be cool, and the period would be just before rutting time.

112

Early fall is a good time to hunt because the males of big-game species begin to lose a bit of caution as the rut approaches. They're looking for distractions, and aren't thinking as much about their individual safety. That makes it much easier for a stalking hunter.

Incidentally, there are several licenses required for big-game hunting in British Columbia. My basic license fee (resident) to hunt all game animals and gamebirds is $4. Then I have to buy tag-licenses for the species of big-game that I choose to hunt. Resident tag-licenses range from 50 cents for black bear up to $10 for grizzly bear. The nonresident tag (termed trophy fee) ranges from $5 for black bear up to $75 for mountain sheep. The non-resident's basic license costs $25. [*Editor's note:* Comparable 1980 fees are about triple these amounts.] All nonresident big-game hunters must be accompanied by a licensed British Columbia guide. You can get details on license costs and hunting season dates by writing to The Ministry of Recreation and Conservation, Fish and Wildlife Branch, 1019 Wharf St., Victoria, B. C. Canada VBW 2Z1.

I was primarily interested in a trophy mountain caribou, but I also had tags for moose, grizzly, and black bear. It would take three days of horseback riding and packing to reach our very remote hunting area, but we would be in top caribou country when we arrived.

Though my pre-hunt luck had been generally bad, I knew that Gene was the type of man who could change it. In fact, it was extremely good luck that had enabled me to meet him six years earlier. I was hunting another area by myself. Gene was passing through and stopped to rest at my camp for a while. We hit it off right away, and a warm friendship developed. We've hunted to-gether every fall since.

You can't do better than to hook up with a guide such as Gene. He's an expert at his business, and he lives in hunting country year-round. He's wiry and middle-aged. He raises horses on his ranch, does some farming, and drives water trucks for a gasoline company. His pack string and camping equipment are tops. He's hard-working and honest, and he's a great woodsman. In short, he's the type of guy I want to hunt with.

Gene was disappointed when I drove up to his ranch alone, but he was philosophical too. "Well," he said with a smile, "those other fellows are going to miss out on seeing some beautiful country."

Gene's ranch is nestled in spectacular wilderness. It's on the edge of a large flat in a long valley in the rugged Peace River country. Coniferous forests, poplar, birch, alders, and brush roll across enormous hills that climb to the sky. The scenery is especially gorgeous in fall when, as Gene says, "All the gold is in the trees."

When we rode out of the valley, our pack string consisted of two saddle horses and five pack horses. Included in our gear was a 9-1/2x12-foot wall tent, down-filled sleeping bags, air mattresses, a two-burner white-gas stove, a gas lantern, aluminum pots and pans, plastic cups and plates, and personal gear. Major food items for the first few days of our planned two-week hunt consisted of steaks and chicken. When those items were gone, we'd live on canned and dehydrated foods.

The caribou area we were headed for was about 40 miles away in a straight line, but it's impossible to travel a straight line in that country. We crossed rivers and creeks, circled swamps, rode across beaver dams, and skirted along rock-shale slopes. We had to go around one chain of mountains that was too high and difficult to cross.

We spotted several bears, moose, and deer on the way in, but nothing in the trophy class. After two and one-half days of riding, we came into an open-range grassy flat that would make an ideal campsite. It was early to quit traveling for the day, but we had been riding in rain since dawn and we needed a rest. We were in a beautiful setting. The lush, grassy flat stretched three quarters of a mile beyond us. It was 200 yards wide and bordered on the far edge by a small river. Beyond the river a wide ribbon of willows covered foothills that edged a steep mountain range. Green pines and spruce tried to conquer the slopes, but the timberline was far below the crest of the mountain.

"There's a caribou mountain if I ever saw one," Gene said. "Let's make camp. Then we'll see what we can find with the spotting scope."

We put the tent up and then sprawled on the carpet of grass. I opened a pack, picked out the 30x60 Hudson Bay scope, and

114

pointed it toward the mountain across the valley. I spotted a moving object almost immediately. I adjusted my focus, and a giant bull caribou jumped into clear view. He was 3,000 feet up on the mountain, but the powerful optics made him appear to be almost in my lap.

The sudden and unexpected sight of the bull's monster rack and massive white neck almost choked me. I managed to elbow Gene and point to the mountain. His "cool" always amazes me. He calmly looked through the scope as if he expected to see something as ordinary as a squirrel. He studied the bull for a long time before pronouncing his verdict.

"Well, that's a fine animal," he opined when he finally turned from the scope. "He'd be worthy of a closer look. But it's too late in the day to get up there. He'll likely be in the same area tomorrow."

I took over the scope and watched the bull for a long time. He grazed slowly along a crest and then finally walked out of sight. I calmed down from my initial burst of excitement and lounged against a grub box while Gene glassed the mountain for other signs of game.

Gradually, I became aware that I was watching the hobbled horses. It suddenly occurred to me that most of the animals were alerted to something and that they were staring toward the far end of the flat.

Curious, I turned and looked at the willows edging the clearing. At first I saw nothing out of place. Even when I zeroed in on the object of the horses' attention, nothing registered. Then, more than half a mile away, the dark object moved slightly. When I realized what I was looking at, my stomach seemed to jump to my ears.

"Gene," I stammered, "there's a bull moose down there that's so big he can't be real."

My partner didn't answer until he found the object with the scope. Then his body seemed to go rigid. "Pete," he replied with real excitement, "you ain't said nothing but the truth. That's the biggest bull moose I ever laid eyes on."

The thing about an unexpected situation like this one is that it momentarily stuns you. We knew we were in moose country, but our thoughts had been on caribou. It's likely that the enormous bull had been aware of us ever since we rode into the clearing. We'd certainly made enough commotion setting up camp. The bull probably had no intention of leaving unless we showed signs of approaching him.

None of this occurred to us at the time. When our initial shock wore off, we literally bumped into each other as we rushed to unpack and prepare the hunting gear. It seemed to take me forever to assemble my 60-pound Grove's Spitfire Magnum bow, a 56-inch-long take-down model. Somehow I got my Microflite glass-shafted arrows tipped with Bear razorheads into my bow-mounted quiver. Gear was scattered everywhere as we searched through packs for what we needed. At one point, while I was pulling on my camouflage suit, I realized I was standing on my Bushnell 9x36 binoculars.

During all this scrambling, the bull didn't seem to move an inch. Once Gene said, "I've got to take another look. There almost have to be two bulls down there. That rack is too wide for one moose."

My guide glassed the scene again and exclaimed, "Nope, he's all one animal, one enormous moose. Let's go."

Our camp was in an ideal spot for beginning the stalk. The grassy flat dropped down into dense willows behind the tent. Beyond the willows were low hills covered with alders, poplars, birch, and some needle timber. It was all thick stuff that we could stay in while we stalked a semicircular route around the edge of the flat to the bull. At first we stayed behind the bigger trees because they offered a solid screen and we could move through them silently.

As we closed the distance, we had to maneuver through thinner cover. We could now see the bull. He was unaware of our presence and completely absorbed with watching the horses. Each time I looked at him, he seemed to grow in massiveness. He apparently had just shed his velvet and his huge, light-colored rack contrasted sharply against the green background. Antler points seemed to branch out in all directions.

The taller tree stands ended 130 feet behind the moose. From that point I was on my own. "Don't rush it," Gene whispered. "He won't move unless you make a mistake."

The last few yards of any stalk produce an excitement that

Peter Halbig (left) and guide Gene Boring pose with Halbig's trophy moose.

borders on complete nervous frustration. I've been through the thrilling anxiety many times, but I'd never had that "chance in a million" that was offered to me now. My mouth went dry, my boots seemed to fill with lead, and my pounding pulse was trying to blow through my temples.

I literally walked ahead on my knees, snaking my way silently through the willows. The biggest challenge was to get behind and slightly to one side of the bull. My arrow would have to enter behind the last ribs in order to slice forward to the heart area. I was within 70 feet of my quarry now, well within deadly range, but I didn't dare shoot until I could find an open path for my arrow's flight through the willows.

I finally found a narrow avenue through the branches; my moment of truth had arrived. The strain of the stalk had left me perspiring profusely. I was out of breath and trying desperately to control a building case of shakes. I don't recall pulling the weight of the bow. I don't even recall seeing the arrow go. But I do remember hearing a "thunk" and spotting my shaft buried to its orange feathers in the bull's massive left side.

I remained motionless and intensely awed when the moose showed no immediate reaction. Then he grunted and began stomping back and forth in small circles. I released a second arrow as soon as I had another clear shot. That one sliced into his right side.

His hind legs began to buckle. Then his head sagged as if the enormous antlers were too heavy to hold high. I was so excited that I was just about paralyzed. The bull began to sway. With an extreme effort, he briefly pulled himself together. Then he crashed to the ground. He managed to lift his head. But then the last of his life drained away and the massive antlers dropped to the ground.

I don't know how long I stood in silence. My mind and body were separate entities. My mind told me to rush in for a close-up view, but my body didn't want to move. Suddenly I was aware of Gene's understanding hand on my shoulder. We were both very proud and happy.

We gutted the bull and returned to camp for an ax, cameras, knives, pulleys, and rope. We chopped the antlers out of the skull, but we didn't have time for much butchering. We finished the cutting job the next day. Then we hung the meat from tree branches near our tent.

Back at camp, the successful bowhunter hefts the huge moose rack.

Our campsite was a half day's travel from the area Gene had originally planned to hunt, but there was no sense in moving on now. The caribou bull we had scoped would be hard to beat anywhere. We decided to stay in the area and try to find him again.

The next morning dawned clear and cool. We rode across the flat, crossed the river, and got one quarter of the distance to the top of the 3,500-foot mountain before our route became too steep to ride. Then we dismounted and led our horses up brushy and rocky slopes that were almost impossible to climb. We had to stop frequently to blow the horses and give our own racing lungs a rest. Eventually we tied our horses to some low brush and crawled and pulled ourselves above timberline. Then we broke out onto the edge of a huge, rocky, bowllike area that stretched a couple of miles in length.

"We better look this over closely," Gene said. "It's a perfect setup for caribou."

We sneaked down a narrow lane leading into the bowl. There we flattened behind rocks and went to work with our binoculars. We spotted several caribou at various places on the slopes, but none were in the trophy class.

After half an hour of glassing, I saw a flash of movement 800 yards away that seemed to disappear immediately. A caribou can blend almost perfectly with rocky background, so I kept my glasses glued to the spot. I saw the movement again. Now everything jumped into focus. Could I believe my eyes? Could it be possible that I was looking at another outstanding trophy?

I touched my guide's shoulder and said, "I think I've found another bruiser. See the truck-shaped boulder off to our right? Now look in front of that . . ."

"Got him," Gene interrupted. "Whooeee, is he nice! Same one we saw the other day, or his big brother. He's going to move and feed. Let's sit tight and see which way he travels."

A few moments later Gene looked up from his 8x40 Leitz binoculars and remarked, "That big brute is coming this way, and he's angling up to the crest. If we can get in the right spot in a hurry, he'll walk right into our laps."

I looked at the edge of the bowl and immediately understood Gene's plan. The side of the bowl ahead and to our right sloped

The moose's rack nearly dwarfs the happy guide.

up to a narrow crest about 20 feet wide. The crest flared into a wide slope between ourselves and the bull. Gene reasoned that if we could find an ambush spot along the bull's narrow travel route, he would have to pass us within easy arrow range. On the other hand, if the caribou reached the wide slope at the end of the crest, he could travel off in any direction.

We shed our jackets, binoculars, and cameras, then took off as fast as we could scramble over the almost straight-up route. We ran behind boulders to conceal ourselves. We had to travel only a few hundred yards, but it took more than half an hour of puffing and gasping to reach the crest. Then we found a pitlike nook eight feet below the narrow trail. It was barely deep enough to hide us, but we fell into it and tried to catch our breath.

We had made the last part of our dash while the bull was out of sight in a dip of the trail. After a few moments, I pulled my camouflaged cap over my forehead and risked a peek down the crest. My luck was holding. The giant was still coming straight toward us. He was moving slowly, grazing occasionally, looking about, obviously completely unaware of our presence. Time seemed to stand still while we waited in our extremely cramped quarters.

As the long minutes passed, I risked a few more peeks that Gene didn't approve of. The monster bull was closer each time I looked. I watched him disappear into another dip in the trail just 40 yards away. The tension now was tremendous because I wouldn't be able to see him again until it was time to shoot. We would have to wait for the sounds that would tell us he was only feet away.

Each passing minute seemed like a lifetime. My muscles were becoming so cramped that I felt like screaming. Could it be possible that the strong wind would wipe out the sounds of his approach? Then I heard the faint, spaced-out cracklings of the bull's joints, sounds that are unique to a walking caribou.

My second moment of truth was close at hand. The torturous wait was over when the enormous rack of antlers suddenly seemed to be floating in the sky just above my head. They were shockingly close even though the sight was exactly what I had expected. I drew my bowstring and leaped upright in a single fluid motion. The bull's eyes bulged with terror, and he reacted with

After his bowhunting success on this big caribou, Halbig poses with it in the Mt. Lady Laurier area of northern British Columbia.

This is the view from camp toward the hunting area. Halbig killed his giant moose in the distant brush at the far right. He bagged his caribou at top of mountain peak visible in center-right.

The packstring navigates past a beaver area. That's guide Gene Boring up ahead of the moose antlers.

On way back to Boring's ranch, the packstring fords a river.

Back home, Halbig relaxes beneath the antlers of trophy moose on his den wall.

astonishing speed. I shot as fast as I could select an aiming point. Even so, the bull was hunching to leap when my arrow sliced deep into his chest cavity. It seemed to have no effect whatever. The caribou made it to the open slope with a couple of unbelievably long and fast leaps. He disappeared over the rim before I could nock another arrow.

Gene and I ran to the end of the crest. Then we slammed to a halt when we saw the bull standing 30 yards below us. He was swaying badly, but I ran closer and put another arrow into him. He went down dead in his tracks.

Gene walked up and said, "Man, I got about 14 knotted cramps in my legs. I didn't think that critter would ever get to us."

So ended my luckiest hunt, but I wasn't to discover the extent of my luck until months later. Both of my trophies were scored for the Pope and Young Club by taxidermists Al Rand and Ed Kirchner of Prince George, British Columbia. In March of 1970, I learned that my Canada moose was a new world record for archers. The official score for the 55-2/8-inch-wide antlers is 201-4/8.

My mountain caribou nearly won new world-record recognition too. The 28-point trophy placed second in its category during the Pope and Young Club award period that ended June 30, 1969. The greatest spread of the bull's rack is 29-3/8 inches, and it officially scored 288-2/8, exactly 9-7/8 better than the previous record established by Fred Bear.

But my bull pales in comparison with the magnificent caribou that my good friend Dr. Lowell Eddy of Seattle, Washington, took in British Columbia during the last Pope and Young Club award period. Dr. Eddy's trophy scored 374-1/8. His caribou's antlers measure almost a foot more than mine in both length and spread. That's amazing. When I jumped upright in that cramped pit along the mountain crest, I thought I was staring at the biggest caribou in the world.

(EDITOR'S NOTE: *Halbig's Canada moose is still the world record for archers. His mountain caribou now ranks No. 6. See Dr. Lowell Eddy's story beginning on page 35 in this book.*)

"Shoot! He's Gonna Fight"

By Robert B. Peregrine

(EDITOR'S NOTE: *The original version of this story appeared in the September 1968 issue of* Outdoor Life.)

Ojibway Indian Andrew Ogemah's whisper hissed with excitement. "Bull. Big bull! Feeding at end of bay. Get rifles ready!"

My guide's abrupt statement startled me. I'd been watching the tree-lined shore 50 yards to the left of our 18-foot outboard. Now I quickly shifted my attention to the far end of the bay, which was 400 yards in front of us.

I expected to see a huge bull standing in plain sight, but I couldn't spot anything that even resembled a moose. I glanced at my hunting partner in the bow of the boat. Andy Andrews' face was a study of concentration.

"I don't see him," Andy muttered. "I don't see anything except trees and marsh grass."

Our guide was paddling furiously for the shoreline. Suddenly the rhythm of his paddle strokes ceased, and he nudged me with the dripping blade. I whirled toward the stern.

"There," he gasped as he pointed toward the back of the bay. "Big bull. Stand up! Look through scope!"

We were in one among thousands of bays along the shoreline of Lac Seul Reservoir, a huge body of water in northwestern On-

129

tario. We couldn't travel closer to the unwary moose. Our way was blocked by a solid mass of floating, deadfall trees. Our guide maneuvered the boat around stumps, drove us between floating logs, and pushed against his paddle with unbelievable strength.

I turned my Weaver V8 scope up to 8X and anxiously scanned the shoreline at the back of the bay. Through the optics I quickly zeroed in on a black object. My heart jumped, but then I realized I was looking at just an outcropping of rock.

All of this excitement lasted only a few moments, but in a way it seemed like hours. Then I heard the Indian whispering, "Don't look for moose, look for horns. Only horns show. Moose feeding behind high grass."

Suddenly I noticed a movement behind some tall marsh reeds that bordered the end of the bay. Then the picture through the scope became clear. I saw part of a rack of moose antlers moving above the dead-still reeds.

"Andy," I said, "there's the bull. It's your shot. You take him."

By now our frustrated guide had pushed our boat to a dead end in the maze of floating deadfalls that edged the shoreline. We were 15 feet from the beach, but we'd have to make the rest of the distance on foot.

Andy tried desperately to find the bull in his scope, but he had no success. Then he lowered his rifle. "Bob," he said dejectedly, "I just can't spot him. He's all yours."

I jumped out of the boat onto semi-floating deadfalls. They made a precarious shooting platform, but I wasn't about to waste time dashing for shore. I jacked a 220-grain cartridge into the chamber of my 30/06 and raised the rifle to my shoulder. The Remington Gamemaster was sighted-in for 200 yards. I leveled the scope's crosshairs two feet over the area where I figured the bull's back should be. Then I squeezed the trigger.

The moose began moving immediately after the roar of my rifle. He walked from behind a hummock of marsh grass. His massive antlers and the top half of his black body emerged into clear view. I held above his shoulder and touched off a second shot. Surprisingly, he began quartering slowly toward us through spires of dead trees standing at the back of the bay.

"You hit him," our guide said. "He doesn't know where we are. Shoot again."

The logs I was balancing on were moving around in a staggering pattern. It was tough enough finding the moose in the scope, let alone trying to settle the crosshairs above his shoulder. I fired the last three shells in the clip, but the bull never missed a step.

I reached into a pocket, grabbed another clip of cartridges, and pushed it into the rifle. By now the moose had reached the beach and was walking into a spruce thicket. I crashed away two quick shots before the animal was swallowed by the bush. "My gosh," I groaned, "how could I miss an animal that big?"

"No miss," said the guide. "Hit good. If missed, he'd run like deer. We'll find him dead in bush."

This moose hunt had its beginning on the patio of Andy's lakeshore home near Oconomowoc, Wisconsin. That was in July 1966. Andy and his wife had invited my family and me for a weekend of swimming. At 53, he's a veteran outdoorsman and owner of a refrigeration retail business. After a session of swimming, Andy began telling me about a bull moose he'd killed in Ontario.

"That one had an antler spread of 52-1/2 inches," he said. "I had the thrill of a lifetime when I lined my rifle on that monster. He was as big as a horse."

"Sounds great," I'd said. "I'd like to try it sometime."

"Like this fall?"

"Sure, if we can line up a hunt."

Andy had walked immediately to his telephone and placed a call to outfitter Irv Fivek's base camp near Sioux Lookout, Ontario. The call went through in minutes. "Irv," Andy had said, "put me down for another hunt this year. I'll have a partner. And I hope you can get Andrew to guide us. Fine. We'll see you in October."

Just like that. One moment I was enjoying a summer swim, and half an hour later I was scheduled for a week of moose hunting in the remote bush of Canada. I didn't have the slightest idea of what I was getting into.

I'm an attorney in Milwaukee, Wisconsin, and I've spent most of my 35 years in a big-city atmosphere. The first contact I had with hunting came after I was married. My wife's father and brothers are lifelong outdoorsmen, and I was impressed by their absorbing interest in hunting and fishing.

131

In 1964, I formed a law partnership with veteran sportsman Mathias G. Schimenz. His vivid descriptions of his hunting adventures fired a desire in me to share his excitement. On our first duck hunt together, I killed a coot and a mallard.

Then we went pheasant hunting, and later in the fall I tried deer hunting. I didn't get a buck, but by then I'd been hooked for life on the unique appeal of the outdoors. I learned a lot about hunting during the next two years. By the time Andy suggested the moose hunt, I was raring to go.

We left Milwaukee at 3:00 a.m. the morning of October 8. We drove straight through to Irv Fivek's base camp. Though we pulled a rental trailer (for hauling meat home), we made the 850-mile trip in 17 hours.

The next morning, a floatplane ferried us to Chamberlain Narrows on Lac Seul. It was a short flight through a cloudless sky. Below us, birch and other broadleaf trees exhibited dazzling displays of fall colors. Reds and yellows and greens mingled with an endless panorama of sparkling blue lakes.

We landed near Irv's outpost camp, then taxied to shore and unloaded our gear. Camp Ojibway is a neat-looking arrangement of furnished cabins, a large mess hall, and a guides' building. All of the buildings nestle in clearings in a thick forest of spruce, tamarack, pine, and birch.

There were 15 other hunters and eight guides operating from the camp when we arrived. All of the other hunters had reserved package-price hunts identical with Andy's and mine. Our full week's hunt cost us $450 each. That includes a $101 nonresident moose-hunting license, guide fees, boats, motors, fuel, lodging, and meals. The package-price includes everything except rifles, cartridges, clothes, and personal gear. [*Editor's note:* A similar package in 1980 was priced at more than $1,100.]

After we were organized, Andy told me more about our hunt plan. "We won't see another group while we're hunting," he began. "Each guide works a separate area. They're all Ojibway Indians, and they live in this section year-round. They spend the summer guiding fishing parties, and the moose season is open here from October 1 to early January. They know the country, they know where the moose are, and they know how to hunt them."

The bush in northern Ontario is so thick and tangled with dead-falls that it's impractical and almost impossible to hunt on foot. In addition, moose in this area feed on succulent water plants along the shorelines of lakes and streams. The best way to find the animals is by boat.

"Our guide will run the boat into bays and up streams and creeks," Andy explained. "He'll shut the motor off when we come to a good spot, then we'll drift and paddle around points and islands. The idea is to spot a feeding moose, then hope to stalk close enough for a shot."

I learned that our outfitter furnishes his guides with 18-foot aluminum boats and 20-horsepower outboard motors. Lac Seul Reservoir is nearly 100 miles long, and its shorelines are frequently more than 10 miles apart. A seaworthy boat is the only answer for safety and fast travel. Besides, the big boats are ideal for transporting moose meat.

Lac Seul, incidentally, is a man-made reservoir. Its waters are backed up behind a dam constructed in 1929 at Ear Falls, Ontario. As the waters deepened and spread through the years, they flooded vast areas of forest. Countless trees died, and many of the naked trunks were toppled by wind storms. Some of the reservoir's bays are choked with solid masses of floating timber. Submerged stumps are everywhere.

"We'll be hunting some of the best moose country in Ontario," Andy said that evening. "But it's possible to hunt for many days without even seeing a moose."

"I'll be happy just enjoying a new adventure and seeing the country," I replied. "But in case we get lucky, let's flip a coin to see who gets first shot."

Andy won the toss.

A blanket of frost covered the ground the next morning. The sky was turning cloudy by daybreak, but the temperature was approaching the thawing mark. We placed our rifles and lunches in the boat, scraped frost off the seats, and motored away.

The first bay we checked was five miles from camp. I spotted an enormous beaver lodge and dozens of ducks. A loon shrieked his eerie cry. We paddled around the bay for 10 minutes. Then our guide started the outboard and we took off down the shore.

The fourth bay we entered was about 300 yards wide by 600

yards deep. Andrew paddled along the right-hand shoreline, and then turned the boat left and started across the bay. We were almost to the opposite shore when he suddenly spotted the big bull I told about earlier.

As I mentioned, I was crestfallen after the excitement of the shooting. I was positive I'd hit the bull with my first two shots, and our guide reassured me.

"Hit good!" the Ojibway insisted. "He probably dead now. We'll find him dead in bush!"

I jumped across the unsteady logs until I got to the beach. There I stepped into 10 inches of black muck. The Indian passed me as though walking on pavement. I looked back at Andy. "You young guys go find the moose," he said. "I'll take it easy and bring your camera."

It was impossible to run through the swampy tangle of logs, deadfalls, and marsh reeds. I had more than 300 yards to go to the spot where the moose had disappeared into the bush. When I got there, I was soaking with perspiration. Andrew wore a grin that split his face, and he was pointing at the ground. Huge moose tracks in the muck were splattered with blood. "Moose didn't go far," he said.

I knew I had too many clothes on for hiking, so I peeled off my heavy coat and hung it on a bush. Then I followed the Indian into a jungle of spruce, alder, tamarack, and a maze of windfalls.

I thought I was in good physical condition, but I just couldn't keep up with my guide. The only thing that slowed him was his constant checking of the blood trail. We struggled through a mile of almost impenetrable thickets before we came to a clearing. Forty feet of ferns, moss, and small pine seedlings separated us from an edge of bushes and clumps of spruce. The Indian stopped in his tracks, pointed toward a thicket across the clearing, and excitedly yelped, "Horn. There he is!"

Then I saw part of a moose antler near the ground in the bushes 15 yards ahead. I marveled at Andrew's eyesight. If I'd been alone, I probably would have walked up to the animal before realizing he was there.

The bull was obviously down. Though we couldn't see any part of his body, we were sure he was dead. I pulled my knife from its sheath and said, "Andrew, show me what to do. You start field-dressing chores."

The Indian's grin of satisfaction was amazing. He'd achieved his goal of getting his hunter a moose, and he was bubbling with happiness.

After Andrew took my knife, I leaned my rifle against a birch tree. In front of us lay a spruce windfall that blocked our way to the moose. The Indian started around the windfall, then had second thoughts. He turned to me and said, "Give me gun."

As I handed him the rifle, Andrew stepped on some dead branches of the windfall. They broke with sharp cracks, and set off the fastest chain reaction I've ever seen.

I'd been shocked with surprises before, but nothing could ever compare with the impending disaster I now witnessed. Even though I'd been looking straight at the moose, he jumped to his feet so rapidly that all I could see was an enlarging blur of black. Suddenly, the bull was facing us head-on. His antlers were lowered in charge position, and he was uttering spine-chilling snorts. I could hear his heavy hoofs ripping through ground and underbrush.

I stood transfixed with horror. Then I saw Andrew throw my rifle to his shoulder and pull the trigger. The rifle didn't fire. (I didn't know it at the time, but the Indian didn't know how to release the safety.) The bull charged as Andrew whirled, pitched the rifle at me, and began running off into the bush. As he flashed past me, he screeched, "Shoot! He's gonna fight!"

I dodged behind the birch tree and shouldered the rifle all in one motion. I've never seen anything as terrifying as that enormous animal zeroing in on me. Though everything was happening too fast for rational thinking, one terrible thought flashed through my mind. "My God," I thought, "I'm spending my last moment on earth. That moose is going to kill me!"

The enraged bull was 30 feet away and coming like an express train. I pointed the barrel shotgun-style at his head and snapped off two shots as rapidly as I could work the slide action. The moose went down as if some giant had knocked his legs out from under him. He didn't get up, but I stood there paralyzed with fear.

Then I was aware of Andrew running up to me. He threw his arms around me with an excited bear hug and yelled, "Good shooting! Now fill clip."

Though the bull was down, he certainly wasn't dead. Grunting-like wheezes were coming from his throat. He was only 15 feet

135

Robert Peregrine (left) and guide Andrew Ogemah pose beside Peregrine's bull moose where it fell.

Across one knee, Peregrine supports the rack of the big Canada moose he shot in Ontario.

away, which was much too close for comfort. I didn't take my eyes off his huge bulk as we began backing away. I climbed a big windfall, and had a clear view of the bull's head. At that moment he raised his antlers and tried to get up. I was all done taking chances. I fired two slugs into his neck. The massive head fell to the ground. "Don't shoot horns," the Indian said. "Fill clip."

I stared at the motionless animal for a few moments.

"Well, Andrew," I said, "I think he's dead. Let's check him out."

Andrew looked at me with a grin. "I'm ready," he said, "You go first."

We walked up to the animal, and I nervously jabbed his rump a few times with my rifle muzzle. He was stone dead. Andrew shook my hand in congratulations and said, "Giant bull. He'll weigh more than 1,500 pounds."

We walked back to the boat to get an ax. Then we field-dressed the bull and chopped out his antlers. Andrew wanted to let the meat stiffen before we cut it up, so we left the carcass and spent the afternoon trying to find a moose for Andy. We spotted a cow feeding in a bay on our way back to camp, but she saw us and spooked into the bush before Andy could get a shot.

We were back at the kill site the next morning. It took most of the day to chop the bull into sections, carry the meat to the boat, and transport it back to camp.

We were hunting again the following day. Late in the afternoon Andrew paddled the boat up a creek flowing through a wide area of dead trees that stood in shallow water. We were drifting silently when our guide suddenly whispered, "Moose ahead. Cow."

This time Andy and I saw the animal immediately. It was feeding in shallow water beyond a stand of dead trees 200 yards ahead. Andy began stepping out of the boat, but our guide whispered, "No. Wait. We get closer."

The Indian silently maneuvered us within 100 yards of the moose, stopped, and motioned Andy to get out. Andy waded about 50 feet. Then the cow whipped her head and stared directly at us. With one burst of speed she was running for the beach 50 feet to her right. Spray flew from her hoofs, and I could hear her heavy legs crashing through windfalls. Andy's Model 70 Winchester 300 Magnum blasted the stillness. I saw his shoulder jerk from

138

As his guide holds the boat steady, Peregrine maneuvers a slab of moose ribs into position for loading.

recoil, and then he was sighting through his Weaver K4 scope for a second shot. The rifle roared again, the moose went down in a heap, and our hunt was over.

Though I was a novice moose hunter, I'd read a great deal about big-game hunting. I was aware that the Boone and Crockett Club measured and cataloged outstanding big-game trophies. I couldn't wait to have my bull's antlers scored.

Two months later, I learned that my 31-point trophy had a total score of 200-3/8 and a widest spread of 58-3/4 inches. According to the Boone and Crockett Club's book, *Records of North American Big Game,* my trophy is the fourth-best Canada moose ever taken in Ontario. Though I didn't kill an all-time record, I sure had a world-record thrill when Andrew threw my rifle at me and screamed, "Shoot! He's gonna fight!"

(EDITOR'S NOTE: *Peregrine's trophy currently ranks as the ninth best ever taken in Ontario.)*

The First of Its Kind

By James F. Tappan

(EDITOR'S NOTE: *The original version of this story appeared in the February 1972 issue of* Outdoor Life.)

When it comes to hunting, the seemingly best plans may go up in smoke when a better opportunity presents itself. That's what happened to my two hunting partners and myself.

During the fall of 1966, Jim Bean and I were planning to go after deer in Montana. One night while we were working out details, my uncle returned from the Ungava region of Quebec with a fine caribou bull. When he phoned me about his success, I couldn't wait to see the animal. Jim and I left for Uncle Wat's home immediately. On the way we picked up Fran Johnston, the third member of our hunting trio.

I'd never seen a caribou before. To say that I was impressed by the bull's long, wide, multi-pointed rack would be the understatement of my hunting career. Jim and Fran were amazed too. As outdoorsmen who considered a 6-point whitetail buck an outstanding trophy, we were justifiably astonished. Our plans for a western hunt began to seem less enticing. They were swept from our minds when Uncle Wat mentioned some details of his hunt.

"There are good caribou camps in the Ungava region," he told us. "I flew past one operated by Whale River Outfitters Ltd. My pilot told me that hunters working out of that camp were almost always successful. The guy who owns the outfit also runs an off-season business in Parish, New York. His name is Stan Karboski. You might be able to track him down by phone."

That turned out to be an easy job. I discovered that his home was only a three-hour drive from where I live in Sayre, Pennsylvania. Jim and I couldn't wait to talk with the outfitter, so we drove up to Parish.

Karboski told us he was booked solid for that fall. He said that the caribou season usually runs from late August to late September. We promptly made reservations for September 15 to 22, 1967. Stan's price for a seven-day package hunt was $450 per man. [*Editor's note:* A comparable 1980 price: $1,450.] We also learned that our nonresident big-game licenses would be good for caribou, moose, deer, and bear. But moose, deer, and bear don't range the area we were to hunt. We estimated that our travel, motel, and incidental expenses would run $125 apiece.

I'm 35. My wife Charlotte and I have a 16-year-old son. I earn my living as a heavy-equipment operator on construction jobs. My big-game hunting experience previous to the Quebec trip had been limited to deer hunting in Bradford County, Pennsylvania, and one unsuccessful bear hunt in Canada.

Jim went with me on the bear hunt in 1965. Before that, he had hunted moose in Newfoundland and killed a fine bull with a 52-inch spread. He is 33, married, and the father of four children. He's an iron worker on construction jobs.

Fran had hunted deer with us for years, and was as anxious as we were to find new big-game hunting adventures. He is a 29-year-old bachelor, and works as a machinist in Athens, Pennsylvania.

We left Sayre at 7:00 a.m. on September 12 and headed for Sept Isles, Quebec, which is as far as you can get into that hunting country by car. Our scheduled arrival was September 14, but we left early in case of travel trouble. We took turns driving and drove straight through to Sept Isles in 27 hours.

The next morning, after a night's rest in a motel, we boarded a Quebec North Shore Railroad train and settled down for the scenic 364-mile run north to the mining town of Schefferville. The slow trip ended in early evening. Our first job was to line up a hotel room. Then I tried to call Ted Bennett, owner and operator of Laurentian Airlines. Our plans called for an early-morning

142

flight to the Whale River camp, but I wanted to make sure everything was in order. To my surprise, Stan Karboski answered the phone.

"Everything's ready to roll," he told me. "I just flew in from one of my salmon camps to get organized for you men. I'm going to Whale River with you. Be ready to fly at dawn."

The next morning we bought our nonresident big-game licenses from a game warden and then met Ted Bennett. My partners and I had never done any flying, so we were as excited as kids around a Christmas tree. We helped load a pile of gear and groceries into the plane, then sat on top of the pile as Ted taxied the twin-engine Beechcraft down the lake.

In minutes we were cruising smoothly above a wilderness broken only with shimmering lakes and streams. After 45 minutes in the air, Ted began his approach down the shoreline of Lac Champadore. I spotted our camp on a little bay off the big lake: It was a splash of color in a clearing among jack pines. I saw a blue tent, a yellow tent, several white tents, and a pile of bright-red gasoline barrels.

We unloaded our gear in a hurry after landing since other hunters, who had finished their week's hunt, were waiting on the sandy beach to stow their equipment in the plane and return to Schefferville. Stan assigned us to the blue tent and told us to get unpacked and ready to hunt.

Our wall tent measured 12 x 14 feet. It contained four bunks made from jack pines, plus a small wood-burning stove. There were four other sleeping tents similar to ours, plus one cooking tent that was erected over a wooden platform.

As soon as we were organized, Stan introduced us to our guides. Bob Crim was 46 years old, and is a lifelong friend of Karboski's. He lives in Williamstown, New York, where he works as a carpenter during off-season months. In hunting and fishing seasons, he guides for Stan's clients in any one of three caribou camps, one trout and ouananiche camp, and two Atlantic-salmon camps.

Bob's assistant guide was a 24-year-old Cree Indian named Sidney. I didn't understand the pronunciation of his last name and I neglected to ask him how he spelled it. He told us that during winter he ran a trapline that covered 100 square miles. He looked the part—rugged and tough as rawhide.

143

Our hunt began when Fran, Jim, Bob, Sidney, and I piled into a big 20-foot freighter canoe and motored to a point of land three miles down the lake. Once there, we beached the craft and climbed a mile to the top of a barren ridge. The terrain made it quite a climb. Thick jack pines and swamp gave way to small bushes, outcroppings of rock, and thick caribou moss.

"We'll glass the surrounding area from here," Bob said. "If we don't spot game, we'll move southeast along the top of this ridge. The trick in hunting caribou is to keep walking and glassing until you find some animals."

We pushed ahead to no avail for several hours. Then Bob suggested we hike down off the ridge to get out of the strong wind and take a break. Right after I flopped down, I discovered one of the reasons why it's tough walking in caribou moss. I had a wet behind almost as soon as I sat down.

"A handful of that stuff can hold a quart of water," Bob said with a grin. "You have to look for dry spots by . . ."

"Caribou on ridge," Sidney interrupted.

The rest of us were facing downhill, but we whirled around quickly. For a split second we had a skyline view of two respectable bulls, a small bull, and two cows. Unfortunately, the animals saw us as soon as we spotted them. They reacted by dashing down the opposite side of the ridge and disappearing.

We jumped up and ran to the crest, but there were no caribou in sight. Bob finally found them with his binoculars. They were almost a mile away and traveling fast on another ridge. Try as we may, we couldn't catch up to them or see them again before we had to begin the long hike back to the canoe.

Supper that night was one of the best I've ever eaten. The main course consisted of freshly-caught salmon that Stan had brought in from one of his fishing camps. We met seven other hunters who had flown in while we had been out looking for caribou. We all gathered in one tent and hunting stories flowed freely, but my partners and I were beat and we left early. It seemed as if I'd just crawled into my sleeping bag when Bob came to our tent and announced that breakfast was ready.

It was a frosty and clear dawn when we started up the same ridge we had hunted the day before. We walked and glassed various barren areas until noon without seeing any sign of caribou. For lunch, Bob boiled a pot of tea to go with sandwiches, apples, oranges, and cake packed by the camp cook. Then he sounded us out on traveling farther into the backcountry.

"The caribou may have moved out of this area," he said. "I think our answer is to cover more ground. Are you fellows game to put more miles on your muscles?"

"We came to hunt hard," Jim answered. "You lead the way and we'll go anywhere."

I don't know how far we actually walked, but late in the afternoon Bob said that the canoe was about six miles away and that we'd better start back. An hour or so later, we were following the top of a barren ridge when Bob stopped suddenly and pointed ahead. We stood just long enough to count 17 caribou crossing the crest a quarter mile in front of us.

"I don't think they've seen us," Bob said. "Stand dead still until they're out of sight. They'll probably work down through that ravine on our left. We'll try to intercept them."

As soon as the animals disappeared, we ran full speed for the ravine. We picked a good vantage point, but it soon became obvious that the caribou had changed their route. Then we walked to the ridge top 300 yards away and tried to figure out where the herd had gone. The problem was soon solved when we heard the sounds of hoofs clicking on the rocks behind us. We spun around, and there were the caribou staring at us. They had circled through a stand of thick jack pines and come out almost on top of us.

There was plenty of time to shoot, but nobody raised a rifle. We all wanted good bulls, and there wasn't a better-than-average rack in the herd. We watched them bolt and disappear into a forest of pines 200 yards away.

When we got back to camp, we admired two big bulls killed by camp members Harvey Stace and Bob Oliver. Both men are from Camden, New York. There was a lot of handshaking and congratulating, but I couldn't take my eyes off those magnificent animals. Caribou fever really had me hooked now. I vowed to myself that I'd walk hundreds of miles over the roughest country in Quebec for just one shot at a good bull. Bob must have read my mind.

"If you fellows are willing, I'd like to try a new territory tomorrow," he said. "We'll go farther down the lake and look for a high point we can use for glassing. It will be a gamble because none of us have hunted those hills."

The gamble turned out to be a flop. When we climbed to the

top of our first high ridge, we couldn't see much open country at all. We then hiked on through thick stands of pines, across bogs, and up other ridges. We were disappointed time after time when we peaked out on high spots and only saw more endlessly rolling pines and bogs with few or no openings. And time after time Bob would tell us that the area was too thick with trees for caribou, and that we should hike to the next ridge. We were always more than willing to keep going, but by early afternoon we knew our efforts were wasting our time.

We hiked back to the canoe, ate a late lunch, and motored across the lake to the area we had hunted before. Many more miles of tough walking followed until dusk finally forced us to turn back toward the lake again. On the way back, we approached a ridge approximately 500 feet high and 200 yards across the top. We split up to cover more ground. Bob headed for the far side, Fran and Sidney walked to the top, and Jim and I started along the near side.

Though my partner and I didn't know it, we eventually got about 300 yards ahead of the rest of the group because we had relatively level walking while they had to cross some ravines. Suddenly, we heard Fran's Marlin 444 roar behind us. We turned, looked toward the top of the ridge, and saw a maze of caribou antlers moving across the skyline. The animals' bodies were hidden behind the barren ridge top, but they were only 50 yards away.

We ran full speed and were puffing hard when we reached the crest. The caribou had already run past our position, and were totally unaware of our presence. Four bulls stood within easy rifle range, but none of them met our requirements. We watched them run on, then headed back toward Fran's position. We found him admiring a fine 19-point bull.

"Sidney and I were walking up out of a ravine when the herd popped into view on the open ridge above us," Fran said, beaming. "This bull was far larger than the others, so I dropped him."

It was after dark when we arrived in camp with the caped-out head and quartered meat. Three of our other hunters had also scored on bulls that day, and we had a fine supper of caribou tongue, heart, and steaks. We headed for our bunks right after eating. We were so bushed that we couldn't stay awake.

146

The next morning, our guides took Jim and me into some open country to the west of where we had been hunting. It didn't take long for Bob to find some sign.

"Look," he said while pointing to two crossing caribou trails, "those trails are deep and well used. It takes a lot of animals to wear a trail that deep in this hard ground. I've noticed a lot of fresh caribou droppings too. But, best of all, we've also passed some fresh wolf droppings. Where there are wolves, there are caribou."

We followed a trail that took us up on a small ridge spotted with occasional jack pines and dwarf aspens. The ridge eventually widened into a large plateau that was whipped with such a strong west wind that our eyes began to water. We wanted to cross the plateau, so we turned south, lowered our heads against the gale, and took off.

We'd traveled only a few hundred yards when I turned my head for a quick glance directly into the stinging wind. For a moment I wondered if I were looking at a mirage. I was staring at what appeared to be only the head and antlers of a giant bull caribou. My eyes were watering badly and my vision wasn't clear, but I finally discerned that a single jack pine hid the rest of the animal's body. He wasn't more than 125 yards away.

My breath went out with a gasp and, for a split second, I couldn't talk. Then I grabbed Bob's arm and wheezed, "Bull!"

Confusion reigned for a moment. The bull was now hidden behind the tree and my partners couldn't locate him. I kept pointing to the exact spot, until Bob finally zeroed in on the enormous rack.

"A giant," he blurted. "Don't take a chance on shooting a bullet through those branches. Wait until he steps out."

It seemed like hours passed before the bull decided to move. The pressure of wondering what was going to happen wrecked my nerves and I developed an awful case of buck fever. My 308 Remington Model 760 Gamemaster felt almost useless in my sweating hands. Then I came apart even more when the bull ended his waiting game. I had expected him to bolt with a running start; instead, he stepped calmly toward us and stood still in the clearing.

I found him immediately in my Weaver K-6 scope. I couldn't

steady the crosshairs and I touched the trigger too soon. As the rifle roared, I knew I'd missed the wide-open target.

A change came over me with the suddenness of an explosion. The thought flashed through my mind that only an idiot would blow the chance of a lifetime. My buck fever disappeared as soon as the bull reacted and shifted into high gear. He was running full out toward a ravine of pines about 200 yards downhill. But the tan and white giant was moving broadside to me, and his route was over open ground laced with rocks and caribou moss.

Now my scope was steady. I held ahead of his chest and squeezed the trigger with precision. The bull never knew what hit him. His legs buckled as if they had been knocked from under his body by an invisible fence. He went down in a heap and didn't move again.

We ran to the bull and I heard Bob saying something about a real fine trophy as everybody excitedly began counting antler points. The rack had double shovels—16 points on the right side and 19 on the left. A check with Bob's tape showed the greatest spread to be 50 inches. My 150-grain hand-loaded slug had caught the bull squarely behind his shoulder.

"This is better than a real fine trophy," Bob exclaimed. "It may even be better than an excellent trophy. I've seen a lot of caribou, but I don't think I've ever seen more outstanding antlers."

The next day Fran and I decided to rest in camp while Jim went hunting with Bob. Our rest turned into a nightmare that didn't end until the next day.

The problems began when one of the other hunters in camp knocked down a big bull a short distance from the tents. We heard his two shots; then, half an hour later, he showed up at the cook tent and said he needed a canoe to get across the river to the spot where the bull had dropped.

Fran and another hunter who had already killed his bull accompanied the man across the river. They discovered that the caribou had only been wounded and had disappeared. Then they split up and looked for blood trails. It was a sunny and warm day at the time, but by noon a cloud front rolled in with rain and fog. The two hunters returned in late afternoon and said that they couldn't find Fran.

By now the weather was really foul. The sky was spitting snow and the temperature had plummeted into the 20s. There was no one in camp familiar with the area where Fran was lost, so we had no choice except to wait until the experienced men returned. When Stan got back, he went across the river with the guides. They built a huge fire and kept running chainsaws in hope that Fran would hear them.

Shortly before midnight, they returned with glum expressions. We were all very concerned now because the weather was turning steadily worse and we knew that Fran was dressed with only a light shirt, Levi pants, and leather boots. There were four inches of snow on the ground, and it was still coming down.

Several of us went back to the search area and kept the fire going. Sidney took off on his own. He returned at 2:30 a.m. and said he'd seen no sign of Fran. There was nothing more we could do except wait for dawn.

At first light, we all loaded into canoes and headed down the lake with intentions of searching a new area. We had traveled a couple of miles when Stan threw up his arm, signaled for a stop, and grabbed his binoculars.

"Something moving way down the shore," he said. "Could be a caribou. Nope, there he is! It's Fran!"

When we reached him, we found his clothes half frozen and his body beet red. We ripped the garments off, wrapped him in blankets, and rushed back to camp. After we got some hot soup into him, he told us what had happened.

"I found some drops of blood from the caribou and tried to follow them," he muttered. "My mistake was that I didn't pay attention to where I was going because it was such a clear day. I was so absorbed with trying to find the bull that I didn't notice the fog rolling in. Then it was too late. By the time it started raining, I was hopelessly lost. I didn't even have any matches.

"I heard the chainsaws, but each time I started toward them the sounds seemed to come from different directions. I decided it was best to spend the night under a tree. At dawn, I climbed a ridge, spotted the lake, and headed for a shoreline. This country is sure beautiful, but it's terribly cruel when you make a mistake. I'll never pull a dumb stunt like that again."

Our scheduled week's hunt was over, but Jim decided to stay in camp another week since he still hadn't scored. He made arrange-

Caribou hunter James Tappan, flanked by guides Sidney (left) and Bob Crim, grasps the antlers of his trophy.

ments for a ride home with a hunter from Delaware. We learned later that he missed long shots at two fine bulls and a pure-white wolf. He had chances at several average bulls, but he held out unsuccessfully for a real trophy.

After I had my bull's head mounted, a local sports writer took some pictures of it and asked if I were going to have it scored by the Boone and Crockett Club. I wasn't familiar with the club's activities, but I finally got in touch with Keith Hinman. He's an official measurer who works for the Pennsylvania Game Commission. Keith measured the rack in March 1969 and came up with a total score of 390-4/8.

In January of 1971, I received a letter from the Boone and Crockett Club requesting that I ship the head to the club's headquarters in Pittsburgh so that a panel of judges could check the score. It was then that I realized my trophy must be truly outstanding.

Several months later I received an invitation to attend the club's Awards Banquet, where winners of their 14th big-game award period covering the years 1968-1970 would be announced. There I learned that the club had established a new big-game classification for Quebec-Labrador caribou. I was astonished when I learned that my trophy officially scored 394-1/8, and that it was established as the world record in its category.

(EDITOR'S NOTE: *Tappan's trophy now ranks No. 21 in its category.*)

Instant Record

By Robert V. Knutson

(EDITOR'S NOTE: *The original version of this story appeared in the July 1967 issue of* Outdoor Life.)

My guide, Fred Thorne, and I were standing on a Newfoundland hillside glassing a valley covered by pine and spruce. Fred called our spot the "Lookout." It was a good name. We could see for three miles in 180 degrees.

A small bull moose was feeding in sparse ground cover below us. He was 600 yards away, in clear view, and I'd been watching him for five minutes through my Empire 7x50 binoculars. I'd already told Fred I wasn't interested in stalking the animal, but I was getting a kick out of observing his feeding antics.

That all changed with Fred's startled whisper. You can tell when Fred is excited, because he always begins his statement with a special form of address.

"My son," he exclaimed, "two giant bull moose are on the hillside above us. You can take your pick if we can get close to them!"

Fred pointed toward the animals, but I couldn't see anything that even faintly resembled a moose. It was a dark day with a light drizzle, and that whole mountainside looked like a puzzle of muddy green and brown. Then I picked out two black spots near a marsh-grass bog 1,000 yards away.

I lifted my binoculars and zeroed in. The two bulls were side by side, standing still and looking down into the valley. Even in the poor light, their heavy-beamed brown antlers burst out in clusters of points. This was the sight I'd dreamed of for years.

"That's my bull," I exclaimed. "Either one of them."

"They'll spot us if we try going straight up," Fred cautioned. "We'll have to go back into the brush, around the mountain until we get behind them. Then we'll work through the timber coming up to the lower end of that bog. We'll have to make a couple miles. Let's hustle!"

It's impossible to hike rapidly in that area of Newfoundland. Thick spruce branches and tangles of berry bushes make the going really tough. Much of the area has been logged, and lumbermen's slashings add to the maze of ground cover and windfalls. I'm only 32 and in good condition, but I was hard pressed to keep up with 38-year-old Fred. He seemed to float through that jungle like a deer.

We stayed in thick cover all the way. It took two hours to reach our destination. When we neared the edge of a spruce thicket, Fred motioned me to move ahead. Those two bulls couldn't be more than 100 yards away now. I'd just slip the rifle through the last of the branches and nail the trophy of my choice.

I saw part of the bog first, then all of it, and finally the whole mountainside. There wasn't a moose in sight.

"That's moose hunting," Fred said matter-of-factly. "They're unpredictable critters. But I had a hunch those two old boys would stay put. Must have heard us."

I had never shot a moose, so I suppose I should have been disappointed. Strangely, I wasn't. I'd seen a lot of moose in the last couple of days, and I'd seen some fair bulls. From a trophy standpoint, this had been the best opportunity yet. I reasoned I'd get another chance.

"Fred," I said, "I've come a long way to hunt moose and caribou. From what I've seen so far, I'd guess I can get a moose most anytime. I'm not so sure about a caribou, and I want a good one. I've only got four days left. Let's forget about moose and get on with the caribou hunt!"

A statement like that sounds a little crazy, but as it turned out, that judgment was the most important big-game decision I'll ever make.

153

I'm a heavy-equipment operator in Janesville, Wisconsin, where I live with my wife Norma Jean and our two boys and three girls. I was born on a nearby farm, smack in the middle of squirrel, rabbit, and pheasant country. In those days, my brother didn't care much for hunting and my dad couldn't spare the time. I had all that game to myself, but I had to learn how to hunt the hard way. On my 10th birthday, my dad bought me a new 22 rifle. That was like buying me heaven on earth.

I killed my first Wisconsin whitetail with a 16-gauge slug when I was 14. I've added 13 more since then, including two 12-point bucks.

I made my first out-of-state hunting trip in 1953, when I went to Wyoming for mule deer and pronghorn. That kind of hunting really opened my eyes and I went back for nine straight years. I became trophy conscious after that. I wanted to shoot a representative head of every big-game species I could afford to pursue.

In 1963 I hunted elk in Montana and was fortunate enough to take a fine 12-point bull. The next year I shot a wild boar on a shooting preserve in Indiana. My oldest son, who was 10 then, went with me on that trip and killed a boar also. I was mighty proud of that accomplishment.

My 1965 hunt was a by-product of a family trip to the West Coast. I'd read an *Outdoor Life* story about Spanish Goat hunting on Catalina Island, off the southern coast of California. I made a reservation to hunt on the island and I enjoyed a fascinating experience. I bagged a regular brown-coat billy, and a rare silver-tip.

That trip was actually a substitute for a hunt I'd set my heart on. I'd planned on going to Newfoundland. This dream began with another article in *Outdoor Life*. That story dealt with a Newfoundland moose hunt, but it also mentioned caribou. If a guy could hunt moose and caribou in the same area, I reasoned, he could add two new species to his big-game list. I was especially excited about the thought of bagging a caribou. I estimated how much a trip like that would cost, and I decided I'd better wait awhile.

My lucky break came in October 1965. Maynard Peck, a 56-year-old Janesville taxidermist, got the ball rolling. "Bob," he said over the phone, "four Rockford, Illinois, hunters were just in here with moose heads they want mounted. They shot them with ar-

154

rows and they got 'em in Newfoundland. They recommended an outfitter named Harry Newhook. I'm going to check it out."

Maynard called Harry in February of 1966. He found that non-resident caribou licenses cost $100 [1980 cost, $200] and were issued on a quota basis to first-come, first-served applicants. Moose licenses were also limited and were priced at $75 [1980 cost, $150]. Harry suggested applying for our licenses immediately. He said he could book six people for a September hunt, at $150 a week per man [similar 1980 fee, $375]. This included everything except sleeping bags and personal gear.

That price was too good to pass up, so we began organizing our trip. Besides Maynard and myself, our group included Bob Bartell, 31; Larry Kettle, 28; Gary Huber, 33; and Dr. Don Springer. Don is a 42-year-old surgeon from Monroe, Wisconsin. The rest of us are from Janesville. Bob and Larry are both single and work at the local Chevrolet assembly plant. Gary heads a family, like Maynard and myself, and makes his living as a stock chaser at a Fisher Body plant.

In a way, we were a strange group to go hunting together. Maynard limits his hunting to archery. He's a crack rifle shot, and proves it by winning trophies in statewide target competition, but he thinks taking game with a rifle is too easy. His arrow kill to date includes 30 deer, five pronghorn, two bears, a wild boar, dozens of pheasants, and hundreds of rabbits.

Gary Huber is an archer too, but he isn't a purist. He will spend most of his time on a trip hunting with arrows, but if he doesn't bag his game he'll make a last gasp attempt with his Winchester Model 70 30/06. The rest of us are riflemen.

We spent the summer ironing out details. Don and I could spare only a week of hunting, so we decided to make the trip by plane. The rest of the group scheduled a two-week trip in Larry's pickup camper. We constructed a 6x12-foot box trailer for hauling meat back home. We lined it with plastic (for road dust protection) and fitted it with a snap-down canvas cover. By early fall, we were packed and ready to roll.

The boys in the pickup pulled out of Janesville on September 7. Don and I boarded a jet in Chicago three days later. Seven and a half hours after that, we were in a hotel room in Gander, Newfoundland.

155

We met our outfitter the next morning. Harry, 48, is a New-foundland native and has never been off the island. His main occupation is guiding hunters. He works as a carpenter in the off-season. His cousin, John Newhook, and another guide named Fred Thorne were scheduled to meet the rest of our group in Millerstown, a small village 135 miles from Gander. All of us would rendezvous there, then drive another 50 miles to Harry's camp, an abandoned logger's cabin smack in the middle of our hunting area.

Newfoundland roads are a far cry from superhighways, and we had plenty of time to discuss our hunt during the ride. Harry told us that killing a bull moose with a rifle would be no problem at all. "But caribou come harder," he added. "They're up in the muskeg plateaus and they're tough to stalk."

That caribou talk was dream material. I'd read a lot about the big-antlered brutes and I wanted to be sure I killed one. I could go moose hunting within 700 miles of home, but I might never get another chance at caribou.

I was joking when I said to Harry, "I want a double-shovel rack with about 40 points. Something like that would be a real trophy."

Harry's answer was surprising, and it fired my anticipation to new heights. He wasn't kidding a bit when he said, "There are double-shovel racks in the area we'll hunt. They're scarce, but a few are taken every year. I'd say that if you get a bull with 30 points, you're doing as well as you can expect."

The last few miles of our journey to camp shot the rest of the day. A logging company owns all the surrounding property and there's only one way in and one way out. That's by tramway across the company's dam on the Red Indian River. It's only 800 feet across, but you make the trip by railroad flatcar—and you have to wait until the small diesel locomotive has a break in company business. We waited four hours to make the 10-minute trip. After that, we drove 45 miles on a rocky bush road that was no more than two tracks winding through dense wilderness.

We rolled out of our sleeping bags at 4:30 the next morning. Outside, a drizzle and 40° F. temperatures promised a dreary day. By 5:30 a.m., Bob Bartell, John Newhook, and I were deep in the bush. For Bob and myself, it was tough going the first couple of

After a long wait by the hunters, the train of flatcars arrives to take vehicles on short but crucial crossing of the Red Indian River.

hours. We had to learn how to walk and maneuver across the tangled ground cover and through the dense conifers. We couldn't see 20 yards ahead of us for most of the time, but once in a while we'd break out on a point or a ridge and be able to glass the countryside for miles around. That was the hunt plan—hike and glass new country for moose. Around 8:00 a.m. we spotted a small bull and a cow on a hillside 700 yards below us. "Forget him," John said. "We'll find better racks."

We spotted a bigger bull that afternoon, but it wasn't big enough to interest either Bob or me. John guessed his antler spread at a little better than 30 inches. Everybody in the group saw bulls that day, but nobody fired a shot. Harry and Maynard stalked within point-blank arrow range of a better than 30-inch bull, but Maynard decided he'd take his chances on something better. All of us had entertained the same thoughts.

The next morning dawned bright and clear. Fred accompanied Bob and me this time. We hadn't walked 200 feet from the road when we came out on a hillside vantage point. A big valley spread out 1,000 yards below us. We began glassing the terrain and spotted game within minutes. "There we go," Fred said. "That's a good bull. Look him over."

Fred pointed to an open hillside near the bottom of the valley. "There's a cow with him. They're moving this way, toward that marsh-grass flat. Let's just sit down and see if they keep coming!"

We watched those animals for 10 minutes. They kept feeding toward us, moving slowly. I guessed the antler spread of the bull at more than 45 inches.

"Good guess," Fred said. "He's a big one and we'll get him. When they get in the brush, we'll sneak down there and . . . My son, my son, look right here below us!"

I dropped my eyes from my binoculars and looked straight down the hillside. Two bull moose were in plain sight, no more than 75 yards away. They were completely unaware of us. They appeared huge at first glance, but a second look told me that the best bull's antlers measured in the 40-inch class. "Up to you, Bob," I whispered. "Take him if you want him!"

Bob's answer was the act of raising his scoped 300 Weatherby magnum. His rifle roared and the moose went down in its tracks.

158

We caped out the head, cleaned the animal, and spent the rest of the day hauling moose meat back to camp.

The next morning Fred and I encountered the action I described at the beginning of this story. By now I'd passed up three bulls and had come within a whisker of getting a shot at two others. You can see why I didn't think bagging a moose would be much of a problem, and why I wanted to get on with the caribou hunt.

Back in camp, at noon, we all discussed the situation and my partners agreed with my caribou thoughts. We packed Larry's pickup with sleeping bags, cooking gear, and a few days' supply of food. With four-wheel drive, we managed to get a mile up the mountain on a long-abandoned logging road. From there, it was a four-mile uphill hike to an outpost cabin that Harry had built a few weeks before on the edge of plateau country.

We were nearly up to tundra altitude when John Newhook turned to me and made a suggestion. "Let's drop our packs right here and hunt a while. There's some valleys and ridges off to our left. It's all top game country."

What started out to be a short hike turned into a cross-country exploration. Each time we glassed a valley, we'd move on to another ridge. Finally, John mentioned we were running out of time. "Let's stake one last look over that next hill," I said. "Then we'll go back."

We went down into a cut of thick brush and scrambled up a hogback ridge of pine. When we topped out, we were looking over a broad valley of relatively open country. A forest fire had swept that valley years before and fire-blackened spires of pine trunks contrasted with green ground cover. A river wound through the bottom of the valley, and knolls of rock showed patches of white and gray.

I caught the flash of movement before I'd raised my binoculars. I didn't say anything because the movement had been gray and white and I thought my eyes might be playing tricks on me. Then, when I found the object in my glasses, I couldn't say anything; my breath simply choked up in my throat.

I'd never seen a caribou before. I knew they had great beams of antlers, but the sight I was looking at just couldn't be true. The

159

animal was 200 yards below us, broadside, but he seemed composed more of antlers than body. The brown rack burst out in every direction. I couldn't tell where the points began or where they ended. Finally I stammered, "Caribou down there!"

"Rock," John answered. "It fooled me for a minute too."

That answer was enough to shake my breath loose. "Rock, hell," I whispered. "That's a bull caribou and he's as big as a barn!"

Then John looked in the right spot. "My God, Bob," he wheezed, "shoot!"

I'd already leveled my Model 721 Remington 300 magnum. The crosswires of the 8X Weaver scope wavered, then settled on the bull's shoulder. I touched the trigger and the 180-grain factory-loaded bullet was on its way. I was sure my aim was true, but the caribou reacted to the roar of rifle as if he weren't even scratched. He bolted to our right and ran straight out with full power. I remembered to lead him with the second shot, but he never missed a step.

"Slow down," John yelled. "Take your time. You're missing him!"

I knew I hadn't missed that first shot, and I didn't think I missed the second one. I held in the same place and fired again. This time the animal piled up like he'd been sledged. He never moved a muscle after he hit the ground.

We didn't go down there right away. We wanted to be sure he was dead. Once we started down through the brush, we would lose sight of the animal. Suddenly, there was more excitement. Another bull caribou walked into sight from behind a knoll within 75 feet of my trophy. He stopped dead still and stared in our direction. We watched him for a few minutes until John yelled and clapped his hands. The heavy-antlered bull bolted and disappeared behind a knoll. We didn't see him again.

We went down the hill through a jungle of brush, windfalls, and rocks. I thought I was moving fast, but John ran right away from me. He reached the caribou, lifted the antlers, and began shouting. "This is the biggest bull I've ever seen. Isn't this something, though. Isn't this something!"

John kept saying that over and over. I was so excited I didn't know what to say. We finally calmed down enough to discover

160

The smile of success on Robert Knutson's face is nearly hidden behind the massive antlers of his caribou.

that all three of my bullets had slammed into the heart area. We took some photos, then raced for the outpost cabin for help.

When we got there, I told Harry I'd shot my caribou. "Fine," he exclaimed, "is it a good bull?"

"It's got 52 points," I answered. "We counted them three times."

Harry looked at me with a disbelieving stare. "Fifty-two points," he echoed. "There ain't no such a thing. They don't get that big."

John verified my count, but Harry still wasn't convinced. "Let's go look at that animal," he said.

Everybody made the three-mile hike, and then there was a lot of handshaking and picture taking. Harry couldn't take his eyes off my trophy. Finally he said something that made me realize the magnitude of my accomplishment.

"I've seen thousands of caribou," he exclaimed. "I've seen many of the best heads ever killed in Newfoundland, but I've never seen anything like this. I'm guessing you've got a world record."

As far as I was concerned, my hunt was over. I was too excited to think about moose hunting. By the next day, however, I had begun to calm down. I still had three days to hunt. Fred and I went down to the main camp while the rest of our group stayed up in caribou country.

The next morning was as clear as a bell, the temperature was in the high 40s, and I almost lucked out on a trophy bull moose. We'd hunted most of the day without sighting game. Late in the afternoon, we walked into a valley and glassed the hillside above us. The sun had dropped behind the western ridge, making it difficult to inspect the shadowed timber. But Fred caught a flash of movement. "My son," he exclaimed, "there's one as big as a mountain!"

The bull was standing in brush 900 yards away, alternately grazing and lifting his head to survey his surroundings. The hillside was so dark that it was hard to see his body. But when that bull threw his head up, I could spot the mass of brown antlers with no trouble at all. That was a tremendous rack, 50 inches or so, by far the best I'd seen.

From left, guides John Newhook, Fred Thorne, and Harry New-
hook. They all said the Knutson trophy caribou had the most mas-
sive antlers they'd ever seen.

Lumbermen built this bridge across raging river. Knutson and his party used it to reach moose hotspots.

If it had been earlier in the day, we could have made a proper stalk. As it was, daylight was fading fast and Fred decided on a shortcut route. We went down a hill, across a creek, through a valley, and up another hillside. We sneaked around a knoll and inspected the area where the bull should be. He was still there, but he'd grazed in the wrong direction. Fred figured our cause was lost.

I guessed the range at 500 yards. I knew I could drop the bull if I could put a bullet in the right spot. "This is a big rifle and my scope is eight power," I told Fred. "I think I can kill him!"

"Try if you want. We can't get any closer."

My rifle was sighted for 250 yards. I held a foot over the bull's shoulder and fired. The big animal wheeled and disappeared into nearby brush. I knew I'd missed, but we walked over and examined the area where the bull had stood. It wasn't as far as I'd figured. I'd held too high and the bullet had gone over his back.

The next day we passed up some small bulls. After that, I had one day left and knew I couldn't be choosy any longer. I killed a young bull the following afternoon. Fred and I had watched him bed down in the thickets of a small valley. I sneaked down there and was wondering what had happened to the animal when he suddenly jumped up and bolted away. I dumped him with one shot in the heart area.

On the overall hunt, everybody in the group filled their licenses. Maynard killed his bull caribou with a single 700-grain fiberglass arrow fired from a 55-pound Bear bow. Gary Huber whanged an arrow into the heart of a huge trophy caribou. That one bolted 20 yards, then piled up dead. Its antlers officially scored 310-1/8 in Pope and Young Club awards, and the trophy ranks well up in the archers' record book. [*Editor's note:* Huber's woodland caribou ranks No. 3 in current Pope and Young Club records.]

I had my giant caribou scored by two official measurers of the Boone and Crockett Club. Their separate total scores came out only 2/8 of a digit apart. The lower total was 405-1/8. That score was verified by a panel of judges on December 31, 1967. I was notified by Boone and Crockett Club officials that my trophy ranked No. 3 in all-time records.

The present world's-record woodland caribou scored 419-5/8.

165

That animal was killed before 1910 by an unknown hunter, so mine is the second-best ever taken by a known hunter. When I consider that I killed the giant within a few hours' plane trip of New York City, I'm amazed to realize that nothing is really impossible in the exciting sport of trophy hunting.

(EDITOR'S NOTE: *Knutson's trophy still ranks No. 3 in its category.*)

The Tigre is Behind Us

By C. J. McElroy

(EDITOR'S NOTE: *The original version of this story appeared in the January 1967 issue of* Outdoor Life.)

March in a Mexican jungle is an eerie world of singing mosquitoes and crawling insects. During the day, the temperature hovers around 100°F. There's usually no wind and the humidity is like a wall of moisture. In the evening, the temperature drops slightly. But the humidity doesn't change, and the insects become almost unbearable. If you're a jaguar hunter, you expect this and you don't complain.

I couldn't have been happier at any other spot in the world. Darkness, now only an hour away, would find my companions and me waiting for El Tigre from a machan eight feet off the ground. We had good reason to believe that we would see action, and that was excitement enough. If I could have known all that would happen that night, my excitement would have been uncontrollable.

We finished our preparations for the arrival of the night-prowling cat in the last golden glow of sunset. Our arena of action had been planned to the last detail. The platform had been built near the conflux of two well-beaten cattle paths that wandered through thick jungle. A 60-foot circular clearing had been hacked out of the green thickets in front of the machan. Near opposite edges of the clearing, just inside the fringe of jungle, we staked out two live goats as an attraction for the killer cat.

Our machan was five feet wide by eight feet long, and made from cut sections of limbs tied between two trees and two posts. Hugo Castellanos, my guide and outfitter, climbed to the platform first. I handed up a blanket, mosquito netting, a water jug, and my rifle. Hugo spread the blanket (used to keep mosquitoes and other insects from coming through the floor) and erected the netting in a tentlike shape. Then Roy Partida and I climbed to our positions. Last to come up was Manuel, Hugo's second assistant and the fourth member of our night-hunting group.

"We must be very quiet," Hugo cautioned. "This tigre is a big one and will be very wise. He will not come close if we make the slightest sound. We may have a long wait. Are you all set?"

"All set," I answered.

Dusk was accompanied by the cries of big white cranes going to roost. A bull bellowed on open range somewhere in the distance. After that, a black world came quickly, disturbed only by the buzzing of mosquitoes and the bleating of our two kid goats. As time passed, I glanced occasionally at my companions. Their dim silhouettes were like statues, but I knew they were as alert as I was.

Darkness was two hours old when Hugo and Roy stirred slightly, noiseless reactions that charged the air with apprehension. I suddenly was aware that the goats had stopped bleating. I zeroed my eyes toward the blackness of the small clearing. I had assumed that if a jaguar approached, he would move silently into the clearing, then make a move to kill the goat of his choice. My guess was wrong.

I've heard the voice of many dangerous wild animals, but I'd never experienced the wave of chills that swept over me when the jaguar grunted directly behind the machan. It's an eerie sound, something similar to the cough of a lion, except not as heavy. It starts higher and ends higher, like a foreboding of complete destruction. The unnatural *Wowwww-ooh-uhh* is terribly unnerving, especially when it erupts directly behind while you're straining your ears for the slightest rustling of leaves.

I fought the temptation to leap upright and swing my Winchester 270 toward the sound. Instantly, I knew I'd bungle everything if I made the slightest move. The spine-tingling grunt came again, then silence. Minutes passed. Was he gone? Did he wind us or suspect something? Seconds seemed like hours. I don't believe anyone has thoughts at a time like this. You just wait and hope that nothing has gone wrong. Suddenly, I heard a rustling of leaves almost directly below us. After the previous silence, the unmistakable tread of the heavy body seemed almost too loud to be real. Dry leaves crinkled, and nobody had to guess that the tigre was moving toward the goats. I slowly and silently lifted my rifle off the blanket and eased it to my shoulder. My left hand moved out along the forearm. I had to be ready to shoot instantly.

The footsteps stopped directly in front of the machan, and a ray of light stabbed the solid darkness.

Hugo's aim with his four-cell flashlight was dead center. The big cat was bathed in a yellow beam that froze him in a posture of suspicion. He stood with one foot off the ground, head held high and looking up at the machan. Somehow, he'd been alerted. Now he was momentarily surprised, and I had the most perfect opportunity a man could ever hope for.

The range was 25 feet. In a single fast flow of motion, I moved the rifle, found the cat's chest across my open sights, and triggered an explosion that shattered the stillness. The jaguar reeled back, the same way any animal will recoil when hit in the chest at close range. But he didn't go down. He staggered, then recovered and started running across the small clearing, heading for thick jungle to my right.

Suddenly he stopped, apparently confused and not knowing quite what to do. Hugo's light was on him perfectly. The cat was broadside now, and I fired another bullet at his shoulder. My second slug staggered him again, but he refused to collapse. Then El Tigre seemed to regain his senses completely.

He whirled around and dashed back across the 60-foot clearing. I fired a third time as the big cat was swallowed by the jungle. The action was over as suddenly as it had started.

Pandemonium reigned on the machan. All of us started talking at once. Hugo and Roy yelled at each other in Spanish, and I tried to make myself heard in English. Apparently, Hugo, Roy, and Manual were discussing what happened instead of what we should do next. I stopped that waste of time in a hurry.

"Let's get down from here and get after him," I shouted. "I'm not going to lose that cat!"

My companions stopped talking at once. Hugo fixed me with a surprised look. "You realize," he said, "that this is a giant of a tigre. To follow him in darkness is very dangerous."

I hadn't even considered the possibility of not following him. That jaguar was a prize worth any effort. But Hugo was my outfitter and guide, and I'd been on enough big-game hunts to know that good guides should be listened to.

"We can find him tomorrow if you hit him good," Roy commented.

"I know that," I replied, "but this hot weather will ruin the skin if we don't get him tonight."

"He moved out of here pretty fast," Hugo cautioned. "Who knows how hard you hit him!"

I was almost ready to take "no" for an answer when Hugo made his decision. He knew how disappointed I was, and it was this knowledge that caused him to relax his guard.

"It's your party," he said with a weak grin. "If you say 'go,' we go."

The four of us, armed with one rifle and three flashlights, climbed down from the machan and walked over to where the jaguar had stood when I fired my first shot. We found some big splotches of blood on the leaves. With Hugo and myself leading the way, and all three flashlights combing the jungle, we followed the trail of red spots to the edge of the clearing. Short minutes later, the thick jungle swallowed us like ants in a sea of grass.

To understand the nature of my disappointment, it is necessary to know something of the quarry I was pursuing. The jaguar is the largest of the North American cats. Worldwide, only the lion and the tiger are larger. The jaguar resembles the leopard, but is heavier and has markings in the form of large black rosettes with one or more black spots in each center. Generally, the jaguar does not stand as high as a cougar, but he is heavier and much stronger.

Jaguars are reasonably plentiful in parts of Mexico, Central America, and Brazil. They are night marauders, and hunt and live in the most inaccessible tangles of jungle. If you want to shoot one, you must go to the jungle and hunt in the midst of myriads of insects, ticks, and chiggers, and not a few snakes. You put up with oppressive heat, foul and stagnant swamps, poor accommodations, and companions who generally don't speak your language.

Besides hunting a rare and exotic animal, you are also matching wits with a vicious killer. Common jaguar victims are horses and cattle. Unlike the dog-fearing cougar, a jaguar will often stop after a short chase and tear the life out of hounds that pursue him too closely.

There are several well-authenticated reports of jaguars making unprovoked attacks on humans. A mistake in judgment by a hunter could very well be his last mistake.

I knew all these things before I insisted on following that blood trail. I've been a big-game hunter for a long time, and I've always been particularly fascinated with cats. Before this hunt, I'd taken lion, tiger, leopard, lynx, bobcat, and mountain lion. All cats of the wild, in my opinion, are clever, extremely fast, and tough to kill. Many of the professional hunters I know dislike hunting cats, and are mighty happy when they are finished with them.

My hunting career began on a farm in Denton County, Texas, where I was born in 1913. I learned my first woodlore from a man named Walter Prather, a dedicated outdoorsman who enjoyed letting small boys tag along while he ran his trapline on Denton Creek. I learned a lot from Walter. By the time I was 10, I was hunting and trapping on my own. I bought my first 22 rifle with money I earned by selling a healing ointment to neighbors. Before I was a teenager, I was running my own trapline before and after school. Money from trapping sales enabled me to buy plenty of ammunition for my gun, and I hunted anything and everything at every opportunity during all open seasons.

I'm 53 now and own a flooring company in Inglewood, California. I use every free moment I can spare from my business to hunt selective trophies all over the world. My wife, Alvina, likes to hunt also, but she stays home when I get involved in the rugged stuff.

I have hunted in all the western states, Mexico, South America, Canada, Alaska, India, and several countries of Africa. I have hunted polar bear at 40°F. below zero in the arctic, and tiger at 120°F. in India. My trophy room has 63 different species of big

171

game. I get around quite a bit, but nothing ever excited me as much as the prospect of bagging a jaguar. In my opinion, it's the most prized trophy in North America.

This trip was my third attempt at jaguar hunting. In January 1963, I hunted the Nayarit area of Mexico for 10 days. We used dogs in the early mornings and ran several cats without ever sighting one. That's an awfully tough way to hunt. You try to follow the dogs through thick brush, tangled jungle, and the ever-present swamps of dirty water. You are soaked with perspiration, and insect repellent is washed away in minutes. A strong man, in top physical condition, is hard put to last even a few hours on this kind of a hunt. You have to want a jaguar in the worst way to plan a second trip.

I went back in March 1964 for another 10 days of the same kind of torture. After it was over, I still hadn't seen a jaguar. I was more determined than ever. I figured that if I tried hard enough, the odds eventually would turn in my favor.

I originally came in contact with Hugo through a friend who had hunted with him. After that, Hugo guided me on two Mexican hunts for deer and javelina. We spent some time running jaguars with dogs on both of these trips, but the animals eluded us. In Mexico, the jaguar is considered a killer. [There was no closed season on this magnificent animal when McElroy made his hunt. Now the open season on jaguar in all of Mexico runs from December 1 through March 31.—*Editor's note.*]

Hugo is 40 years old and makes a living guiding hunting parties in Mexico. Though he is a Mexican citizen, he lives with his wife and children in National City, California. Good outfitter-guides for the Mexican jungles are hard to come by, but Hugo's knowledge and ability is tops. In January 1965 he visited me in Los Angeles. We talked jaguar hunting and I said, "Hugo, if you hear of a good bet for a hunt, phone me right away."

He called early in March. "I have heard of a giant jaguar," he said. "The tigre is killing cattle and goats near the small town of Cienega in the state of Sinaloa. He is very aggressive and unafraid, sometimes taking livestock from corrals. I think this is your opportunity."

I'd learned from my previous trips to Mexico that it's best to leave all hunting arrangements to your outfitter. If you go through customs with nothing more than your field clothes and personal gear, you will have no delay. If you try to bring guns, ammunition, and other gear, you will be faced with a myriad of questions, forms to be filled out, and all types of time-consuming bottlenecks. If you hire a man such as Hugo, your cost for a 10-day hunt will be about $1,000 [*Editor's note:* Similar 1980 charge, about $2,500] and he will furnish everything, including your rifle. It is much too difficult to do it any other way.

On the 19th of March, I boarded a plane to Mazatlan on the Gulf of California. Hugo met me at the airport with a jeep. We drove northwest through the small town of San Jose, then turned south as the thin growth gave way to thick jungle. Late in the afternoon, we came to the village of Cienega. Leaving this small cluster of houses, we drove another 12 miles to the San Blas River. Roy and Manual (natives of the area) and 12 assorted hounds of mixed breeds met us at the river's edge. We used dugouts for the last phase of my journey, which was a short trip to Tacula Island.

The island, which is the largest in the river in that area, had been selected as a choice spot to set up camp. In contrast to the high banks along the river, the 100-x-300-foot island was flat, and the low sandy banks offered ideal beaches for loading and unloading our dugouts. While Roy and Manual organized our headquarters base, Hugo filled me in on our hunt schedule.

"I heard about the giant jaguar from Roy," he said. "The animal frequents a ranch area eight miles upstream. I think our best chance to get him will be from a machan at night. Roy and Manual built a platform a few days ago. But we should let the tigre get used to the construction before we hunt from it. We'll give him a few more days. In the meantime, we'll use dogs in the mornings and try calling at night. If we're lucky, we'll get our jaguar without having to use the machan."

We weren't lucky. We hunted hard for the next three days without success. During the early mornings, we tried running the cats with our pack of hounds. We jumped jaguars four times, but never caught up to any of them. The dogs either lost the trails or began staggering from exhaustion. You hunt early in the mornings because by noon the oppressive heat is unbearable for dogs or men.

During the nights, from darkness until around 2:00 a.m., we

173

drifted downstream in a dugout and tried calling the tigres. Our call was a native-made device of tight skin that resembled a drum top. A leather thong pulled through a hole in the skin produced a sound that was amazingly like that of a jaguar. We had answers from cats on two occasions, but they didn't come close enough to be seen.

The morning of March 24th dawned like every other day in the jungle: cloudless, hot, and humid. We took it easy most of the day because that night we were going to hunt from the machan. It was a long day for me. My inner feeling that our luck would change grew stronger as the day wore on.

Our camp came alive as the broiling sun settled to the jungle in the west. An hour later, our outboard-powered dugouts had moved us eight miles upstream. We pulled into a high bank, then walked a short distance to a small farmhouse surrounded by ramshackle buildings and corrals built of poles. A few scrawny cows and calves looked at us without interest, and three goats started a conversation with our kids. An old man came out to meet us. Hugo spoke rapidly to him in Spanish. When they finished, we circled the corrals and walked across dry pasture toward the machan, two miles away in thick jungle.

"What did the old man say?" I asked.

"We're in luck," Hugo said, grinning. "The big tigre was calling close by the house last night. The old man wished us success and he hopes we kill the cat. He has lost a lot of livestock."

Four hours later, after the machan action I described in the beginning of this story, I was fervently hoping that the jaguar's list of victims would be terminated before he added lives much more valuable than those of livestock.

It was touch and go in the ebony jungle. Nobody said a word. We were all well aware that the cat could easily spring on us without a breath of warning. I held the rifle at instant readiness, and I closely watched the beams of the flashlights as they darted into thickets ahead. For a while, I had the feeling that my two bullets had seriously wounded the tigre; I didn't think he would try a counterattack. But Roy's and Manual's actions indicated that they put no stock whatever in that theory. They were extremely edgy, acting as if they were ready to leap aside at any instant.

By the time the trail was 10 minutes old, I began to share their apprehensions. Maybe my bullets hadn't hurt that cat badly after all.

The blood trail was easy to follow. The spots of red glistened like jewels in our flashlight beams. The cat had started through the thickest growth he could find, and then switched directions and went down a hill into some high grass. Hugo seemed to sense that the jaguar might have chosen that grass as a fine spot from which to watch his backtrack.

We moved slowly now. Everybody was very grim. My pulse thudded with building tension.

One of the lights flickered past a light spot in the brown grass. Then the beam immediately backtracked. Thirty feet ahead of us, the light spot trembled slightly. Suddenly, two yellow-green spots glowed at us as the cat turned his head. Maybe I shot too fast but, whatever the cause, I missed the target. With the roar of the rifle, the tigre vanished in a single bound.

We now knew that the cat could move quickly. Nobody said anything, but I knew my companions were extremely disappointed that I hadn't put an end to this spooky business. The cat hadn't given me much time, and I hadn't seen more than a spot in the high grass. Yet I'd had a good opportunity to kill him, and I knew it.

The tigre was still bleeding quite heavily, and his trail led out of the grass and into thick jungle. About 100 yards later, Hugo made a discovery that really shook us up. The trail of blood had circled and we had crossed the original trail. There was some conversation in Spanish, but I didn't understand it. Then Hugo looked at me and said, "He has been behind us!"

Hugo's grim words hit me with full impact. I knew that wounded animals considering attack will often double back and ambush their victims from the rear. I still had enough confidence in my ability with a rifle to believe I could kill the cat quickly if I had any chance at all. I said as much and waited for Hugo's reaction. He shrugged his shoulders and turned back to the trail of blood.

Fifteen to 20 minutes passed without incident. By now we had trailed the cat for more than 300 yards. We still moved slowly, letting the lights explore every inch of thick cover before we moved forward.

175

Suddenly, we saw the tigre again. He was no more than a flash of movement as he jumped from a maze of thickets. I snapped off a shot, but I knew it was wasted. Now, for the first time, I was tempted to give up. I didn't say anything, however, and we kept moving ahead.

Another 10 minutes went by, one step at a time. The flashlights kept tunneling their beams into each suspicious thicket. We came to the thickest jungle we had encountered, and Hugo was forced to part the branches before I could step ahead with my rifle. Then I saw the huge cat again.

He was 25 feet away and half hidden behind the protruding roots of a big tree. But I could make out his head and part of his shoulder. When the lights zeroed in, he remained still for a split second. I shot quickly, and the bullet slammed into his neck. He collapsed in a spotted heap. We moved up slowly, but the tigre was dead. Four mighty relieved men suddenly jumped and yelled with exultation.

I examined the cat carefully and discovered that my first two bullets, fired from the machan, had slammed into him at my precise points of aim. The first had opened a gaping hole in his chest, and the second had broken up on his massive shoulder bone. The bullets I used were 100-grain. They were light for such a big job, but it was still hard to believe how the tigre had been able to lead us on such a long chase. The vitality of these beasts is phenomenal. Hugo guessed the tigre's weight at 270 pounds, and his age between 12 and 18 years.

Though I'm an official measurer for the Boone and Crockett Club, it didn't occur to me at the time that my jaguar might be a new world record. I was more than pleased that I'd finally killed the giant cat. Hugo was happy because he had succeeded. The native rancher was joyous because he could sleep more soundly at night and have more beef and lamb to sell.

A few months later, after the skull had dried, I made some preliminary measurements. I was astonished. I had thought my trophy would easily make the record book but now, if my measurements were confirmed by the panel of judges at the Boone and Crockett Club's headquarters, I knew I had a new world record.

That's the way it worked out. On May 4, 1966, at the Club's

C.J. McElroy grasps a foreleg of his big jaguar as the trophy animal hangs from pole. Local ranch hands carried the cat out from thick jungle.

12th biennial awards dinner at the Carnegie Museum in Pittsburgh, my jaguar was officially recognized as the best ever taken in North America. He scored a total of 18-7/16. [*Editor's note: The official system used to score jaguars is identical to the system used to score bears.*] I had the animal mounted in a full lifelike pose. He is now the feature attraction in my trophy room.

(EDITOR'S NOTE: *McElroy's jaguar may never be surpassed. It still retains its No. 1 ranking.*)

The Rage of a Bear

By W. L. (Tommy) Cave

(EDITOR'S NOTE: *The original version of this story appeared in the August 1967 issue of* Outdoor Life.)

As far back as I remember, I longed to kill a bear. My grandfather started the whole thing, and he did so in dramatic fashion.

In his youth, Grandpa left his Missouri farm and drove a wagon to California during the gold rush of 1849. He didn't find much gold, but he got mixed up with a grizzly bear. He shot the critter with an old muzzleloading rifle.

Later he brought some of the claws back to Missouri for souvenirs. When I was five years old, Grandpa gave me one of those claws, and I'd never seen anything in my life that so excited me. That claw was three inches long. I figured the rest of the bear must have been as big as a house.

Back in those days, times were mighty tough on our Missouri dirt farm. I was one of 13 children, and I was doing farm chores as soon as I was big enough to be useful. If ever a kid had a bleak future as a bear hunter, it was me. There wasn't a bear within 500 miles of our farm.

But times change, and 45 years later I was going to have my chance. All through those years, ever since I bought a 22 rifle with money I earned by stoking school furnaces, I hunted every time I could. For the last 10 years I've traveled to Colorado for deer and

179

elk hunts. Actually, on those hunts I spent most of my time following bear tracks. But I was never lucky enough to get a shot.

After my 1963 trip, I made some decisions. I'd bought 10 bear licenses, but still hadn't killed a bear. There seemed to be only one answer: hire a professional guide. I began corresponding with guides whose ads appeared in *Outdoor Life.*

I've hunted enough years to be particular about what I shoot. I wanted a bear big enough to make a rug, a large rug. I'd read about bears killing livestock and I reasoned that if a bear were big enough to kill sheep and cattle, he'd be big enough to be a real trophy. I told those guides not to call me until they located a bruin turned killer. I mentioned one other condition, too. I knew a late summer or fall bear would have a better coat than a spring bear. Though the Colorado season runs April 1 through September, I specified a hunt no earlier than August.

So it was that Walt McCart, an outfitter operating out of Fruita, Colorado, called me on the evening of August 8, 1964. "Tom," he said, "I've heard of a monster black bear that's killing sheep up around Steamboat Springs. I think we can get him."

I'd been waiting a long time for that call. "I'll be there in 36 hours," I answered. "I'm bringing my brother Andy along. We'll have to find a bear for him too."

Our trip plans were in motion within minutes. I immediately called Andy and told him the good news. Andy, 37, is a farmer and part-time carpenter with a growing family. He lives a few miles from my home town of Fulton, Missouri. I'm married, 51 years old, and make my living as a housing contractor.

We pulled out of my driveway at 3:00 a.m., only four hours after Walt had called. We drove as far as Estes Park, Colorado, then curled up in the car and slept for six hours. That's Rocky Mountain country, and the miles go by slowly. But we met Walt in Steamboat Springs at 10:00 a.m. on August 10.

Walt is 35 and has the lean, hard appearance of a man who spends his life outdoors. He's a full-time outfitter, guiding hunters in western Colorado and Utah. Bears and mountain lions are his specialties, but he also operates elk and deer camps. His charge included everything except sleeping bags and personal gear.

Walt had five hounds in the back of his pickup, and I looked those dogs over mighty close. I didn't know anything about bear

180

dogs, but I've owned coon and coyote hounds for 40 years. I like to think that I can tell a good trailing dog when I see one. I liked the looks of those dogs. I knew that my lifelong quest for a bear was getting down to its final hours.

We bought our nonresident licenses, then left Steamboat Springs on one of the roughest roads I've ever seen. We drove 30 miles north, then turned right on a two-wheel track that served as a ranch road. We rattled across a wooden bridge above the Little Snake River, then turned into a mountain valley.

A few minutes later we spotted Walt's sheepherder wagon parked under a stand of cottonwoods. A green wall tent was set up nearby. Two hobbled horses looked at us with disinterest. Three chained hounds bawled a chorus of welcome. I readily recognized them as a bluetick, a black and tan, and a Plott.

It was too late to hunt that afternoon. We spent our time organizing camp, catching trout from a willow-lined creek, and soaking in the scenery of choice big-game country.

"Plenty of deer and elk up here," McCart told us. "But it's top black bear country too. It's loaded with berries, and bears are great berry eaters. There are lots of ant logs, which are great bear attractions too. In addition, it's sheep country. When a local bear turns sheep killer, he can live in paradise. There are no humans in these mountains except isolated sheepherders and a few families living on summer ranches."

We talked bear hunting until nearly midnight, when Andy came up with a final question. "Are these black bears dangerous," he said. "I mean, are they likely to attack you?"

"I've read a lot and I've heard a lot," Walt began. "But I have to go by my own experience. I personally think a black bear is terrified of human scent. I don't think they'll attack a man unless they're crazed by pain or sickness. I once had a bear run right over me. I was in a position where I couldn't shoot him. If conditions had been different, and if I had shot him, I'd probably have figured he was charging me."

Andy and I couldn't let that gem of a story slip by. We pressed for details. Walt then told us the story from its beginning.

"John Wright, a state trooper, and I went bear hunting for fun. My dogs hit a smoking-hot track around noon and lit out at full speed. We followed on horseback, and four hours later I saw the bear cross an opening of thick tangles. That mass of brush reached the belly of my horse and I'd seen the whole bear as he charged through there. He was big, and I wanted him bad. The rug from a critter that huge would carpet a small room.

"The big black never stopped running until almost dusk. Then he took a stand in dense brush and started fighting the dogs. I got within a few hundred feet of the ruckus, and then the thickets became so tangled that I had to crawl and part the brush with my hands.

"Suddenly, a dog went darting past me. I looked through the thickets and saw a wall of black coming toward me. The brush was so thick I couldn't tell what part of the bear I was looking at. Then he dove at the rest of the dogs and disappeared from my view.

"I shoved my 44 Ruger handgun in the brush and started crawling ahead again. I made about 10 feet when, all of a sudden, that bear was all over me. I didn't have a chance to do anything except flatten out on the ground. He went over me like a bulldozer, pinning brush against my back so tight I couldn't move. If he knew I was there, he gave no sign of it. I think he was just getting the hell out of there, and getting out as fast as he could go in the easiest direction."

Andy and I didn't get much sleep that night, but we were wide-eyed and ready to go long before dawn the next morning. Walt cooked a breakfast of pancakes and bacon and eggs on an outside camp stove. A canopy of stars hung in a clear sky. The hounds strained at their chains and whined in eagerness to start hunting.

We left the horses in camp, put five dogs in Walt's pickup, and bounced eight miles through rocky canyons to an area where a Mexican sheepherder was grazing 3,000 sheep. Walt talked to the herder in Spanish. He discovered that a bear had killed three sheep two days before. The Mexican pointed to the pine-covered mountainside a mile away. Walt and Andy took the dogs and hiked up there, but the trail was too old to start.

We drove close to another sheepherder's area that afternoon. This fellow was a Basque, a native of the rugged Pyrenees Mountains bordering France and Spain. He could only speak in Basque, a language unrelated to any other European tongue. American ranchers hire Basques (under U.S. Government control) because of their incredible capacity to endure hardship and solitude. Their stay is limited to two years and they are paid well. Many sheep ranchers are glad to get these fellows, and there are hundreds of them in the West.

Our Basque was a friendly young man in his early 20s. Walt had a tough job trying to tell him we wanted to find a bear. He finally got the idea across, then' the Basque pointed down the valley.

I visited with our host while Andy, Walt, and the dogs took off on a scouting trip. An hour later I heard the dogs strike a track, but the occasional yelps didn't promise much. I tried to ask the herder which way the bear would go, but I couldn't make my question understood. After that, the Basque made finger and mouth motions indicating we should eat. He fed me baked bread, potatoes, and powdered cheese. We enjoyed each other's company, though neither of us knew what the other was talking about.

Andy and Walt came back two hours later. "We found a track," Walt said. "But it was old and the dogs couldn't work it out."

It was near evening when we got back to camp. Bob Evans, a friend of Walt, was waiting for us. McCart had asked him to join the hunt because we could use his four-wheel-drive pickup. Bob, 36, is a full-time guide from Baggs, Wyoming, and he often joins Walt in working with hunters. He's a happy-go-lucky guy, and I measured him as another veteran outdoorsman.

Andy and Walt left camp before dawn the next morning. They headed up the valley on horseback, accompanied by seven dogs. Bob and I washed breakfast dishes, loaded two dogs in his pickup, and took off after our companions. Daylight was breaking when we passed them and first-geared Bob's truck up the dusty two-wheeled track angling along the mountain.

We hadn't made a quarter of a mile when my eye caught a disturbance in the roadside dust. I'm always alert for animal tracks, and I knew exactly what I was looking at. "Whoa!" I exclaimed. "There's a bear track!"

We stopped the truck and examined some pretty exciting evidence. The impression in the dust looked like the barefoot print of a huge man. A pre-dawn sprinkle of rain had dimpled the dust,

183

but there were no raindrop marks in that print. "That's the biggest bear track I've ever seen," Bob said. "I think you're going to get a crack at that sheep killer!"

Walt and Andy arrived a few minutes later. Walt's lead dog, Belle, scented the fresh track long before she was near it. The hairs on her back bristled like a wire brush and she turned and looked at her master. Walt glanced down at the track from his horse, then fixed me with a knowing grin.

"Tom," he said, "that bear's as good as dead as far as my dogs are concerned. They'll run him up a tree somewhere. You just better hope you'll be able to get there!"

At that moment, Belle opened up with a long, loud bawl that sent shivers down my spine. In a moment, Walt and Andy and the pack of yelping hounds were gone. Dog music began to fade in the depths of the canyon.

The sun was just rising, and its early light accentuated the wistful look on Bob's face. I knew he wished he were on horseback, following the hounds. I wished I were, too. I wished with a passion that I could have been charging a horse through the brush, following the dogs to certain action. But I didn't have any choice.

I guess I better stop here and explain a few things. When I was 11 years old, I slipped on some ice while running a trapline and broke my right leg. Maybe the doctors didn't set it right, or maybe I was just unlucky, but bone infection set in and stopped normal growth. By the time everything cleared up, my right leg was three inches shorter than my left. Horseback riding was a thrill I'd never experience.

But I'd like to say loud and clear that I don't consider my physical defect much of a handicap. In fact, I think I'm a better hunter because of it. If I had the two best legs in the world, I still wouldn't be able to outrun wild game. I realized long ago that the best hunter is the guy who can outthink and outsmart his quarry. I get more game than most hunters, and I'm successful because I've taken the time to learn and interpret the reactions of wild animals. I can't move very fast, but I've learned how to be in the right spot at the right time.

Now, standing there in the mountains, I knew I was in the wrong spot. It was a situation I couldn't control. All I could do was hope for the best.

There wasn't much time to think about it. We listened to the dogs cold-trailing for a few minutes, then suddenly heard a burst of loud hound music.

"Jumped him," Bob bellowed. "That bear better run in the right direction."

Bob didn't have any particular direction in mind; he was thinking about where we could go with the pickup. If we lost hearing of the chase, our part in the hunt would be over.

I've been on wild vehicle rides before, but I'd never seen anybody handle a truck like Evans did. We bounced and slid and clawed over mountain terrain that would tax a horse. We stopped six times in the next couple of hours. Three times we could easily hear the dogs and three times we thought we had lost them. The first time that happened, my hopes dropped to near despair. Then, far in the distance, a faint yelp or two came through the still air. We roared away in a new direction.

Our fifth stop found us on top of a ridge overlooking a canyon. We heard the dogs putting up a wild ruckus of yelping and snarling that rolled up the mountainside.

"Bear's stopped to fight," Bob said with a grimace. "A bear that size will kill some dogs. Nope. They're moving out. He's running again."

The last time we stopped, we listened to the distant dogs for 15 minutes. They were running the bear around a bowl-shaped canyon. Then the barking sounds changed again. I recognized the new chop-mouth tempo. "I'm no bear hunter, Bob, but I'd say those dogs are barking treed."

"Maybe you're no bear hunter, but you're right," he replied. "Well, we're on foot now. Let's hustle."

Bob released one of his dogs from the back of the pickup, and that black and tan headed for the action like a race-track greyhound. Though I didn't know it at the time, this maneuver had important significance. When Walt noticed Bob's dog join the rest of the pack, he'd know we were aware that the bear was treed and that we were on our way. Without this signal, Walt would know we'd lost hearing of the chase.

I forgot about my bad leg. The bear was on the mountainside across the canyon in front of us. We went a mile along a ridge to a point opposite the action. Then we half slid and half ran down a steep grade of loose shale, windfalls, pine, and thick brush. We made it to the bottom of the canyon in quick order, but going up the far side was another story.

When I get involved in tough walking, I use my rifle as a cane. It's a J. C. Higgins 30/06 fitted with a HVA Swedish bolt action. It will hold five cartridges, but I keep the chamber empty because of that cane business.

Right now, the magazine held four cartridges loaded with 60 grains of 4831 powder and 150-grain Herter bullets. That's a hot handload, and I didn't have any other cartridges with me. After all, there was only one bear to shoot, and I'd never seen anything yet that wasn't knocked flat out with just one of those loads.

My heart was pounding from excitement and exertion by the time we made 100 yards uphill. Then I found a gully wash that was free of brush. Loose rocks and windfalls were bad enough, but I struggled along at a faster pace. The dogs were raising an unbelievable racket, and I knew we were getting close. I looked up the mountainside and the little breath I had left rushed out of my lungs in a throaty gasp.

Seventy yards away, I saw a mass of black high in a big pine. Maybe it was the exertion, but I would have sworn I was looking at three bears. Then the sight focused in. The monster bruin was lying across a web of branches with a front and back leg hanging loose. At first glance, those legs had appeared to be separate bears. I was puffing so hard that I wondered if I was seeing things. "My God, Bob," I stammered, "is that all one bear?"

Bob was breathing hard too, but he sputtered out an answer I'll never forget. "Hell, yes—but they just don't get that big. You're the luckiest hunter that ever climbed a bear mountain!"

I couldn't see Walt or Andy and the dogs. They were screened behind low brush. Then suddenly I was aware of Walt hollering, "Hurry up. Kill that bear before he comes out of that pine and smashes up my dogs."

I got up near the tree; I've never heard such a collection of vicious sounds in my life. The dogs were a blur of frenzied yowling. The bear was slobbering at the mouth, clicking and popping his teeth like pistol shots. He was mad at the whole world, and it didn't take any expert to know he wasn't going to stay in that tree much longer. Then I heard Walt talking.

186

"Soon's he's rested," McCart said, "that big old boy will come down faster than you can turn around. Take him in the throat and break his neck. But take it easy, and don't miss!"

I wasn't worried about missing. As far as I was concerned, the show was over except for one easy shot. That bear was only 40 feet away. His neck almost filled my 2-1/2X Weaver scope. I moved uphill so the animal would be below me when he hit the ground. Then I settled the crosswires and squeezed the trigger. I heard my slug slam into the animal with a distinct *Whomp!*

What happened next just didn't make any sense at all. That bear went into a rage. He acted as if the bullet never fazed him. He started smashing branches in all directions. He grabbed a limb as big as my arm in his jaws and snapped it like a dry twig. I was dumbfounded. Then I became nervous. If a 30/06 bullet just made him mad, what would it take to kill him?

I didn't know if anybody else had a firearm. It crossed my mind that nobody knew I had only three cartridges left. From what I could tell, that bear could come down and kill dogs and men anytime he got the notion. I decided a neck shot wouldn't do the job; I'd have to shoot him in the lungs and bleed him to death.

All these thoughts went through my mind in split seconds. My second bullet slammed into his lung area, and again the bear didn't seem to notice the slug at all. He kept smashing around up there, and twigs and branches rained to the ground. When he turned around, I sent another slug into the lung area. Nothing happened except for more branches being smashed apart. Walt was hollering, "Shoot again, give him another one!"

Maybe Walt thought I was missing accurate bullet placement, but I knew those slugs were going right where I aimed them. I was really shook up now. I had one cartridge left, and I wasn't about to use it. I wanted to save it in case I had to shoot that bear off one of my companions.

I guess 15 or 20 seconds had passed since my first shot. The bear seemed dazed now, like he was trying to make up his mind what to do. Then down he came. He didn't jump; he just seemed to slide off the limbs. He hit an eight-inch pine deadfall and smashed right through it.

The dogs were all over him when he smacked the gound. There was a violent uproar of barking and snarling, and I thought for a moment that the bear was fighting. Then Walt's voice topped the clamor of the dogs, "That bear's stone dead. He ain't going nowhere!"

Now it was all work. Andy went after the horses while Walt, Bob, and I began skinning chores. We got one side skinned and found we couldn't roll that huge bulk over. When Andy returned, we all grabbed handfuls of fur, set our feet, and heaved in unison. On our fourth try, the bear finally tipped over. I'm only five feet four inches tall but I was able to stand up and work on that critter. I wouldn't know how much he weighed. Walt guessed 600 pounds. I guessed a lot more than that. I was probably wrong, but I've butchered a good many cattle. That bear looked as big as a full-grown steer.

I stayed in camp the next day while Walt and Andy rode out after another bear. It didn't take long. They were back at noon with the hide of a big female. That one had run five miles before it treed. Andy shot twice with his Remington 760, 30/06, and our bear hunt was over.

We broke camp quickly so we could get our trophies to a taxidermist in Denver that same day. I'd heard of the Boone and Crockett Club method of scoring big-game animals, and I figured my bear might make the record book. People at the taxidermist studio assured me I was right, and they offered to score the skull after the required 60-day drying period. That was on August 14, 1964.

In the spring of 1966, I got a letter from the Boone and Crockett Club headquarters. When I read that letter, I couldn't believe my eyes. My bear, with a total score of 22, had been officially recognized as the new world record. I've got the skull hanging in my gun cabinet. Whenever I look at it I can't help but wonder how a guy with a crippled leg could ever be fortunate enough to kill the best black bear ever taken in North America.

(EDITOR'S NOTE: *Cave's trophy now holds the No. 6 ranking, but the current world-record black bear has a total score of only 22-6/16. That's less than one half of one digit better than Cave's bruin.*)

188

Three Bucks for the Book

By Ed Morgan

(EDITOR'S NOTE: *The original version of this story appeared in the November 1967 issue of* Outdoor Life.)

I've been on a lot of deer hunts in the past 20 years, and I've been fortunate enough to find areas with plenty of bucks and few hunters. But nothing will ever top the stroke of luck that set the locale of my 1966 hunt. My son, Ed Jr., decided the issue when he was six months old. That was in the summer of 1965.

My family and I were driving home to Nacogdoches, Texas, after a vacation in Colorado. We stayed on the road too late that night, and we had trouble finding a motel with a vacancy. The baby was worn out, and I had to find some kind of a room without delay.

We were desperate by the time we drove up to the Elk Horn Lodge in the small town of Chama, New Mexico. While registering for the last available room, I noticed a framed photograph on the wall. I couldn't believe what I saw. It was a picture of the two largest mule-deer bucks I'd ever seen.

"Good gosh," I said. "Where did those bucks come from?" The motel owner looked me over and smiled quizzically. "Right around here," he answered. "Lots of big bucks in this country. Take a look at the wall behind you."

189

I turned around and saw a mounted mule-deer head that took my breath away. The antlers were so massive it seemed impossible they could belong to a deer. I knew right then that I'd found a premier deer-hunting area.

Six of us hunted the Chama district in October 1965. Our camp was near the eastern boundary of the Jicarilla Apache Indian Reservation, a 758,000-acre chunk of north-central New Mexico wilderness. We had a good hunt, the weather was beautiful, and we enjoyed a fine week of camp life. Two of the fellows killed monster bucks. I had chances at average bucks, but I never fired a shot. I wanted a real trophy or I didn't want anything. The three other unsuccessful hunters felt the same way.

The most impressive thing about that hunt was the mystery of the Jicarilla Reservation. The area was out of bounds for our hunting, but it didn't take us long to suspect there were plenty of big bucks in there. We spotted some wide-beamed trophies while scouting the day before the season opened. But those bucks vanished when rifles began cracking in the ranch country. I guessed that they'd slipped into the reservation, where they wouldn't be bothered.

During the following year, I couldn't get that reservation out of my mind. Then, in August 1966, Parrish Cox, a Nacogdoches insurance agent who was a member of my hunting group, showed me a clipping from the *Dallas Morning News*. The clipping was about deer hunting in the Indian territory. It mentioned that Melvin Vincenti, Chief of the Jicarilla Apaches, would supply more information to interested hunters.

Less than an hour later, I was talking to the Chief by telephone.

"We're offering two hunts," he said. "The early hunt begins on October 30 and lasts two weeks. You can kill two deer, either sex. There will be 200 permits at $100 each in the north hunting zone, and 500 at $30 each in the south. [*Editor's note:* These costs have more than doubled in recent years.].

"Our late hunt runs from December 3 to 10," Vincenti went on. "During this period you will be limited to one buck, and your permit will cost you $150. You can rent horses from the Indians. They'll cost you $10 each per day, and that includes riding gear and services of a wrangler."

Though most hunters would choose the early season, my gang

190

decided on the December hunt. We figured the rut would be on then, and that the big bucks would be more apt to be moving about. This decision was a group endeavor. We've made our hunting-trip decisions in this way for years.

There are 10 of us. We're all lifetime friends, and most of us are related. We're all in our 30s, we were all raised in Nacogdoches, Texas, and we've been hunting since childhood. Dick Ferguson, an insurance salesman, and Roy Tidwell, an orthodontist, live in Tyler, Texas; the rest of us still live in nearby Nacogdoches. Charles Wright has a laundry; Harold Muckleroy is in the ice-cream business; Ken Sutton operates a cattle ranch; Vyrne Shofner is a dentist; Dick Wright owns a feed business; and my brother, Charlie Morgan, is a doctor. I'm 36, and I operate a gasoline wholesale business. We are all married, and when our families get together there are 30 children to boast about.

We left Nacogdoches on the last day of November, and drove 1,000 miles to Chama, New Mexico, where we had stored some of our camping gear after the previous fall's hunt. We had five vehicles: my one-half-ton pickup, Ken Sutton's three-quarter-ton four-wheel-drive pickup, my brother Charlie's one-half-ton pickup, Charles Wright's station wagon, and a Jeep that belonged to the group.

We collected our gear in Chama and then drove 40 miles to Dulce, which is a small town in the extreme northern part of the reservation. Nathan Vigil, a 25-year-old Apache wrangler, was waiting for us. I'd made previous arrangements for Nathan to supply our horses. Though it was the first day of December, the weather was like summer. The sky was cloudless, and the air was hot and dry. Dust swirled as we drove over tribal dirt roads leading to the hills.

An hour later, I was looking at the most beautiful wilderness I've ever seen. This is a country of high mesas, sheer rimrock, rolling ridges, and draws that break away in every direction. From the tops of the mesas, you look down on thick pine forests, beautiful oak basins, and sagebrush flats. In the distance, jagged mountain peaks rest in a blue haze. I think the best description would be to say that it looks like Indian country—awe-inspiring in dimension, undisturbed by man, and locked in solitude.

We selected a campsite below a rock bluff. An acre of flat

191

Members of the party look over some rugged hunting country.

brown grass, nestled in thick pines and oaks, served as a floor for our 16x32-foot sleeping tent. Right next to that, we pitched a 16x16-foot cook and supply tent. A small creek ran below us, and beaver activity was much in evidence.

We spent a day and a half arranging our camp and scouting the surrounding territory. By now, the weather had changed from wonderful to awful. When we rolled out of our sleeping bags at 4:00 a.m. on opening day, it was pitch black outside, and a mixture of rain and snow promised miserable hunting conditions.

Our hunt plans followed the normal technique used in the wilderness areas of the Southwest. We would hunt from horseback, riding slowly from ridge to ridge, glassing the rims and pockets of brushy draws. Normally, two hunters work together, riding parallel a few hundred yards apart. I chose to hunt alone that first day.

By noon, I had seen five bucks. They were all accompanied by does and they all had good racks, but not one was in the trophy class. Three of those bucks were aware of my presence, but they didn't appear unduly concerned. The woods seemed alive with deer.

After I saw the fifth buck, the mixture of snow and rain changed to all snow. In minutes, big, wet flakes turned the sky to a ceiling of white. It was snowing so hard that I could hardly see my horse's ears. I dug my thermos of coffee out of a saddle bag, slid off my mount, and waited for the storm to slack off.

Fifteen minutes later the snow had changed to rain. I mounted my horse and turned him up a sagebrush ridge. Below me, on my right, a shallow draw separated me from a high hill. There was thick cover in that draw, including tangles of oak brush and scattered pines and cedar. I glanced at those thickets, then turned my face away from the rain and continued up the ridge.

Suddenly there was a commotion 25 yards to my right. I knew what was happening before I could turn my head. A heavy buck, lunging to his feet, makes a peculiar stomping noise. I'd heard the same type of racket before, and I reached for my rifle at the same time I looked for the deer.

By the time I spotted the buck, he was running straight away in full view. The first thing I noticed was a tremendous maze of thick antlers. They extended far out beyond the buck's ears, and beyond both sides of his body.

193

While setting up hunting camp, the party gets into an earnest discussion.

My horse saw that muley almost as soon as I did, and he didn't like the sight a bit. He humped his back, snorted, and began pitching a fit. I no more than had my hand on my rifle when my mount decided to unseat me and leave the country. Somehow I hit the ground on my feet.

By now the buck was nearing a thick patch of pines 50 yards away. I jacked a 180-grain handload into the chamber of my converted sporter 30-06 Springfield and threw the rifle to my shoulder. I found the buck in my scope, but he disappeared before I could get the shot away.

Though I couldn't see him, I could discern his travel route from the sounds of snapping brush and clattering rocks. He was running up a steep mountain covered with thick pines and oak. I spotted a small clearing ahead of the sounds, about 125 yards from my position. The buck went through that clearing as a gray-brown flash. I didn't have time to pick a precise aiming point; I just shot at the deer. The monster muley never missed a step.

I turned and saw my horse going over a ridge, running full out. I never felt so alone in my life. There wasn't a sound of any kind. I was sure I'd missed the buck, but I wasn't about to take anything for granted. I wanted to follow his tracks, but I figured I'd better get my horse back first. I removed my heavy outside clothing, piled it on the ground, and took off in a trot.

Two miles later I topped a ridge, and saw my mount grazing with two wild horses. By the time I got within 100 yards, the wild animals snorted and galloped away. My horse glanced at me, wheeled, and ran after his new companions. By now I was completely frustrated.

There wasn't anything to do except climb back up the mountain to where I'd left my gear. By the time I got there I was completely wet from snow and rain, and chilled to the bone. I struggled into the wet coat and raingear, picked up my rifle, and headed for the clearing where I'd shot at the buck.

I searched the area for any sign of a hit, but I found nothing. The buck's tracks were easy to follow for a half mile, but then I lost them in an area of rain-washed rocks. I made a wide circle, but to no avail. I said to myself, "Old buddy, you'll have a great story to tell in camp tonight, but that's all!"

I gave up the search and started down the mountain. I hadn't

195

made 50 yards when I glanced across a draw of oak brush. I couldn't believe my eyes.

A big buck was partially hidden in thickets 65 yards away. He was standing still, looking straight at me. His rack seemed every bit as massive as the one I'd seen before, and I didn't hesitate a second. Through my Lyman 4X scope, I found a small opening in the brush that centered on his right shoulder. I touched the trigger, and that muley went down in his tracks.

Elated, I ran across the draw like a jackrabbit. When I reached the buck, I stared at a massive 17-point rack. Over and over I muttered to myself.

"My gosh, what antlers!" I figured I was looking at my goal of a lifetime.

I finally started the field-dressing chores, and then discovered why that buck had offered such an easy shot. This was the same deer I'd shot at before, and my first bullet hadn't missed. The slug had slammed through both hind hams, but had missed hitting bone. The shock would have knocked an ordinary deer off his feet.

I finished my job, then took off for camp. It was snowing hard now, and I was still dripping wet. Darkness was closing in fast by the time I had walked three miles. Then I topped a ridge, and looked down on one of the greatest sights I'll ever see. There was my horse, with his bridle firmly tangled in thick brush. He pitched another fit when he scented buck smell on me, but I wouldn't have let loose of that bridle for $100.

It was long after dark when I got back to camp. Nathan, Ken Sutton, and I piled into the four-wheel-drive pickup and took off to get my buck out of the woods. By the time we got back, it had snowed six inches. We hung my buck alongside a big 8-pointer (4-point western count) that Parrish Cox had killed. Then we discovered that Harold Muckleroy had not returned from his hunt.

Six of us jumped into the pickup and drove the tribal roads in a blinding blizzard. We'd stop every mile or so, blow the horn, and holler into the driving wind. We were extremely concerned when Harold suddenly rode into our lights out of a curtain of white. He was exhausted, and his horse looked half dead.

"Man!" he said. "I'm sure glad to see you boys!"

196

The next day, Dick Wright shot a buck that made mine look undernourished.

Dick and my brother Charlie were miles from camp by the time the rising sun and a foot of new snow turned the wilderness into a glistening wonderland. The welcome sunlight didn't last long, though, because the sky soon clouded and the temperature dropped well below freezing. About mid-morning, Dick jumped a 10-point buck. He had a good chance for a shot, but he decided the antlers weren't thick enough for trophy material.

"It's an enormous thrill to pass up a big buck," Dick told us when he rode happily into camp. "But I forgot all about the animal as soon as I crossed the next knoll. There below me was a flat of sagebrush running between two foothills. Out in that sagebrush, the biggest mule-deer buck I ever hope to see was walking slowly away from me. He hadn't noticed me top the ridge, he was only 75 yards away, and I thought I could kill him with no trouble at all.

"That dream blew up in a hurry," Dick continued. "By the time I yanked my 270 Weatherby from my saddle scabbard, that buck had glanced over his shoulder, spotted me, and bolted to his left. He disappeared in thick brush before I got my scope on him. Those oak tangles were too thick to run a horse through, and the only chance I had was to circle the thickets and hope I'd get another glimpse of him. I kicked that quarter horse, and he really took off. Snow flew higher than my head, and we went 400 yards at full tilt."

Dick went on to tell us how he pulled the horse up at the base of a hill, scanned the countryside, and saw no sign of his deer. He moved on for another 300 yards and found tracks in the snow near a house-size boulder. The tracks led around and across a ridge, and Dick suddenly found himself looking down into a small canyon of scattered spruce and snow-covered thickets.

"There was a doe and a 10-point buck down there," Dick recalled excitedly. "They were 200 yards away and looking up at me, but I knew in a flash I wasn't looking at my trophy buck. This fellow's antlers weren't as massive, but he was a good one and I decided to take him.

"I'd had my rifle in my lap during that wild ride, and it was

197

covered with snow. When I dismounted, I dropped to one knee. I couldn't see a thing through my 6X Redfield scope. The lenses were iced over. I frantically tried to wipe them clean with my gloves while I kept my eyes on those two deer. They ran around some brush, then stopped.

"I suddenly realized they weren't looking at me at all," Dick continued. "They were watching something to my right. I turned and spotted the big buck I'd seen before. You just don't mistake antlers like that. He was unaware of me, and he was walking down into the canyon. By now I'd worked a dime-size hole through the ice on the scope. The range was 125 yards, but I had a clear shot. I touched the trigger, and that buck piled up dead in a cloud of snow."

Ken Sutton accompanied Dick to pack out his trophy. They took off in the four-wheel-drive pickup, and they got stuck three times. They made it back to camp, but they were darn lucky to get there. The temperature had suddenly warmed, and it was raining again. Melting snow turned the countryside into a sea of gumbo mud and slush.

The next two days were awful. It rained and snowed continuously. There was some hunting done by the seven men who hadn't filled their licenses, but no shots were fired. Most of us spent our time digging out stuck vehicles. The tribal roads were virtually impassable. Our Jeep went down into the black gumbo so far that we couldn't jack it up. It finally froze in and stayed in the same spot all winter. Our Jicarilla friends pulled it out in March 1967.

Everything went from bad to worse. We had a real scare one night when Harold and Dick Ferguson failed to return from a horseback hunt. We tried to search for them. But every time we'd get a vehicle moving, it would slide off the road and become stuck again. We gave up late in the night and trusted in the Lord that Harold and Dick were all right. They were. They spent the night on a comfortable bed by a roaring potbelly stove in a sheepherder's line cabin. When we learned the details the next morning, we didn't know whether to be glad or mad.

The transportation problem was bad enough, but our living quarters became almost unbearable. Both tents began leaking. Our bedding was wet, our groceries were wet, and our tent floors

From left: Dick Wright, Vyrne Shofner, Kenneth Long (local Indian agent), and Ed Morgan display three bucks that qualified for the record book.

turned to masses of mud. We kept our butane stove going full blast in an effort to dry things out, but it was a losing battle.

Though we had originally planned to hunt seven days, we decided we'd better break camp. That morning, the fifth day of the season, a news broadcast on our portable radio warned of a severe snowstorm heading our way. We knew we couldn't get out if new snow drifted over the mud, so we began a session of frantic packing.

When the snowstorm didn't show, we decided three men could make a last hurried hunt. The seven unsuccessful hunters drew straws, and Charles Wright, Roy Tidwell, and Vyrne Shofner lucked out. They took off on horses while the rest of us finished breaking camp and getting one of our trucks out of the mud.

After lunch, Parrish and Nathan climbed into the truck and took off for Dulce to arrange for a tribal roadgrader to return and pull out our other vehicles. When those two men returned, they were as happy as a couple of kids in a candy store. I couldn't figure out what was going on until I looked in the back of their pickup and saw a monster 17-point buck.

"You better wait until Vyrne rides in," Parrish said with a big grin. "He'll tell you the story."

"There's a lot to tell," Vyrne said an hour later. "I think the Lord was guiding us because I just happened to be in the right spot at the right time. I was riding down a mountainside when I spotted a buck coming toward me down another mountainside about 600 yards to the west. There was a valley of thickets between us, but I was in thin cover so I stopped my horse dead still.

"The deer was so far away that I couldn't tell much about his antlers. When he stopped and put his head down in some brush, I eased off the horse and steadied my Bushnell binoculars. I got a real shock when I picked him up in those 7x35 optics. That buck looked as big as a horse, and his massive antlers looked as if they belonged to an elk.

"I sneaked away from my horse and ran toward the buck while screening myself behind a cedar tree that stood between us," Vyrne continued. "When I got to the tree, I peered around it and . . . no buck. I figured he must be in an arroyo 200 yards below me. I didn't think he could have crossed it in the short time it took me to make my run. For a moment I panicked. Then I spotted

Dick Wright with his mule-deer buck, the best taken by any member of the group.

movement only 100 yards below me. There he was, trotting up toward me, but he was in brush so thick that I could hardly see him. I picked a tiny clearing 60 yards ahead on his likely line of travel, leveled my 257 Weatherby Magnum, and waited. My heart was going like a trip-hammer by the time I realized that the buck had changed directions.

"Above me, 125 yards away, a road ran along the side of the mountain. I figured if I could get up to that road fast enough, I might spot my trophy when he crossed it. When I turned around, I noticed my horse alerted to something behind him. I saw the buck almost in the same instant. He'd already crossed the road and was hurrying into thick brush. I found him in my 3-9X Weatherby scope, and touched the trigger. I don't think I ever fired a rifle as fast in my life. The next thing I noticed was the buck's rear legs kicking air. By the time I got there, he was dead.

"Well," Vyrne said, "I was a pretty happy guy. By the time I dragged that monster 25 yards to the road, I heard a truck coming toward me. Nathan and Parrish couldn't have timed their arrival more perfectly."

Vyrne didn't have all the luck that day. Charles and Roy knocked off big bucks too. Roy dumped a fine 10-pointer that was running full tilt at a range of 200 yards. Charles spotted his 10-pointer grazing in sagebrush 400 yards away. He dropped off his horse, got into a sitting position, leveled the crosswires of his scope over the buck's back, and squeezed the trigger of his 270 Winchester Model 70. The buck hit the ground as if he'd been slammed by an invisible club.

All of us were familiar with the Boone and Crockett Club's method of measuring trophy deer. We were also familiar with the club's book, *Records of North American Big Game.* We'd all dreamed of the day when one of us would kill a buck good enough to be registered in that book. We knew we'd killed some top trophies, but we weren't prepared for the shock we got on March 3, 1967, when our bucks were scored by W. R. Long, an official Boone and Crockett measurer from Tyler, Texas. Of the six bucks, three of them scored higher than the 185 minimum required for typical mule deer to make the record book.

Dick Wright's monster totaled 203-7/8, a score equalling 12th place in the current edition of Boone and Crockett records. My buck scored 192-7/8, and Vyrne Shofner's totaled 186-2/8.

Though we had fantastic luck on our hunt, the same adventure is available to anybody. You can get details by writing to the Jicarilla Apache Indian Tribe, Department of Fish and Game, Dulce, New Mexico. There is a motel in Dulce, but accommodations and guide services are limited. If you don't plan on camping and hunting on your own, you'll have to make arrangements months in advance of the hunting seasons. In addition to buying a hunting permit issued by the Indians, you'll also need a nonresident New Mexico deer-hunting license. There's a lot of planning that goes into a hunt like ours, but I know 10 Texans who can't wait until the December snow flies again on the Jicarilla.

(EDITOR'S NOTE: *Wright's trophy currently ranks No. 48 in the typical-mule-deer category. This large drop in ranking highlights the astonishing fact that 36 better bucks have been entered into the Boone and Crockett record book in the intervening 14 years.*

When this book went to press, hunting on the Jicarilla Reservation had been greatly curtailed.)

Don't Shoot the First Buck

By Harvey P. Olsen

(EDITOR'S NOTE: *The original version of this story appeared in the July 1979 issue of* Outdoor Life.)

When I set out from Tom Martin's farmyard near Elkhorn, Manitoba, I felt certain I was beginning a hunt that would produce a giant whitetail buck. It had taken me years to narrow down my trophy search to this immediate area, but now the moment of truth could be almost at hand.

Though dawn was still more than an hour away, I was already jumpy with anticipation. While scouting the previous afternoon, I had spotted nine whitetails. Four were bucks. Three of the four wore fine racks. One buck was a monster, with antlers so massive that they looked like a bushel of brush. Though I got a good look at that brute, he didn't see me. I built a blind in a spot where I figured I had a good chance of seeing him again. Now that blind was one and one-half miles ahead of me.

There were six inches of snow on the ground, but my mind was so preoccupied with big bucks that I scarcely noticed it as I began my hike. The weather was perfect—no wind and no clouds. Overhead, stars glittered like jewels in the 10°F. temperature. There were still 30 minutes before full light when I reached my destination. I had camouflaged my sitting spot on a deadfall log by jabbing branches into the snow.

My stand was 30 feet off a runway that routed through the edge of woods bordering a marsh. The marsh was 250 yards wide, and loaded with thick cattails, high grass, and scattered red-twig dogwood. A creek about six feet wide ran through the middle of the marsh. As the eastern sky began turning yellow, I realized that the creek could cause me some problems.

Fog hung over the running water. It was so thick I couldn't see the beaver dam 150 yards away. I knew that deer used the beaver dam for crossing the marsh enroute to bedding areas. I also knew that, once they crossed the marsh, they would be hidden in the woods before reappearing much closer to my stand. I had hoped I'd be able to nail a buck as he crossed the marsh. The fog was fouling up that plan.

Three does suddenly appeared on the runway. They passed me without the slightest suspicion. That fact really built my confidence because now I knew I'd picked an ideal spot for my blind. A spike buck then traveled along the same route. He also passed me with no inkling of trouble.

About the time the fog began to thin, I spotted movement in the marsh near the beaver dam. Wisps of fog cleared enough so that I could make out one deer, and then another. They had already crossed the beaver dam and were in high grass and cattails near the edge of the woods. Just before they disappeared behind a rise of brush, I got enough of a view to know I was looking at two huge trophy bucks.

If the bucks came my way, they should appear on the runway in about four minutes. Those few minutes were some of the longest of my life, but not nearly as long as those I began experiencing shortly.

When the two bucks crossed the marsh, they were almost side by side. But when they showed up on the runway, they were 30 yards apart. My nervous system hit high gear when I got a clear view of the first buck at a range of about 70 yards. He wore a typical rack that spread far beyond his ears and reached high above his head. He was walking slowly down the runway, and I had every intention of shooting him . . . until I got my first good view of the second buck.

This one wore antlers that astonished me. Tines as thick as small branches seemed to be sprouting out in every direction above his head. I wondered how a deer wearing so many heavy tines could hold his head up. "Don't shoot the first buck," I said to myself. "Wait for that big brute!"

I fully expected the leading deer to pass my blind just as the others had done, but he had different plans. When he got almost in front of me, he veered off the runway and began walking straight toward my blind. I fervently hoped he would change course, but on he came. By the time he was within five yards of me, his 11-point rack with at least a 20-inch spread looked twice that big.

I had become totally unglued inside, but somehow I managed to remain motionless. On came that 11-point monster. He was only a few feet away when he finally noticed me. His body went rigid. We stared at each other for what seemed to be forever. I wondered if he could hear my heart banging against my ribs. Then he snorted, whirled, and bolted. By now I had become so excited that I'd lost track of the bigger buck. He also spooked when the buck in front of me began crashing through the thick brush. Both bucks were gone in split seconds. I was numb with disappointment.

The only thing I could figure out was that the first buck had decided to bed down in the immediate vicinity of my blind. He wasn't alert to danger or he never would have walked so close to my blind before spotting me. I'm sure that the weather conditions prevented him from picking up my scent. In that kind of windless situation, scent goes straight up with thermal currents that always rise just after dawn on clear days. Since my stand was above the runway, there was no way that buck could have winded me.

My nervous system was so shot there was no way I could continue sitting on stand. I walked off through the woods to Jack Cliff's blind. I told him what had happened, and then we still-hunted until noon. Neither of us saw another deer.

This hunt had its beginning in 1970 while I was working at Engle Chevrolet in Utica, Michigan. Bill Bevens ran the body shop there, and he had just returned from a deer hunt in southeast Saskatchewan. He'd scored on the biggest 10-point buck I'd ever seen. He thought his typical whitetail would make the Boone and Crockett record book, but it didn't.

I didn't know anything about the record book, but I sure wanted to see a copy. If Bevens's buck wasn't good enough to make the book, I wanted to find out how big a whitetail had to be to get listed in its pages.

I visited several libraries, but none had a copy. Then I learned that there were some copies in Birmingham at the "Sportsman," a very fine outdoorsman's shop owned by Erwin Wilson.

I visited with Wilson and learned that he is an official measurer for the Boone and Crockett Club. Little did I realize, when I bought a copy of the record book from Wilson, that three years later he would score my trophy as one of the best whitetails ever taken.

I began hunting deer with my dad in 1956, when I was 14. I got a fine 5-point buck that fall with my 16-gauge shotgun. For several years after that, I got my deer every fall in southern Michigan's shotgun zone. The first time I got skunked was in 1965, when my brother Frank, Bill Park, and I tried deer hunting on Beaver Island in northern Lake Michigan. We all got skunked, mostly because we were hunting new country we hadn't scouted.

We hunted nearby Garden Island the next year. We paid a commercial fisherman from St. James on Beaver Island to get us to uninhabited Garden. We camped there for 10 days, then did the same thing for three years in a row. We enjoyed some fantastic deer hunting, but those are other stories in themselves.

When 1970 rolled around, I was very interested in trophy hunting. That big buck that Bill Bevens killed in Saskatchewan really added fuel to my trophy fever. I was even more fired up after I got my copy of the Boone and Crockett record book. My three hunting partners were just as excited.

At that time, we were all in our early 30s. My brother Frank is now a general supervisor in a manufacturing plant. Bill Park works for the Ford Motor Company, while Jack Cliff is a builder. I'm a professional landscape contractor (Designed Landscape) in Royal Oak, Michigan.

The four of us got together and went to work with the information we found in the record book. We bought maps and made Xs

207

on the areas where record-book whitetails were taken in Manitoba and Saskatchewan. We were surprised to discover that most of those big bucks were downed in a 150-mile-wide area that stretched across southeastern Saskatchewan and southwestern Manitoba.

In 1971, we joined Bill Bevens's group on a combination moose and deer hunt near Hudson Bay, Saskatchewan. There were nine of us on that trip. We planned on hunting moose for a week, then moving south for a week of deer hunting in the area we'd mapped. Moose hunting got into our system pretty strong after Bill Parks got a fine bull with a rack measuring 59-1/2 inches. Our luck with moose was zero after that, but we all got fine whitetail bucks.

Frank, Bill, Jack, and I planned our own hunt for 1972. Again we scheduled our first week for moose and our second week for deer; and again the moose hunting came up bad. We saw only one cow moose in more than a week of hard hunting, and that cut down our time for going after deer. We managed to get only three bucks, but they all had nice racks.

By now we were convinced that if we were going to get trophy bucks, we'd better concentrate on deer hunting. We decided that our 1973 hunt would start in the trophy-rich area we'd mapped three years before. If we got lucky, and filled our deer tags in a hurry, then we'd head farther north and try for moose.

We left our homes in southern Michigan on November 9 and drove straight through to Brandon, Manitoba. We had my 11-1/2-foot DelRay camper that sleeps six, my pickup truck, two snowmobiles, Jack's snowmobile trailer, and snowshoes. We also had assorted clothing, hunting equipment, and camping gear.

We headed west the next morning. We bought our nonresident Manitoba deer-hunting licenses in a small diner and discussed our scouting plans over breakfast. We had allowed two days for scouting before deer season opened.

Our scouting work is fairly elaborate. The system involves driving back roads while looking for good deer habitat. On the prairies, good habitat means a proper balance of woodlands, food, and water. What looks like good habitat may not be. One area may be loaded with deer sign, and another equal area of identical terrain may show little or no sign.

When we spotted an unposted area that looked as though it had possibilities, we'd stop and spend an hour scouting. We'd spread out and cover most of the area, then meet back at our vehicle. We have a rating system that works on a 1-to-10 basis: 1 is the worst, and 10 is the best. A low-rated area is one that shows few tracks or other sign. We are very critical. One of us would almost have to get run over by several deer of sizable proportions before we'd give an area a 10 rating. After we rated each area, we'd mark its score on a map and then drive on.

We didn't find any high-ranking areas until we got close to the Saskatchewan border the second day. This area harbored about 300 acres of dense woodlands, which is a big chunk of forest in a region that is mostly cleared for grain farming. We found lots of deer tracks in the fields around the wooded areas. We also found several well-used runways, some recently used beds, and some rubs and scrapes. The area obviously harbored quite a few deer, and the rubs and scrapes told us that at least some of those deer were bucks. This area got a rating of 9.

We drove to the closest farmhouse, introduced ourselves to Tom Martin, and asked if we could hunt on his property.

"That will be okay," Martin said. "Where are you fellows staying?"

"We've got a camper," I answered. "We figured on parking it along the road."

"Tell you what. You can park it in my farmyard if you want to. And you can plug into my hydro."

"Great," Frank said. "We looked around your woods for a few minutes. Lots of deer sign. We found some rubs and scrapes. Have you seen any nice bucks?"

"I suppose you fellows want trophies," Martin said. "We call those big bucks 'jumpers' up here. I'm not much interested in 'em. I go for meat. But I saw lots of jumpers when I was harvesting my wheat and barley. They're using my place. You ought to be able to find 'em."

We had about three hours of daylight left, so we went scouting for places to be on stand the next morning. We split up. I headed into the largest area of thick aspen. Once in the woods, I jumped two bucks that were bedded within a few yards of each other. They were both 6- or 8-pointers, and they really blew out of there.

Though Manitoba farming country might not look as if it would hold many deer, Harvey Olsen found that headquartering in this farmyard was the key to enjoying his greatest whitetail hunting ever.

As they went crashing away through the brush, they put another buck on the alert.

I think this one heard the two other bucks running, and he just stood up in his bed to see what was going on. He was more than 100 yards from the two animals I jumped, but he was only about 80 yards from me. This probably was the buck I described in the very beginning of my story, the one with antlers so massive that they looked like a bushel of brush.

I stared at that rack for several moments, and then realized the buck was unaware of me. He didn't spook; he just walked away in a northerly direction. By the time he melted from my view, I had already decided to backtrack him from his bed.

When you know where a buck beds, you can get a pretty accurate picture of his habits when you backtrack him. A lot of hunters believe it's best to follow a jumped buck in order to discover his escape routes. This tactic doesn't make sense to me. A buck that's being followed knows somebody is after him, and he may leave the country. You can learn a lot about a buck's routine by backtracking, and he won't even know you're there.

The backtrack led me out of the thick aspens and alders and down to the marsh I described earlier. The tracks led on across the beaver dam and into a smaller section of woods. This stand of low aspens edged the marsh for about a mile, but it was only 200 yards wide. I found a wheat field on the other side of these woods.

Deer tracks were almost everywhere in that field. So were scratch marks, where the animals had pawed through snow to uncover waste grain. Now I had a clear picture of that big buck's travel routes. I surmised that he fed in the field at night. Then, at dawn, he headed across the narrow strip of woods to the marsh, crossed the creek on the beaver dam, and bedded in the big woods where I'd seen him.

Though there were several runways in the big woods, I wanted to pick a stand site where I'd have a good view of the marsh and the beaver dam. I wanted a blind close enough to the dam to be within fine shooting range, yet I wanted to be high enough to have a good view of the runway areas.

One runway seemed to be more heavily traveled than the others, and it routed through the edge of the big woods bordering the marsh. I walked down it about 125 yards and came to a slight rise on the east side of the travel route. That was important because the predominantly western winds would keep my scent away from passing deer. Up on the rise, I found the deadfall area that would give me good visibility through the 50 yards of woods between me and the edge of the marsh, and limited visibility of the beaver dam.

After I blew my chance at the huge buck the next morning, I was jumpy for hours. Manitoba law limits deer hunting to mornings only, so we were all back in Martin's farmyard shortly after noon. I guess we really hit it off with Tom and his wife Joyce because he said we could stay as long as we wished. Maybe our desire to help with the chores had something to do with his decision. He found lots of chores every day.

Jack, being in the construction business, was elected to fix a cattle feeder that had been damaged by wind. Each afternoon Frank and Bill took hay out to feed the cattle, then chopped open a watering hole in the pond. This was quite a chore because there would be about five inches of new ice every day.

I got all the good jobs, such as feeding the pigs and cleaning the pens. One afternoon I helped repair the roof on a livestock shelter. After being up long before dawn, hunting all morning, and working all afternoon, we hit our bunks early each night.

After the first day of the hunt, we really got socked with bad weather. The wind blew about 30 miles an hour for three days, and it snowed almost continually. Temperatures hit down to 20° below zero every night. We had our bottle-gas furnace turned full open, but the temperature in the camper wouldn't get higher than 45°F.

We hunted each morning of those three days, but we didn't see a single deer. The weather broke on the fifth day, but not until afternoon. We went for a drive around the countryside in brilliant sunshine. There were deer everywhere in the fields. They hadn't fed for three days, and they were making up for lost time. We saw well over 100 deer. At least 20 were fine bucks, but none wore racks as massive as the exceptional trophy that had got away from me opening morning.

Late that afternoon, Frank and Jack went to Moosomin, Saskatchewan, for a bottle-gas refill. On their way back, they spotted an enormous buck crossing a rise along the far side of a field.

*This 10-point whitetail is one that Olsen could easily have downed,
but he passed it up for a chance at a better trophy.*

"We could actually see horns with our naked eyes, and he was a mile away," Frank told me later. "That buck has the best typical rack any of us have seen . . . ever! He must be the biggest buck in Manitoba. Tomorrow, Jack and I are going to get that monster!"

They didn't, but they came close. While still-hunting, they spotted the buck crossing a distant slough in the same area they had seen him in the day before. They stalked him but could only get quick flashes of his body in very thick brush. The animal finally heard or saw his pursuers, then bolted through the slough and ran over a distant rise. Though they trailed him, they never saw him again.

After five days of hunting, we were still scoreless. There's no Sunday hunting in Manitoba, so we went to town and rented a hotel room just to get the use of a shower.

The next morning, Frank downed a big 10-pointer that field-dressed at 185 pounds. He had his favorite spot in a 20-acre woodland that was loaded with deadfalls and thickets. Lots of deer bedded in there, and Frank figured that sooner or later his still-hunting tactics would pay off. They did. Frank's Winchester Model 88 put a 243 slug into the buck's neck, and that was that.

Jack took a fine 6-pointer the next morning. He had a stand on a knoll half a mile west of my site. His blind was right in the center of a huge deadfall. He was so well hidden that he had an easy shot with his Model 99 Savage.

By now it was Wednesday of the second week. I'd mentally kicked myself at least 100 times for not taking that 11-pointer over a week earlier. I had a regular path worn to my stand, and I'd hunted there every morning when the wind wasn't blowing too strong. On windy days, Jack and I would walk and still-hunt up to eight miles. It was the only way we could keep warm.

The next morning came up like the first day of our hunt. There was no wind. The skies had cleared, and the temperature was moderating. It was already up to about 0°F. by the time I reached my blind. A doe walked down the runway right after dawn. A few minutes later I spotted another doe on a runway that joined the one passing my blind. I had no sooner spotted the doe than an enormous deer stepped out of a thicket behind her.

My breath rushed out of my lungs when I got a good look at that whitetail's head. I wouldn't swear that this buck was the same

Olsen poses with his big whitetail buck after it was hauled out of the woods (notice rope and position of forelegs).

one I was hoping to see again for over a week, but he almost had to be. There just couldn't be two bucks in the same area with antlers that massive. I said to myself, "This time you're mine."

Neither deer had any suspicion that there was a human within miles when I lined up the 100-yard shot. The 95-grain slug from my Remington Model 700 killed the buck instantly. He dropped right in his tracks. I ran over there so fast I must have left a trailing cloud of snow. When I got close to my buck, I began getting shaky.

Back home in Michigan, we count a point on a buck's rack if the point is big enough to hold a ring. There were so many points on this buck's antlers, and my adrenaline was flowing so fast, that I lost count several times and had to start all over. I finally made a count of 51.

I hiked back to the farm. Frank and I returned with a snow-mobile and sled. Dragging these big farm-country bucks through deep snow is almost impossible, which is why we'd brought the snowmobiles.

Within hours after we got my trophy hung in Tom Martin's grain-storage shed, word was spreading that an enormous buck had been taken on Martin's farm. People came from all over the region to look at it. That was something because the locals don't get very excited about big bucks. A jumper has to be far better than ordinary to draw much attention.

Bill Park downed a big 10-pointer two days before we were scheduled to leave for home. He was hunting from a blind made of hay bales when he spotted the buck feeding his way across a field.

"He was too far for a shot, but he had a great rack," Bill said as he recounted the action for us. "When he went down into a ravine and out of sight, I worked my way around a knoll to close the range. I got to the edge of some woods that I figured the buck was heading for. Then I hid in thick brush and waited. The big bruiser reappeared out of the ravine and headed toward me just as I thought he might. I rested my 6mm Ruger over a deadfall and put the crosshairs on my scope on his shoulder. I waited until he got within 100 yards, and then I took him."

The next morning we loaded up, thanked the Martins for a great time, and headed for home just ahead of another blizzard.

This view (same as the one on the front of this book) shows the massiveness of Olsen's nontypical-whitetail trophy.

We drove straight through to St. Ignace, Michigan, where we stopped to eat. In the restaurant, I was approached by a man who said he'd give me $1,000 cash for my buck's head. I told the man, "No, thanks!"

Months later, Erwin Wilson measured the antlers and came up with a total score of 252-4/8. That put my buck near the top of all nontypical whitetails listed in the Boone and Crockett record book. In 1977 I was invited to attend the 16th North American Big Game Awards Program (cosponsored by the Boone and Crockett Club and the National Rifle Association of America) held in Denver, Colorado. There, a panel of judges scored my buck officially at 257-3/8. My trophy is now ranked No. 12 out of the 283 entries for nontypical whitetail deer in the record book.

In the Boone and Crockett scoring system, a point on a deer's antler must be more than long enough to hang a ring on before it's counted as a point. Many of the 51 points I counted just after I shot the buck were disallowed by the panel of judges. They recorded the rack as having 21 points on the right antler and 17 on the left. Ten years ago, if somebody had told me that I'd eventually take a buck with antlers boasting 38 points, I would have considered him totally crazy.

Six-Year Chase

By Dwight E. Green

(EDITOR'S NOTE: *The original version of this story appeared in the October 1969 issue of* Outdoor Life.)

My heart almost stopped when I saw the buck's antlers. There couldn't be a whitetail in the world wearing a rack like that. I'd already been amazed only moments before when I caught my first glimpse of the animal's body broadside. The splash of brown behind tangled brush looked big enough to belong to an elk.

I'd walked around the corner of a 10-acre cornfield that nestled in timber on my dad's farm in Clarke County, Iowa. I looked down in a draw covered with buckbrush and second-growth oak about seven feet tall. It was the first day of our December 1958 deer season. The leaves had long since fallen, and three inches of snow covered the ground. But that brush was so thick I couldn't trust my eyes.

A dried-out pond at the bottom of the draw was covered with interlaced thickets. I'd seen a flicker of brown movement in there, only 50 yards below me. I was sure I was looking at a huge deer, but I couldn't tell if it was a buck or a doe. The animal was standing belly-deep in buckbrush, and its neck and head were hidden behind a maze of tangled branches.

I wasn't sure if the deer had seen me, so I froze in my tracks. I stood like a rock for what seemed to be ages. Then I wondered why I was being so cautious. I'd killed a big doe less than an hour before and my numb fingers still had traces of deer blood. As I inched to my right, a small clearing in the thickets offered the most startling sight I've ever seen.

The whitetail was staring at me, and his enormous rack spread out like a three-foot bronze crown. I suddenly became enthralled, extremely disappointed, and sick to my stomach in a succession of seconds. There was the trophy buck of a lifetime, but I couldn't shoot him because I'd already filled my license.

Maybe I wouldn't have been able to kill him anyway. I was still in a state of shock when a shotgun *"whoomed"* 200 yards behind me. I knew dad fired that shot. If he was running true to form, our deer hunting was over for that year.

When dad's gun sounded, the big buck I was watching didn't jump or lurch. He was in high gear as suddenly as an arrow is released from a bow. He went over an oak-lined ridge 100 yards away while my mouth was still hanging open. I made up my mind on the spot that the huge buck would be mine. I'd get him next year for sure.

My plan didn't seem like too much of a project for an 18-year-old with unlimited energy and desire. Iowa's deer aren't roamers, because premium farm-crop foods are everywhere. The big bruiser would be around next December, and I'd scout his movements so thoroughly that I'd have him dead to rights when the 1959 shotgun-deer season opened. Those are the things dreams are made of, but it didn't work out that way.

I'm 29 now, and I have my own farm near New Virginia, Iowa. I'm married, and my wife Patricia and I have two girls: Linda, seven, and Carla, five. When I'm not farming, I'm also a part-time gunsmith. The extra money I earn from gunwork has enabled me to enjoy some fine hunting trips. I make out-of-state hunts every fall when my farm work eases off. I've hunted in Wyoming or Colorado every year since 1960. My best western trophy was a big bull elk I killed in 1968.

I've always been absorbed with any type of hunting, and it all started on the farm where I grew up. Dad's 150-acre section is only a quarter mile from where I live now, and I'm familiar with every swale and ditch in this part of Iowa. That's a tremendous advantage when you're hunting farm-country whitetails.

Our deer are animals of habit. They normally limit their travels to the confines of two or three farms. This means that if you spot a big buck, you can usually get him if you take enough time to thoroughly scout his travel routes. You discover where he feeds, where he beds down, and the cover he travels through. You kill him from a stand along his runways, or by stalking his bedding areas.

The secret of success in farm-country deer hunting is in looking for specific types of cover. Timber laced with thick brush in areas near crop fields are the best spots. Stay away from timber areas used by cattle. The cows beat down the brush and they don't want any part of deer herds. I've watched cattle chase whitetails many times. The deer won't put up with that treatment. They leave the area.

Dogs are a problem too. We have plenty of foxes and coyotes in Iowa, and some areas are great for hunting the varmints with hounds. When deer get bothered too much by dogs, they clear out.

The trick is to find timbered areas that haven't been pastured for several years and are owned by farmers who don't run trailing dogs. If you can locate an area that's so thick with underbrush that you swear you'll never hunt it again, you've found choice deer cover. If a creek or river winds through that brush and there are crop fields nearby, you can bet you're close to a herd of whitetails.

My dedicated scouting enabled me to kill a lot of trophy bucks, but "Old Timer" always outsmarted me. I tagged him with that name because I spent so many years trying to get him.

I did more hunting during my boyhood than many outdoorsmen enjoy during a lifetime. My dad has farmed all his life, and he always had the same desire for hunting and fishing that I have. He began teaching me how to shoot and hunt as soon as I was big enough to carry a gun. I don't have any brothers or sisters, so dad spent a lot of time with me; that meant plenty of hunting.

By the time I was 10, I'd learned a lot about the outdoors on my own. Dad gave me a Marlin 22 rifle fitted with a Weaver 4X scope, and I hunted the woodlots around our farm. I enjoyed watching birds and animals as much as hunting them, and I spent every spare hour I had in the outdoors.

I saw my first deer when I was 12. Back in those days, our

whitetails were just beginning their comeback. They had been almost wiped out by uncontrolled hunting many years previously. There had been no legal deer hunting in the state during my lifetime.

Deer have always been present in Hawkeye land, but back in the 1930s and early 40s the statewide herd was down to about 1,000 whitetails. With complete protection and ideal habitat, they came back strong. The estimated population in the spring of 1955 was 10,684. That sounds like a whale of an increase, but it fails to match the harvest of one recent hunting season. Iowa shotgun hunters in 1966 went home with 10,742 whitetails.

By 1967, every county in the state was open to deer hunting and the herd was estimated at 50,000. The gun-hunting army now numbers more than 20,000. Archers are cashing in on the whitetail excitement too. In 1955, 58 deer were killed by 414 bowmen. Archers now total nearly 5,000, and they rack up a success ratio of close to 20 percent. When I saw that first deer years ago, I couldn't believe my eyes. Local farmers now rate deer sightings as common events. [*Editor's note:* Iowa's current whitetail population numbers about 60,000 animals, and the annual harvest is about 18,000.]

The fall of 1955 seemed to take forever to arrive. That was when Iowa's Conservation Commission decided to open our section of the state for the first modern-times deer season. The only thing that disappointed me was that the law required deer hunters to use shotguns. Though I was only 16 at the time, I'd become a veteran of fox and coyote hunting with high-power rifles. I'd customized a 303 Enfield and restocked it myself. I'd also bought a 257 Roberts, and I handloaded ammunition for both of those rifles. I'd fired thousands of rounds at varmints and targets.

I didn't kill a deer in 1955, '56, or '57. In 1955 there were few deer around dad's farm, and I doubt if I could have killed one with a rifle. But our area has some excellent whitetail habitat, and by 1958 we had deer all over our farmlands. Hunting deer with a shotgun and slugs contributed to my failure to score. I won't shoot at any game with any type of weapon unless I'm almost positive I can make a clean kill. Shotgun slugs are deadly, but they aren't extremely accurate at ranges over 50 yards. I had some reasonable opportunities during those first three years of deer hunting, but I didn't pull a trigger because I didn't want to risk wounding an animal that might escape.

I knew about Old Timer before the 1958 season opened. Dad had spotted him twice from his tractor while working in the fields. "You wouldn't believe the rack on that buck," he'd told me. "He was running with other deer both times I saw him, but he trailed behind and stayed close to cover. I haven't had a good look at his antlers, but I'll bet they're twice as wide as his body."

Some of our neighbors had gotten quick glimpses of the buck too, and they had told their stories with the same degree of respect dad used.

"I'm telling you, Dwight, that deer is big," said one neighbor. "He's big in all directions, especially in the width of that rack. It looks as if it belongs on an elk. The person who kills that buck will kill the biggest whitetail in Iowa."

I got my first look at the giant buck that fall. I described the details at the beginning of this story.

The next year, I began scouting for Old Timer. Those were twice-a-week sessions for two months before the deer season opened. The second time I saw him, he almost ran over me.

I was standing on a hillside of sumac, berry bushes, and scattered oaks. It was late fall, but we still had cattle in a fenced field 200 yards below the hill. The cattle suddenly began raising a fuss and running toward me. Then I spotted the object of their excitement. They were chasing a monster buck, and he was running full speed for the hill I was standing on. I jumped behind a big oak and watched him coming dead on.

When he got within 20 feet of me, I stepped from behind the tree. He slammed to a stop and his eyes bulged while he stared at me. I would have bet my last dollar that his rack had a spread of three feet. I'd never seen another buck's antlers that could come close to Old Timer's spread. The giant buck took my full measure. Then he crashed away and was swallowed by thickets. I could hear him running long after he disappeared.

I didn't see him again that year. But I knew he was still around because I could recognize his tracks. I'd studied those tracks after our second encounter, and I'd discovered that the points of his front hoofs were blunt-edged. He probably had injured them when he was a fawn. Whenever I found a giant deer track with no

223

points on the front hoofs, I knew I was standing on one of his travel routes.

I killed my first buck that fall. My scouting trips were my key to success. Our gun seasons last only three or four days, and that's not much hunting time. You have to know where the deer are, and I knew the feeding and bedding areas of a couple of herds. I waited on stands for Old Timer for two days, but he never appeared. I saw plenty of other deer, including some nice bucks, but I just watched them go by. Finally I decided I'd kill the next buck that offered a shot. I slammed a 12-gauge slug into a big 8-pointer that walked down a runway within 50 feet of my stand.

I killed four more bucks during the next four years; all of them were 8- or 10-pointers. I never did see Old Timer during those deer seasons and, as far as I know, he wasn't spotted by anybody. He seemed to evaporate. But after the gunfire ceased, he'd show up again in the same areas he always frequented.

I lost count of how many times I spotted him on my scouting trips. I saw him often at long distance, but that crafty old buck always seemed to know I was around. I developed the eerie feeling that he recognized me and that he knew I was trying to get him.

I did get close to him one more time on a scouting trip. I'd discovered a runway he used that routed through a draw laced with willows and wild plum trees. I climbed high up in the branches of a giant willow that leaned over the runway. Just before dusk, I spotted him come out of a cornfield and begin grazing in a patch of wild buffalo grass. He had six does with him; one old doe was the cautious leader of the group.

I've watched bucks use smart does for protection on many occasions. They depend on the lead doe to alert them to danger. That doe constantly watches and listens and checks the wind while the rest of the group trails behind and acts as carefree as if nothing could happen. The instant she snorts, stomps, or raises her tail, those crafty bucks sneak away in a backtracking direction.

That didn't happen this time. The lead doe failed to detect my presence, but it took more than an hour for those seven whitetails to travel 100 yards toward me. It was dark by the time they moved under my tree. I heard them walk under me, but I couldn't see

224

more than the dim outlines of their bodies. I enjoyed a tremendous feeling of accomplishment. I'd managed to get within 20 feet of Old Timer and he didn't have the slightest suspicion that I was there.

When the 1964 deer season approached, I had my hunt plans organized around the buck's latest travel patterns. He seemed to be aware that another hunting season was arriving because he never ventured far from thick cover, night or day.

He fed at night in a tangle of thickets a half mile from my farm, but he didn't stay there during the day. He varied his bedding locations and, surprisingly, didn't bed in large thickets. He chose tiny patches of almost impregnable tangles near stands of timber. He selected spots where he could see trouble coming from any direction, and yet be within a couple of jumps of vast cover areas.

The night before the season opened, Max Blair and I held our final strategy session. He's 33, married, and works in the maintenance department of Simpson College at Indianola. He lives a mile from my farm and we've scouted and hunted together for years. Max was well aware that I was still after that special buck, and he was hoping for a shot at him too.

The season opened at 8:00 a.m., but I picked Max up two hours early because we wanted to be on our selected stands long before the first hint of dawn. It had been an unusually warm December. Little snow had fallen, and the ground was bare. The temperature had dropped below freezing during the night, and I knew I'd put in a few cold hours on my stand before the sun rose high enough to offer any warmth.

Shortly after dawn, a big doe walked by my deadfall-elm stand. She came out of the thickets where Old Timer had been feeding for the past week and she was headed toward his bedding areas. The deer was not aware of me and she was taking her time. She acted as if she were waiting for companions.

A few minutes later, six more does stepped out of the thickets and walked up the draw below me. I was so positive Old Timer would be following his harem that I slowly moved my Model 12 Winchester to shooting position. My heart was banging my ribs as I glanced through my Weaver K-1 scope to check shooting light.

I never moved a muscle for half an hour. Then a familiar feeling engulfed me. It was the same one I had had during the previous five years. Whenever I figured I had that crafty old buck dead to rights, he vanished.

I heard a few shots in the distance during the rest of the morning, but none of them came from the area we were hunting. At noon I walked the quarter mile to Max's stand. He'd seen some does and a 4-point buck. He passed them up because of the same premonition I'd felt.

"I figured it was my lucky day," he said with a grin. "I had a feeling I was going to get a crack at that monster buck. I was sure he'd be following those other deer, but he never showed."

We ate some sandwiches and candy bars, and then we decided to still-hunt the timber we were in.

"There hasn't been anybody else in here," Max said. "Maybe that buck decided to sit tight."

We use a system in our still-hunting. We walk into the wind, and we keep each other in sight. We position ourselves about halfway up each side of a draw, walk a few steps, pause and look around, and then walk another few steps. We've killed a lot of bucks that way. When you walk real slow and stop frequently, a bedded deer isn't sure what you're up to. If you walk rapidly in a relatively straight line, a smart buck will lie tight while you travel right past him. But that stop-and-go slow motion will make the craftiest buck nervous. He will usually jump when you get close to him.

The timber we were in is two miles long by one mile wide. Our plan was to work out one brushy draw, move into another, and keep walking upwind. The terrain is a rough, rolling maze of hills, draws, ditches, and thickets intermixed with tall oak and elm trees. We had jumped deer every time we had hunted in there.

The bottom of the first draw we hit was covered with tall grass and briar bushes. Six does flushed out ahead of us and bounded over a ridge. We waited for 10 minutes and watched our backtrack area because bucks often try to sneak behind walking hunters. No buck appeared, so we continued on and worked out other draws. We didn't see any more deer for a couple of hours.

Then we approached another draw with high brown grass. There wasn't much brush in there, but the oak trees grew close together. Those oaks are so big and so closely-spaced that you

226

have to walk a zigzag path to get through the almost solid wall of timber. It was an ideal spot for a big buck to hide, and there was a big buck in there.

When he jumped up 50 yards ahead of us, he went out through the trees like a wisp of brown smoke. He didn't run; he just moved slowly and took advantage of every inch of cover. I had a couple glimpses of his huge rack, but I knew he wasn't Old Timer. His antlers were thick-beamed, but not wide enough to be worn by my dream buck. There was no chance for either Max or me to fire a shot. The timber was so thick that we couldn't find the deer in our scopes.

It was late afternoon by the time we approached the end of the woodlands. Suddenly, I happened to think of a small patch of brush on the next hill. It was the exact type of spot that Old Timer had chosen for bedding locations during the past few weeks. It wasn't more than 12 feet in diameter, but it was a solid tangle of briar bushes and wild cherry trees nestled on a grassy hillside.

I knew I could get close to the tangles by walking around the bottom of the next ridge and sneaking up through some scattered oaks. I'd almost made it through the timber when Max's 16-gauge Remington automatic roared from over the ridge to my right.

I was looking at the little tangle of brush when Max's gun went off. The briar bushes exploded a flash of brown. I've never seen anything happen so rapidly. Though I'd been staring at the buck's bedding location, I don't recall seeing anything except a monster whitetail running full speed up the grassy ridge. He was charging straight away and those enormous antlers spread far out beyond the sides of his body. I knew that Old Timer and I had met again.

I found his back in my scope just before he went over the ridge. The range was about 75 yards when I pulled the trigger and heard my slug smack home. The buck skidded sideways but was still on his feet when he stumbled and melted into the skylined oaks.

I don't think I'll ever get quite as excited as I did at that moment. I didn't know if the buck was down, and I'd have a whale of a job finding out. There was a 10-foot-deep washout between me and the ridgetop. I must have looked like a crazy man after I jumped into that ditch. Its wall was bare ground without handholds. But I scrambled and clawed and jumped and slithered my way to the rim, then ran up the hillside.

Dwight Green stands beside his trophy whitetail. These antlers have the widest inside spread ever recorded for a rack of the typical pattern.

As I neared the top, I could hear crashing sounds. I knew the buck was down and thrashing around in the brush. I spotted him as soon as I burst over the ridge. He was only 20 feet from me, and it was obvious that my slug had broken his back. His hindquarters were paralyzed, but he was up on his front legs and trying to drag himself into some thickets. Almost dead, he suddenly collapsed and a last breath rasped from his throat.

I didn't think about field-dressing him for quite a while. I just stared at those antlers. Then I grabbed the massive rack with both hands and moved it. I still couldn't believe a whitetail buck could grow such wide-beamed antlers.

Finally I started the gutting chores, and that's when Max came over the hill. He saw what I was doing and hollered, "Boy, wait until you see the 10-point giant I killed."

Then Max got a little closer. When he spotted my buck's antlers, he stopped in his tracks. "My gosh," he gasped, "I've never seen a rack like that. You finally got him!"

We dragged Old Timer down the hill, across two large draws, and up another hill before we got him to an area I could reach with my Jeep. Then we hauled him to my farm and hung him in the barn. After that, we went back for Max's buck. That wasn't so much of a back-breaking job because we were able to drive close to the kill site with the Jeep.

I was aware that the Boone and Crockett Club scored and recorded outstanding North American big-game trophies, but I didn't get around to having my prize inspected for more than a year. I finally took it to Ames, Iowa, where it was measured and scored by Dr. Arnold O. Haugen of Iowa State University. He was amazed when he taped the antler's inside spread at 30-3/8 inches.

In the spring of 1968, officials of the Boone and Crockett Club informed me that my buck had won first award as the best typical whitetail taken in North America during the Club's 1966-1967 big-game awards period. He scored a total of 187-2/8.

That was an extremely high honor, but there's another fact that makes me glow with even greater pride. After studying the 1971 edition of the Boone and Crockett Club's book *(Records of North American Big Game),* I discovered that my trophy's official inside-spread measurement of 30-3/8 inches is the all-time best ever recorded. I wonder if there will ever be another whitetail buck

229

with a rack that wide. His mounted head now graces a wall in my den.

(EDITOR'S NOTE: *Green's trophy still ranks as having the widest inside spread ever recorded for a typical whitetail.*)

A Ram for the Records

By Richard Browne
as told to Bruce Hartford

(EDITOR'S NOTE: *The original version of this story appeared in the October 1970 issue of* Outdoor Life.)

I'll never forget that spring day in 1967. My woods crew and I were returning from a tree-planting job in the upper reaches of the Thompson River near Thompson Falls, Montana. We were driving down a road edging the river when I glanced at a patch of white on the mountain slope that didn't look natural. As the scene jumped into focus, I suddenly realized that the white patch was the rump of an enormous bighorn ram.

The sheep was standing less than 100 yards from us. I hadn't spotted his outline immediately because his tan body blended almost perfectly with background rocks. What really confused me was that I never expected to see a giant ram so close to a road.

By the time I braked our vehicle to a screeching stop and grabbed my 7x50 binoculars, he had scrambled up on a ledge. Now the fantastically thick horns were in plain view. I had never seen anything like them.

When I focused my glasses on the ram's head, I stared in amazement. I'd bet my last dollar that those perfectly symmetrical horns curled at least 46 inches in length.

"Boy," I said to myself, "if only there was a bighorn hunting season in this area. You're safe, you big buster. But if you ever become legal game, I'm sure going to match wits with you."

If I'd known then that a local bighorn-sheep season was in the making for 1968, I would have studied every inch of that ram. Even so, my mouth went dry as I watched the magnificent animal head back for the high peaks.

I'm 35 and work as a woods-crew boss for the Thompson Falls Ranger District of the U.S. Forest Service. I've been with that agency for 15 years, ever since I moved to Montana from Sturgis, Michigan. I left Sturgis right after I graduated from high school in 1955. I knew exactly where I was going. My parents had taken me on a vacation trip through this mountain country when I was 15 years old. I couldn't wait to get back when I struck out on my own.

There is no prettier country than Montana, and it teems with fish and game. I've hooked hundreds of lunker cutthroat-rainbow trout crosses. I've killed an elk during each of the 15 years I've lived here. Whitetail deer have fallen to my rifle too. Within the last three years, I've been lucky enough to score on a moose and a mountain goat.

I'll be the first to point out that much of my luck results from my fine physical condition. You harden up in a hurry in my kind of a job. It's no chore for me to walk 10 miles through the mountains to a forest fire with an 80-pound pack on my back. It's rugged hunting in our country, but the guy who can cover miles of ground really raises his odds on seeing game. I think nothing of walking 15 miles during a day's hunt. Many times I've had to pack out elk and deer meat from miles back in the mountains.

My search for a trophy bighorn ram began in the spring of 1958. That's when our local sportsman's club had a meeting with officials of the Montana Fish and Game Department. The meeting was called to discuss the possibility of opening a bighorn-sheep season in Sanders County. Our modern sheep herds had developed from a fish and game department stocking program in 1959. That plant consisted of 14 ewes and five rams.

The stocked sheep found ideal habitat, and their numbers increased each year. Because the animals had never been hunted, it was possible that some of the rams could be at least 10 years old. There was another factor that upped a trophy-hunter's odds too.

Our winters are usually open because the warm Pacific frontal systems that pass over the Cascades of Washington also pass over our mountains.

Such weather means that big, old, toothless rams have a good chance of surviving on the bunch grass and other natural foods that are available year-round. That's important because the horns of a sheep continue growing each year of the animal's life. The older the ram, the better the trophy. When I considered those factors, I realized it was very possible that some of the best trophy bighorn rams in North America were living almost in my back-yard.

The fish and game department decided to open a three-month sheep season in Sanders County beginning on September 15, 1968. The catch was that only three permits would be issued for three-quarter-curl rams or better. I figured I had about as much chance of drawing one of those $25 permits as I did of winning the Irish Sweepstakes. Sanders County is as big as the State of Rhode Island, and it has nearly 1,500 licensed hunters. I knew that about 400 big-game hunters would be trying for those lottery-type permits, but you can bet your grandmother's sweet-apple pie that I applied anyway.

I could hardly believe it when I received my permit in the mail. Then I made some decisions right away. Before sheep season opened, I would spend every spare moment I had scouting the high country for the best ram I could find.

I was well aware that I might never participate in a bighorn hunt again. I couldn't afford a mistake. Unless I could sight my rifle on a ram that met trophy standards, I wouldn't take a sheep. I couldn't forget the enormous ram I mentioned earlier. No effort would be too great in trying to meet him again.

It seemed like an eternity before opening day of the season arrived. With the dawn came some of the foulest weather I've ever seen. Sheets of rain were coming down with such windblown fury that my hunting partner, Melvin Hoy, wondered if we should even try to hunt. He telephoned me and said, "It's pouring buckets out there, Dick. I don't think we can get up in the mountains."

"I hate to admit you're right," I answered. "We'd be crazy to try any serious climbing. We can't do a darn thing except glass some of the more accessible areas from down below."

We didn't find any signs of sheep that first day, but we really didn't expect to. Melvin lives in Thompson Falls too, and he works for the Flodin Lumber Company. He had to go to work the next day, so I was on my own. We didn't hunt together again because Melvin scored early in the season on a fine ram boasting 39-1/2 inch and 40-inch horns.

I had a week's vacation and I'd be hunting every day, so I wasn't concerned about the weather. I knew it would break sooner or later, but I was really surprised when the next day dawned bright and clear. I headed for the Thompson River country because I'd spotted some big sheep there during scouting trips only a few days before the season opened.

As I turned off Highway 10A onto the river road, I glanced at the huge slopes that rise abruptly from the river's edge. I decided to glass the mountain above timberline before going any farther. I pulled off on the side of the road, raised my Navy-surplus binoculars, and immediately spotted two white specks that stood out against gray rocks high up on the fault of a slope. They were the white rump patches of two sheep. Closer inspection showed both animals to be rams with fine heads. "Well," I said to myself, "get ready to climb. It's the steep side of the mountain, but one of those rams might make the grade."

You might think I was lucky to see those sheep only a few miles out of town, but there's a tremendous difference between spotting one and getting close enough to shoot at him. The elevation of Thompson Falls is 2,550 feet, and some of our mountain slopes go almost straight up for a mile and a half or more. There is always loose rock and talus to contend with while climbing. It's hard work, and you have to love the high places and solitude to go up there.

From my scouting sessions, I'd learned that you can't stalk a wise ram unless you see him before he sees you. I'd read that a sheep's eyes are capable of at least the sight a man gains when looking through 8X binoculars. There was no way of knowing if those rams had already spotted me. If so, they'd be long gone by the time I was halfway up the mountain.

An hour later, I worked around a rock ridge and discovered that the sheep hadn't moved. I slowly climbed to their left until I

234

A fair ram in the area that Browne hunted.

was above them. The best way to approach sheep is from above because they don't expect danger from that direction.

The two animals were on a shelf; they were completely oblivious to my presence. One was feeding slowly on dried bunch grass, and the other was gazing down toward the river that looked like a silver ribbon far below me. Eventually I stalked to within 100 feet of the rams. Then I stopped and studied them closely with my binoculars.

Their white rumps stood out like patches of snow on bare ground. Their rough, sparse summer coats were gone, and their flanks looked as smooth as silk. Their bodies were the color of dark-brown sandstone. The larger of the two was the darker. That's true of all bighorn rams.

I'd already decided I wasn't going to take either sheep. Both wore horns well over 3/4 curl and in the 37-inch class, but neither was an outstanding trophy. Still, I was amazed how enormous the horns of the best ram actually were. They made the whole animal look larger than he was.

Through the glasses, I noticed how large his eyes were in comparison with his head. They were a rich, deep brown. The lashes on the eyelids were long but sparse. I grinned when I noticed his nose wrinkle with each passing air current. This was truly a magnificent animal, and I felt enchanted with being in his domain. I wondered if I could actually kill one of those beautiful creatures if I found the trophy I wanted.

Suddenly I felt a puff of breeze on the back of my neck, and I knew the show was over. Both rams whirled toward me and then bolted up the mountain. They were gone in seconds.

That stalk was symbolic of the lure of sheep hunting. Stalking a big-game animal in the up-and-down terrain of high mountain country is a constant challenge. The ever-changing wind currents alone are enough to drive a preacher to drink. Sometimes it takes me a half hour to stalk 20 feet. But the longer a stalk lasts, the better I like it. That's where the excitement is. To me, the wild ram represents the mystery and magic of the rocky crags and canyons, the slide rock, and the clean, thin air.

I climbed on up the sharp ridge and found plenty of sheep sign. A bed here, droppings there, and occasionally what I call a "playground." A playground is usually on a level ledge or ridge that is covered with soil. The soil gives the sheep traction to butt each other, paw at the air, and go down on their knees to play. The ground in these areas will be covered with tracks and gouges.

I continued climbing east toward the Munson Creek Drainage. I planned on working to the top of the range and then following a game trail down the other side of the mountain. It would be an eight-mile walk as the crow flies, but that giant ram I was looking for might be just over the next ridge.

I didn't find him that day, but I did see and count 42 different sheep. A lot of them were ewes, and that raised my hopes. I was almost certain I'd find a big ram sooner or later, because the rut would begin very soon.

I spent the remainder of that week doing a lot of tough climbing. I probably walked about 90 miles, but I didn't see any signs of a really large ram. I did glass three wearing horns that pushed the 40-inch mark, but I passed them up.

Through the rest of September, all of October, and most of November, I hunted sheep unsuccessfully every weekend. I continued seeing legal rams, but I just couldn't force myself to shoot one while there was still a chance of finding that dream trophy.

The last week of elk season was coming up and there still wasn't any game meat in my freezer. I had to remedy that situation. I went elk hunting the weekend before Thanksgiving and managed to take a big cow. I normally hold out for a bull, but there just wasn't time for that this year.

A few days after the close of the elk season, I was bowling at the Thompson River Ranch Lanes when Jerry and Al Wolfekuhle strolled in. They are a father and son logging team and I know them both well. I knew something special was in the air when they walked directly toward me.

"I think we saw that big ram you're after," Jerry said. "He's with several ewes and another good ram. He's really a giant and he didn't act as if he were in any hurry to move. Those sheep are a quarter mile down the road from here and about two thirds up the mountain. We glassed them for 15 minutes and they just looked at us. I don't know if you can get up there, but I'll bet those sheep won't move tonight."

I was ruined for the rest of the evening. My bowling game suffered a horrible slump. I couldn't sleep when I got home, and I

237

was up long before dawn. Though I had checked my gear many times, I was so keyed up that I went through everything again. Daylight wasn't even a promise when I parked my car on the side of the road where Jerry and Al had spotted the ram.

The sun finally began to rise behind the mountains to the east. I went to work with my binoculars and studied the rocks and slopes 1,700 feet above me. I picked out two sheep—a fair ram, and a ewe. Then, higher and to the left, two more sheep showed in my field of view. One was a ram that gave me a jolt. He was so huge I didn't waste time trying to decide if he was the one I had been after for more than two months.

I picked out a spot way up there that I figured I could climb to. Then I hurriedly drove a few miles down the road, turned across a bridge, and drove back to a spot unseen by the sheep. An hour later, I was far up in the mountains.

Now I moved slowly, analyzing each step. I continually checked the wind that was blowing down the river valley to my right. I eventually reached the vantage point I had spotted from the road. I carefully scanned the ridges and pockets below and upwind. Suddenly, as if by appointment, a band of four ewes, a lamb, and three rams moved into sight 150 yards away. They were angling toward me.

I flattened and slid down behind some rocks until I got a rock ridge between me and the sheep. I moved quickly but quietly across a small ravine, and then climbed to head off the animals. I stopped about 60 yards from a rock cut that I felt the sheep would pass through if they stayed on course. The wind was still in my favor. My heart was pounding as I laid my Model 721 Remington 270 on a flat rock and waited.

Suddenly two of the three rams were in front of me, grazing slowly as they climbed through the narrow defile. The lead ram was a peculiar sight. His left horn was normal and in the 40-inch class, but his right horn was deformed. It angled down from his head, and a projection branched off the main curl.

The second ram took my breath away. Both of his horns were very even. Neither horn was badly broomed, and each had to measure at least 45 inches. The horns swept down and then up well past the eye, making more than a full curl. I noticed immediately that they were extremely wide from tip to tip. That both-

238

ered me because I wanted a normal trophy, one with horns that didn't flare to the sides.

I'll never be in another situation quite like that one. I simply couldn't decide what to do. Here was a ram far superior to any I'd stalked yet, but I just didn't like the wide flare of his horns. Then I said to myself, "Use your head. The season will be over soon and you'll never find a better trophy. Take him."

I lined my open sights on his left shoulder, then paused as the third ram moved into view. He was smaller than the other two. Now all the sheep were standing still and staring in my direction. I squinted down the sights, then held up my trigger squeeze at the last instant. I went through that act a couple more times, but I just couldn't decide. The sheep weren't aware of me. They showed no fear. They moved slowly on up around a rock ledge and I watched them disappear without raising my rifle again. When they were gone, I noticed that my hands were shaking.

For two more weeks, I hunted unsuccessfully for a better ram. It was now December and the winter snows had begun. For some reason it was hard to find a ram of any kind, let alone a trophy. I was getting desperate. I could have kicked myself for passing up that big bruiser with the wide-flaring horns.

On Sunday, December 8, I was up in the mountains once more. I hiked to many bighorn hangouts, but couldn't find any sheep. The situation looked really grim. I decided to leave that range, walk back down to my car, and drive to the Koo-Koo-Sint Ridge area near the mouth of the Thompson River. It was noon when I began climbing the 3,000-foot ridge. It was treacherous work because a previous storm had covered just about everything with ice and scattered patches of snow. The temperature was still hanging around 30°F.

Two hours later, I was following a 10-inch-wide sheep trail that was worn in rock on a 70 percent grade. I came around a ridge and spotted a small ram bedded down on some talus 200 yards ahead. The wind was in his favor and I knew he'd scent me. He got up and walked straight away on the game trail.

Where there's one sheep there are probably more, so I slowed my travel to not much more than a step every few moments. On my immediate left was a ledge running up to the peak of the pinnacle I was skirting. Ahead was a draw and another ledge. The

239

talus I was standing on stretched steeply almost to the top of the pinnacle. I was really high in the sky. Clouds were beginning to enshroud the peaks of the mountains. Far below me was the confluence of the Thompson and Clark Fork rivers.

I was almost above timberline when I let myself down over the edge of a 15-foot cliff by hanging onto the top of a limber Douglas fir that arched with my weight. Just ahead was another well-traveled sheep trail. I spotted fresh droppings, and immediately knew that I was close to sheep. They could be anywhere around me.

I carefully moved ahead until I stopped to silently remove some loose rocks from the trail. I'll always do this when I'm stalking to make absolutely sure I don't make any noise. I was bent over when a sudden clattering of rolling stones came from above and slightly ahead of me. I whipped upright and found myself staring dead-on at a ram and a ewe that had obviously been moving down the trail in my direction. The ram and I were 50 yards apart, but even at that range he seemed to be all horns. I didn't hesitate a second, and the rifle flew to my shoulder.

I've never seen a sheep swap ends so rapidly. The big ram exploded past the ewe and raced up a steep talus slope. I was about to squeeze the trigger when the thought flashed through my mind that if I dropped him on that incline, he might roll all the way to bottom of the valley a half mile below. Then he swerved suddenly to my right and topped a rise 80 yards away. The rise appeared to be relatively flat.

I sighted below his spine, and the 270 roared. The ram lurched and dropped from view. Suddenly he stumbled back into sight, slumped forward to the talus slope, and began to roll. He actually tumbled head over heels, landed on his side, skidded, and then began tumbling again. Those beautiful horns! I was frantic. It was a horrible sight watching that trophy animal rolling toward certain destruction.

I dropped my rifle and ran ahead with the crazy idea of trying to stop the plunging body. Then I came to my senses, stopped, and watched in awe as my bighorn rolled past me and bounced over a rise. There was a clatter of rocks, then silence. Was it possible that his descent had been suddenly arrested?

As quickly as I dared, I scrambled to the rise and peered down

240

*At base of mountain, Richard Browne poses with his trophy. Dark-
ness fell by the time a friend had helped him pack huge sheep down
treacherous slope.*

Back home, Browne can't stop admiring the ram's enormous horns.

at the most wonderful sight I ever hope to see. My ram's right horn was wrapped around a downed fir tree. I was jubilant.

I knew I had to have help getting that sheep out of there, so I hurried down the mountain, drove back to town, and found Ira Soule. Ira's a 25-year-old co-worker of mine and he's a top climber. When he saw my trophy, he blurted, "Wow, what a set of horns. They're not damaged a bit."

On March 10, 1969, the head was measured for the Boone and Crockett Club by Jack Atcheson, a well-known taxidermist in Butte, Montana. The length of the right horn was 45-2/8 inches, while the left was 43 inches. The respective circumferences of the bases were 16 inches and 15-6/8 inches.

When Jack added the trophy's total score of 192-2/8, he said, "Dick, I'm sure this is the finest bighorn taken in the United States during 1968. I wouldn't doubt if it's the best taken last year in all of North America."

According to the latest edition of the Boone and Crockett Club's book, *Records of North American Big Game*, my ram ranks No. 27 in the all-time bighorn-sheep records. It was the best taken in Sanders County during either of the three-permit seasons of 1968 and 1969. All six permits were filled, but none of the five other sheep wore horns measuring more than 40 inches.

I'm convinced that the wide-horned ram I passed up was a better-scoring trophy than the one I killed, and that neither could match the giant bighorn I described at the beginning of this story. I'm sure I never saw him again. He may have died of old age by now. But if he's still alive, and if some hunter gets him, that ram can't help but score close to the top in the record book.

(EDITOR'S NOTE: *Browne's ram now ranks No. 44 out of 289 listed in the 1977 edition of the Boone and Crockett record book.*)

A Pronghorn to Wonder About

By Lee Arce

(EDITOR'S NOTE: *The original version of this story appeared in the January 1970 issue of* Outdoor Life.)

I've hunted most of my life and I've seen hundreds of big-game animals, but the sight I witnessed the afternoon of September 21, 1968, actually entranced me. My wife Leona and Jim Avakian were stunned too.

We were driving my four-wheel-drive vehicle along a dry creekbed in a long valley 50 miles southeast of Lander, Wyoming. We were creeping along at about five miles per hour, looking up the valley for distant herds of antelope. To our right, 150 yards away, a sagebrush ridge paralleled our route. On the opposite side of the valley, a quarter of a mile to our left, another ridge rolled against the bright blue sky.

We weren't paying any attention to those skylines, because antelope usually stay far out in bowl-shaped basins. That's why we were caught by surprise when a giant buck suddenly appeared on the ridge to our right. He must have been in a dead run when he came up the other side of the slope because he burst into our view as abruptly as if he'd jumped out of a hole in the ground. The buck spotted us at the same time we saw him, but he didn't change his travel direction one inch. He hesitated a split second, and then jetted ahead, barreling full out diagonally in front of us.

It was his flicker of hesitation and his charge almost straight at us that struck us spellbound. Any antelope is a beautiful animal, but when you see a giant buck, at close range and backgrounded by a sparkling blue sky, you're looking at a fantastic sight. If the sight appears unexpectedly, and you're a trophy hunter, your breath goes out in a gasp.

That's what happened to me. I'm well aware that a really big antelope buck will weigh about 100 pounds, but for a moment that animal looked as large as an elk. The sun caught his glistening tan coat, brown-and-white barred throat, and jet-black horns in a splash of color. Those horns looked unreal, like two enormous lengths of coal jabbing into the sky. The view of that magnificent animal was so spellbinding that for a moment I didn't think of shooting at him. He challenged us with his blinding speed, and he won hands down. By the time I thought about my rifle, I was too late to use it.

Experts claim an antelope can run 50 miles an hour. All I can say is that this buck lined out in what seemed to be at least mile-a-minute speed. He blitzed in front of us and flashed across the valley in almost nothing flat. One moment he was broadside and the next he was going straight away, a speck of color zipping over the distant ridge.

That incident happened back in 1961. I joined my brother Martin for a successful antelope hunt in Fremont County that year, and I've been sold on the area ever since. Its vastness intrigues me. The area is desolate too: no telephone poles, no fences, no trees, no anything except mile after mile of rolling plains covered with sagebrush and meadow grass. Most of the land is open to public hunting, and it's a pronghorn paradise.

I'm 50 and live in Covina, California, where I'm in partnership with Martin in an industrial property-development concern. My wife and I have a son and a daughter who are both grown and on their own now. That means Leona is able to accompany me on most of my hunting trips. She has developed into quite a hunter, and she's as enthusiastic about hunting as I am.

I didn't find time to hunt in Wyoming again until 1967, when Leona and I took fine antelope bucks. Both of our trophies just missed qualifying for the Boone and Crockett record book. We hunted the same area I had explored six years previously. Everything seemed the same—lots of antelope, and plenty of bucks.

By now I'd become fascinated with trophy hunting. It's not just the challenge of killing an outstanding animal that intrigues me, either. Leona and I also know that when we have bagged our game, our hunting for the season is finished. We don't like to rush our hunts since we enjoy every minute of every day afield. If we hold out for trophies, our hunts are likely to last longer. That means we also run a good chance of being skunked. I've been skunked on elk hunts in four different states, and that hurts because we love wild-game meat.

After our 1967 hunt, I became particularly interested in scoring on an outstanding antelope. Pronghorn are pretty special in my opinion. A lot of hunters don't know that they are the only species within their genus, and that it's the only genus within the family. Pronghorn have no near relatives in the world, and they're found only in North America. They are also the fastest four-footed wild animals on this continent. Some biologists claim their eyesight is equal to that of a man using 8X binoculars.

The older the antelope, the larger his horns. Those horns continue to grow throughout his lifetime. This means that a trophy pronghorn has been around for many hunting seasons, and that he knows what the crack of a rifle is. Match that knowledge with his speed, eyesight, and wide-open habitat and you've got a trophy that's extremely difficult to outsmart.

Surprisingly, it's not much of a chore to kill an average antelope. Harvest statistics from the better hunting areas point up hunter-success ratios of more than 90 percent; and most of those animals are taken during the first two days of the season. But you'll find very few really big bucks hanging in cooler lockers. Those wise old-timers normally stay so far out in open country that it's almost impossible to stalk them.

Early in June of 1968, Leona, Jim, and I put in our applications for hunting licenses covering the Fremont County area. There were 1,250 antelope licenses authorized for that area, and applications were accepted at the Cheyenne office of the Wyoming Game and Fish Commission. We mailed our applications and $35 [*Editor's note:* The nonresident fee is now $50] and hoped we'd be lucky in the impartial drawing for permits. We were delighted when our licenses showed up in the mail. Our hunt plans were all settled by midsummer.

Though I was absorbed with the thought of downing a giant buck, I was just as enthusiastic about the prospect of finding a good one for Jim. He's one of my favorite people. He's Leona's uncle, and he's 70 years old. Jim is a retired barber, now living with his wife in Glendora, California. He's had considerable hunting and fishing experience, but he'd never been on a pronghorn hunt.

Jim was very excited about the possibility of shooting a pronghorn, but he had reservations about being able to do it.

"I know they can run like greased lightning," he told me. "And I know that most shooting opportunities are at long ranges. My eyes aren't what they used to be, and neither are my legs. But I'll sure give it everything I've got. I can't think of anything I'd rather do than take an antelope."

Though the 10-day season didn't open until September 21, Leona and I wanted to get to the prairies several days early so we could study the pronghorn herds before they became jumpy from gun pressure. We left home and began the 1,000-mile drive on September 15. We had advance reservations at a motel in Lander, and we agreed to meet Jim and his wife there on September 19.

We drove hard until we reached Wyoming's sagebrush flats, and then we practically crawled. We saw herd after herd of antelope between Big Piney and Farson. Many were within 150 yards of the highway. Some of the animals would spook when we stopped, but others would stand and stare at us. We had two pair of Bushnell binoculars, 9X and 6X, and we studied antelope for hours.

It doesn't take long to discover that big bucks hang to the rear of the herds and that they're usually screened by does. That knowledge gives a good clue about where to look for the best bucks when you're glassing a distant group.

Relaxed herds also offer a top opportunity to judge horns. A general rule is that if the horns are at least twice as long as the ears, and spread out far wider than the skull, you're looking at a respectable trophy. After you've glassed a few dozen bucks, you can pick out the good ones in a hurry.

During those days of studying antelope we spotted one buck

247

that sent shivers up my spine. He wore trophy horns that were surely in the record-book class. We found him by glassing a distant herd of animals that was lying down. I immediately pinpointed this buck because his body was much larger than those of his companions.

He was partially hidden behind several does, and he never moved a muscle during the long time we inspected him. His back was toward us, but his head was turned far enough so that he had a clear view of our activities. His jet-black horns extended far beyond his ears and curved majestically above his head.

"There's one I'd sure like to get a crack at," I said to Leona. "Look at him staring at us. I'll bet if we stepped toward him, he'd be gone like a wisp of brown smoke."

Jim, Leona, and I loaded our gear into my vehicle long before dawn on opening day. We drove southeast out of Lander on Highway 287. We watched dozens of cars ahead of us turn off the main route and follow dirt roads into various hunting areas. Yellow headlight beams flickered against sagebrush and red taillights winked in the distance. It's quite a sight on opening morning to watch the lights of vehicles bounce across the blackened prairies of pre-dawn. It's only a once-a-year show because most of those hunters will down their game before the day is over. Many of the local sportsmen figure their hunt is a bust if they're not back in town with a buck by 8:00 a.m.

By the time we reached Sweetwater River Station, the concentration of cars had thinned. We turned right and drove 20 miles into the Bison Basin area. There I found the narrow trail I was looking for. Our hunt was under way.

Incidentally, there are very few roads in the area we hunted. You won't get very far in a regular passenger car. I'd say the minimum hunting vehicle for this country is a pickup truck because most of your driving is cross-country.

I value my 4WD vehicle for security as much as for transportation in those vast remote plains. Everything looks the same out there. It's all endless rolling prairies of sagebrush. There are few landmarks, and it's remarkably easy to get lost when you continuously drive in various directions.

Our hunting technique is basic: drive slowly and try to read the lay of the land ahead. The trick is to determine which knolls and ridges run along the edges of basins. Then you park far back from a rise, sneak up to its rim, and glass the country beyond. If there are antelope ahead, if they haven't sensed you, and if there's a buck worth taking, you plan your stalk and hope for the best.

The secrets of success are to keep off the skyline and park your vehicle far away from potential hotspots. This means a great deal of walking. But if you alert a wary buck to any hint of your presence—by sound or sight—the odds on successfully stalking him are prohibitive.

You can, of course, get lucky by spotting traveling animals before they see you. Then you try to position yourself ahead of them and hope they approach close enough for inspection. That's what happened with the first buck we found, but a comedy of mixed signals blew the whole show.

Leona and I had previously agreed that Jim should shoot the first good buck we had a chance to take. But some way or another, neither of us had relayed that information to Jim. Anyway, we spotted a buck traveling toward us, and he wore better than average horns. He was unaware of us, and when he disappeared behind a ridge we scrambled out of the vehicle and rushed ahead.

We were all puffing when the buck came busting over the ridge 200 yards away. He spotted us immediately and slammed to a halt. He stared at us and I whispered, "Take him, Jim!"

Uncle Jim's desire must have been tremendous, but he calmly answered, "No, it's not my shot. Ladies first."

Leona just about exploded. "Quick, Uncle Jim, shoot! The first buck is yours. Hurry, he's running!"

Too late. The pronghorn wheeled, shot down the back side of the ridge, and was gone.

Jim's second chance came late in the morning, shortly after we glassed six antelope walking across a small basin 800 yards away. A terrific wind had developed. I'd guess it was blowing 30 miles per hour. The sky was clear, but the temperature had dropped to near freezing. Stalking those animals was the coldest stalk I ever made in my life. We weren't dressed for that sudden change in weather.

The animals were walking diagonally toward a hogback that concealed us while we made the stalk. We knew there was one nice buck in the herd. We inched to the top of the hogback di-

249

rectly in line with the animals' travel route, and peeked over the top. There they were, not more than 100 yards below us. We were well screened by sagebrush, but those animals spotted us immediately, changed course, and started running.

The buck bolted from the herd and lined out broadside to us. Jim jumped upright, shouldered his 308 customized Mauser, and found his target in the 4X Weaver scope. The rifle roared, but the buck didn't even flinch. Then, before Jim could trigger a second shot, the pronghorn suddenly piled up in a heap.

I've never seen a prouder man. Jim ran to his trophy with a speed belying his years, grabbed the horns, and actually kissed them. An enormous grin split his face and he bubbled, "I got one. I did it. I shot a buck antelope."

Had our trip ended right there, it would have been fine with me. Jim's enthusiasm was reward enough and we were all very happy. We field-dressed the buck, and then we each piled on all the extra clothes we had in the vehicle.

We spotted a few more herds after that, but saw no decent bucks. Later in the afternoon, we were almost run over by the enormous buck I described at the beginning of this story. And right after that, we were up to our ears in excitement again.

We drove on up the valley, topped a rise, and spotted a small herd moving toward us up a draw. For some reason they didn't see us, so I backed the vehicle below the skyline. There was a hogback between us and the six animals. As soon as they disappeared behind the rise, Leona and I ran toward it. We found some one-foot-high sagebrush and dropped into prone positions. Minutes later, the herd topped the rise and we immediately spotted a fine buck. Just as immediately, the animals sensed something wrong and began milling around.

It was fantastic how that buck kept himself screened by does. Anxious minutes passed before Leona finally had a clear shot at the animal. Then she shot so fast I couldn't believe she'd had a chance to line up the crosshairs of her Redfield 2X-8X scope. The bullet missed clean, but the buck stood as still as a statue. Leona's 308 Saco Forester cracked a second time, again much sooner than I expected.

In all, she fired four cartridges before the accommodating buck jetted away. Leona was a bundle of nerves. "None of those bullets came close," she blurted. "I've got so many clothes on that I can't get my finger around the trigger. I was shooting before I was aiming."

I've never seen my wife so disgusted. She normally handles a rifle like an expert. The previous year she had downed a bull elk with a single shot, and she's a marksman on our range at home. But with all those clothes on—and in a prone position—she just couldn't reach the trigger in normal fashion.

We gave up for the day. The next morning we were back in the same area before dawn. We spent the whole day spotting and stalking numerous pronghorn, but we didn't find any bucks we wanted even though the herds were settling down. Far fewer hunters were out, and we had the area practically to ourselves. Jim got pretty tired, so he decided to skip the next day's action.

Right at sunup on the third morning, Leona and I spotted a distant pronghorn that was larger than average. The air was still cold and clear, but there was little wind. We made a long stalk, and the animal turned out to be a doe. Then Leona's luck reversed.

I was glassing the area when a feeding buck with 10-inch horns walked into view from behind a bluff 200 yards to our right. I nudged Leona. This time she made sure her finger did not touch the trigger until she was ready to fire. She squeezed one off and the bullet dumped the buck in his tracks.

We couldn't find more than three lonely, curious does during the next four hours. Finally we walked to the rim of a basin and spotted 12 antelope more than half a mile away. My binoculars brought them up much closer, close enough so that I could identify two fine bucks. The distance was too long to accurately judge horns, but I knew both of those bucks were trophies and that one was much better than the other.

We drove below a ridge that circled the basin, and we continued until we reached a point straight downwind from the animals. When I started my stalk, Leona remained behind because it's much easier for one person to make a successful stalk than it is for two. I took off along the side of a 50-foot-high hogback and crawled 400 yards through sagebrush and rocks. At this point I

251

didn't know if the animals had moved or not, but I didn't dare skyline my head to find out. Even if they hadn't moved, I was still far out of effective rifle range.

I kept crawling for half an hour. Then I couldn't stand the tension any longer. I bellied my way to the rim of the hogback and peeked over.

The herd was 300 yards away and unaware of me. I immediately spotted my buck to the right of the herd. I didn't need any binoculars to know that the horns on that buck were unbelievably enormous. I couldn't decide what to do. I hate to shoot at any animal that's more than 200 yards away, for fear of wounding and losing him. Still, I might spook him and miss any opportunity for a shot if I tried crawling closer.

The sagebrush in front of me was pretty thick and about two feet high. I decided to try bellying on, and that's when my heart really began hammering. I'm sure hundreds of rocks imprinted their shapes in my anatomy by the time I'd wormed 75 yards. Suddenly I knew I wasn't going one inch farther. The buck turned broadside, and he sensed something was amiss.

I shoved my arm into the sling of my custom-made 264 and looked through my 3X-9X variable Redfield scope. The first thing I noticed was that the buck was in motion and walking diagonally away. As soon as I was sure my sight picture was perfect, I fired at his neck.

I'll never know what happened, but the bullet missed. The buck wheeled and began running broadside. I bolted another cartridge through the Mauser action, held ahead of the buck's chest, and touched the trigger. The bullet nailed him perfectly. He went down flat and was dead when he hit the ground.

I knew I'd killed an exceptional trophy, and I couldn't wait to break the news to Leona. I ran back to the top of the ridge and yelled, "Honey, I got a beauty. I really got a beauty."

I had no idea that I'd taken a truly outstanding trophy until I took the horns and cape to taxidermist Tom Radoumis in San Gabriel, California. Tom mounts all of my trophies, and normally he's pretty quiet. But when he saw my pronghorn, he couldn't contain himself. Though the horns were still "green," we measured them according to the Boone and Crockett Club system and came up with a total score of 93.

252

Lee Arce smiles, as who wouldn't, when posing with his wondrous pronghorn.

Close-up shows the pronghorn trophy in considerable detail.

"My gosh, Lee," he exclaimed, "do you realize that the No. 2 antelope in the Boone and Crockett Record Book scores 91-4/8 and was killed way back in 1899. You've taken the best antelope ever killed in Wyoming. It's the second-best ever taken anywhere, and the No. 1 buck dates back to 1878."

On December 4, 1968, my pronghorn was scored for the Boone and Crockett Club by Dr. Kenneth E. Stager of the Los Angeles County Museum. He arrived at a total score of 91-6/8, just 2/8 better than the No. 2 buck listed in the Club's current record book.

Though the overall lengths of the symmetrical horns aren't exceptional (each measures 15-3/8 inches), the circumference of the bases (8-2/8 inches) and the length of the prongs (eight inches) are fantastic. There isn't another pronghorn in the record book with measurements of as much as eight inches in either of those categories.

In searching through recent Boone and Crockett Club statistics, I found another amazing fact. At least three other pronghorn that each have a score of 90 or more have been killed in recent years. Bob Schneidmiller won the Boone and Crockett Club's first award for 1964-65 with a Colorado pronghorn scoring 91-4/8. The second-place pronghorn in that competition scored 91 and was killed in Carbon County, Wyoming, by J. Ivan Kitch. In September of 1967, Fred Starling downed a Wyoming pronghorn that had a total score of 91.

Many hunters have long claimed that the big bucks are all gone, killed off years ago when hunting pressure was far less than it is today. Those same hunters say that today's bucks don't live long enough to become outstanding trophies.

Obviously some bucks still live to ripe old ages, and I'll bet plenty of outstanding pronghorn are roaming the prairies today. I'm exceptionally proud that my buck will in all likelihood rate as the second-best ever killed. But I won't be surprised if some hunter moves me down a notch or two within the next few years. I still wonder if the buck I scored on was the same one that shocked me on opening day. Could it be possible there were two giant bucks in the same area?

(EDITOR'S NOTE: *When this story was published in* Outdoor Life, *Arce's pronghorn had not received a final official score from the Boone and Crockett Club's panel of judges. All big-game heads that are considered for high awards are subjected to an extensive rescoring by the panel before the score is allowed to stand. In this case, the judges decided to score the circumference of the bases at 7-6/8 and 7-5/8 instead of each 8-2/8. This difference dropped the final score considerably. Nevertheless, Arce's pronghorn still has the distinction of being the only one ever recorded that has prongs measuring as high as eight inches.)*

The Greatest North American Trophy Ever?

By Ben East

(EDITOR'S NOTE: *This concluding chapter is contributed by Ben East, one of America's greatest outdoor writers of all times. East, now in his 80s, has studied the trophy-hunting picture for more than half a century and has discussed it in many of the thousands of magazine articles he has written. The original version of this story appeared in the February 1980 issue of* Outdoor Life.

(It is appropriate that East should write this chapter because it had its beginning more than four decades ago and its finish in 1978, a span of time during which he was deeply involved with sheep-hunting stories. This story is one that will shock and anger, then finally delight, every sportsman who reads it.)

The ram did not look huge in the spotting scope, but the hunter hoped for the best. The hunting party of four had been on a bacon diet for two weeks, and he was interested in camp meat as well as a trophy.

He and his guide debated briefly whether to try for this sheep or wait for something better. The hunter also wanted movies, and the ram was in the open valley where a stalk within camera range would not be too difficult. In the end, he decided to go after this ram.

The hunter and his guide eased down into the valley. Three rams were feeding in a group, and the two men crept to within 200 yards of them. The hunter ran some film through his camera, then decided to kill the best of the three. By this time he was aware that it carried horns much better than those of its two companions, but he still didn't think it looked too promising as a trophy. Its body didn't seem big enough to carry a head that would stand very high in the records. It didn't occur to the hunter that among wild sheep, as among humans, some individuals have small bodies and big heads, and vice versa.

The time was late August of 1936. The place was the almost unhunted country at the headwaters of the Muskwa and Prophet rivers in British Columbia, 100 miles or more northwest of Fort St. John. The hunter was L. S. Chadwick, a 62-year-old Cleveland tool-and-die manufacturer and a dedicated sportsman who had hunted in Ontario, Alberta, British Columbia, and Alaska. He was also a wild-sheep enthusiast.

Chadwick had three guides, all capable and experienced in hunting mountain game and all having detailed knowledge of the ways of sheep. They were Roy Hargreaves of Mt. Robson, Curley Cochrane of Rolla, and Frank Golata of Dawson Creek.

"It was due entirely to their ability that I took the head," Chadwick would say of them afterward.

He had picked his hunting area for two reasons. First, it was wild and rough country, hard to get into, and consequently hunted very lightly if at all, even by the standards of 1936. Second, one of the guides, Cochrane, had run a trapline there a few years before, and he told of seeing an unusual number of Stone rams with excellent heads.

The party had set out from Pousse Coupe, a hamlet a few miles south of Dawson Creek. They had covered the first 100 miles by car, over what is now the Alaska Highway, to a place known as Bear Flat. There they had picked up saddle horses and their pack train and rode northwest into the mountains.

258

For the first two and a half weeks, nothing much happened. They were in trailless wilderness, and some days they did well to make six or eight miles. Mosquitoes and gnats plagued them mercilessly, and heavy rains delayed them constantly. They made 16 camps in 18 days. It was a hard hunt, as sheep hunts are likely to be.

In early afternoon on August 27, they made camp in sheep country. Curly Cochrane was serving as cook. "Somebody go out and get a sheep," he demanded. "I'm sick and tired of bacon." So was everybody else.

Chadwick and Hargreaves rode out of camp. On a nearby mountain, they spotted a band of 10 or a dozen sheep.

There were rams in the bunch. But the 20X spotting scope showed nothing with horns that would measure better than 36 inches around the curl, and Chadwick had strong aversions to killing a ram of that size, whatever the reason. He figured it meant one less worthwhile trophy in the country later on.

"Too many hunters shoot rams with small horns and then wonder why no big trophies are left," he said a year later in the story of his hunt in *Outdoor Life*. "Big heads are becoming scarce wherever hunters are active, because of this practice."

Despite the need for camp meat, he voted against trying for a sheep from that first band.

But later in the afternoon, when it was time to head back to camp, Hargreaves spotted three more, silhouetted on a high skyline. "One looks as if it might be worth going after," he told Chadwick.

There was nothing they could do in the brief daylight that remained. They rode to camp and ate bacon for supper once more. But they and Golata rode out again shortly after daylight the next morning, so confident of killing a sheep that they took a couple of packhorses along to bring in the meat.

They ate lunch below a high saddle, near where they had seen the rams the evening before. Lunch over, they climbed to the ridge of the saddle and sat down to glass. It took only a few minutes to pick up the three rams on a neighboring mountain about a mile and a half away. One ram looked good enough to qualify as both a trophy and a source of roasted sheep ribs. Chadwick and the guides decided to try for a shot.

259

The behavior of the sheep indicated that they had seen the hunters. One of the guides, Golata, stayed out in the open with the horses to hold the attention of the rams. Chadwick and Hargreaves began the stalk.

They followed the edge of a glacier down a steep ravine, to the floor of the valley that lay between them and the sheep. When they reached the top of the opposite ridge, they saw that the rams had moved on to another valley half a mile away. Chadwick and the guide debated whether to give up. The best of the three sheep hardly looked worth all the effort. But they still wanted meat, so they went ahead.

They crept and crawled to a point 200 yards above the rams. Chadwick took movie film and then decided to kill the best one.

He was using a scope for the first time on big game. His rifle was a custom-made 404 Magnum, the product of Frank Huffman, a Cleveland gunmaker. It weighed 10 pounds, but Chadwick liked it better than any other rifle he had owned. It drove a 300-grain bullet at 2,700 feet per second and had about double the striking power of a 30/06. No big game in North America was too much for that rifle with the 300-grain load, and with a heavier bullet he even rated it adequate for anything in Africa. Chadwick conceded that it was on the heavy side for sheep, but that it had a very flat trajectory and great range and accuracy.

The sheep he was after was now directly below him and almost straight down. He held a bit low, and the heavy bullet hit solidly in the body. All three rams lit out, crossed the valley, and started up the mountain, but the wounded one soon lagged behind.

Hunter and guide were running as hard as they could in pursuit, but Chadwick's 62 years told against him. Hargreaves had to slow down to keep even. Chadwick got in more shots, and one put the ram down. The animal then tumbled into a deep ravine. When the two men got to him, he was dead.

Chadwick instantly saw that he had taken a far better trophy than he'd expected. The sheep's body was small, but his horns were enormous—heavy, incredibly long (more than a full curl), flaring widely, beautifully symmetrical, with unbroomed tips. The hunter had never seen a head to match it. At the moment he was too excited to notice that a small fragment had been broken from the tip of the right horn at some time in the past, and that the break had been worn rounded and blunt.

260

The two men next laid a steel tape on the horns. The left one measured 52-1/8 inches along the outside curve, the right one about two inches less. Each was a little more than 15 inches in circumference at the base. The tips of the horns were 31-1/4 inches apart.

Later, after drying and shrinking, that fantastic head would go into the record list with the following measurements: length of right horn, 50-1/8 inches; left, 51-5/8; circumference of base, 14-6/8 each; tip-to-tip spread, 31. The total score was 196-6/8, still almost seven digits higher than that of today's No. 2 Stone ram, killed on the Sikanni River in British Columbia in 1962 by Norman Blank. Chadwick's was the only sheep ever shot in North America with a horn length greater than 50 inches.

Imagine what L. S. Chadwick's feelings must have been when he and Hargreaves finished taping those incredible horns. He remembered that the best wild sheep head on record up to that time, a bighorn killed in British Columbia in 1920, had horns between 48 and 50 inches long and a spread just under 24 inches. His ram's measurements were well above those figures. Did that mean that he had taken the best wild sheep ever shot in North America? It seemed so and, for a dedicated sheep hunter, that is an intoxicating thought.

Golata came up with the horses, and the three men caped and dressed the ram. They loaded the head and meat and rode back to camp. That sheep, they decided, was 14 years old, about the top figure for a wild ram. Scientific examination later showed its correct age to be 12 years. It was in excellent condition, with good teeth, which would be somewhat unusual for a 14-year-old.

When Chadwick and his guides rode into camp late that August afternoon, they were bringing out of the Muskwa and Prophet River country a trophy that in all likelihood will never be matched by any hunter on earth.

At that time, the sheep was reported to have been killed on the headwaters of the Muskwa. Jack O'Connor, who visited Chadwick's campsite later, said it was taken instead on Lapp Creek, a tributary of the Prophet. That entire area was then one of the best blocks of Stone-sheep range on the continent.

It is very hard to believe that such a magnificent head would later be allowed to fall victim to gross neglect, but that is what happened.

Beautifully mounted by James L. Clark, former director of preparation at the American Museum of Natural History in New York and author of the bible of sheep hunters, *The Great Arc of the Wild Sheep,* the Chadwick head ultimately went into the National Collection of Heads and Horns. That collection had been established in 1907 by Dr. William T. Hornaday with his presentation of 133 trophies. Madison Grant helped make the collection a permanent repository for outstanding big-game trophies. It was housed at the New York Zoological Society's Bronx Zoo in New York City.

In 1922, a Heads and Horns Building was completed on the zoo's grounds, especially for the collection, which now consists of almost 250 trophies from every part of the world. It has outstanding deer, elk, moose, caribou, musk oxen, grizzly bears, and brown bears from North America; deer from Europe and Asia; gazelles, buffalo, rhinos, and elephants from Africa; Indian rhinos; and mountain goats and wild sheep from North America and Asia.

Almost without exception, hunters took it for granted that the trophies they entrusted to the National Collection were well cared for and kept on public display. Not so.

In January of 1977, Lowell Baier, an attorney from Washington, D.C., and a sheep-hunting enthusiast who had long been interested in the Collection, made a trip to New York for the express purpose of viewing what he called the Holy Grail of hunting. He learned first of all that it could be seen only by appointment.

Two weeks later, Baier addressed a bitter open letter "to the leadership of the hunting fraternity."

"The National Collection was created by sportsmen, hunters, and conservationists as a lasting memorial to the big game of the world," he wrote. "I almost cried when I saw the deplorable state this fabled collection is now in. The New York Zoological Society, requiring more office space, has converted the Heads and Horns Building to that use, shutting the trophies from public view with plywood partitions in front of the walls on which they hang.

"The heads cannot be seen by the general public and are no longer maintained. They are dusty, dirty, not humidified, and many of the hides are badly in need of repair. Security is terrible.

A number of record heads have recently been stolen. Two Big-horn heads, ranking among the top dozen on the Boone and Crockett record list, hanging on both sides of the Chadwick ram, have mysteriously disappeared. It seems likely the Chadwick tro-phy was not taken only because the mount includes the shoulders and front legs of the sheep and is too bulky for a thief to make off with. Can you imagine the loss to sheep hunting if this head were stolen and sold on the black market to some interior decorator who thinks it would look cute in a family room!"

Finally, and most shocking of all, the whole National Collec-tion was, as Baier puts it, up for grabs. At the end of 1976, Dr. James Waddick of the Bronx Zoo ran a small ad in the *Journal of Mammalogy* offering the collection or any part of it free to any institution that would pay crating and shipping costs. The only stipulation was that the recipient properly house, exhibit, and uti-lize the collection, something the zoo itself was no longer doing. [*Editor's note:* Recent detailed research by Harold Nesbitt, Direc-tor of Hunter Services, National Rifle Association, indicates that the New York Zoological Society stipulated that the collection must be utilized to its "full scientific and educational purposes."]

Dr. Waddick received 13 inquiries from universities and col-leges "looking for something interesting to display." The list in-cluded a veterinarian school and a dentistry school.

It is hardly a wonder that Lowell Baier concluded his open letter with an urgent appeal to fellow hunters to band together, salvage the National Collection from oblivion, and raise funds to move it and house it in suitable quarters.

"The ideal solution," he wrote, "would be a national museum tied in with the Hunting Hall of Fame, Safari Club International, Boone and Crockett Club, or National Rifle Association."

The Chadwick ram, along with the other trophies in the Collec-tion, had gathered dust in storage for many years. In March of 1978, it finally saw the light of day once more. It was acquired from the zoo on loan, for a fee of $200, and displayed at a meeting of more than 200 sheep hunters from every part of the country, at Dearborn, Michigan.

Frank Bays, a grand-slam holder from Michigan, flew to New York and brought the trophy back to Dearborn, guarding it as if it were the crown jewels. There was good reason. One of the condi-

The fantastic Chadwick ram with Frank Bays, a Grand Slam holder and an official of the Foundation for North American Wild Sheep.

tions laid down for its loan was that it be covered with a $25,000 insurance policy while it was away from the zoo.

At the meeting, Bays told his fellow sheep hunters that he was as shocked as Baier had been at the conditions under which he found the Chadwick ram and other trophies in the National Collection.

"The heads are dirty with the accumulation of many years of dust and grime, and nobody can see them," he reported angrily.

Officials of the New York Zoological Society made no secret of the fact that strong antihunting bias among the society's membership was behind the deliberate neglect of the Collection. Dr. Waddick said candidly that display of trophy heads and horns won the zoo no favor and even undermined its campaigns for contributions.

"The objectives of the North American Sheep Hunters Association and the New York Zoological Society differ," William Conway, general director of the society, told Frank Bays in connection with the loan of the Chadwick head.

The ram stole the show at the Dearborn meeting. It is a trophy so beautiful and perfect that it is almost impossible to believe. Those of today's sheep hunters who have seen it regard it with feelings akin to reverence, a monument to all sheep hunting everywhere.

For me it recalls what another hunter, Texan George Landreth, said long after Chadwick's time, when he finished telling me of the magnificent Mongolian argali he took in the Gurban Sayhan Mountains east of the Gobi Desert in 1965.

"No other trophy in the world can begin to match the great rams that live out their lives on the earth's roof," George said. "The hunter who takes them must outwit the canniest and wariest of all game animals, endure the bitter winds that sweep endlessly across lofty summits, and climb until his legs ache, his heart pounds, and his lungs are ready to burst. He pays dearly for his trophy in hardship and fatigue. That is what makes sheep hunting so great."

Nobody has summed it up better than Jack O'Connor in his excellent book, *The Big Game Animals of North America*, published by *Outdoor Life* in 1961.

"Of all the trophies found on the continent of North America,

I'd put the wild sheep at the top," O'Connor wrote. "The wild ram embodies the mystery and magic of the mountains, the rocky canyons, the snowy peaks, the alpine meadows, the sweet clean air of the high country, and the sense of being alone on the top of the world."

The Dearborn meeting was called by the Midwest Chapter of the North American Sheep Hunters Association, an informal and loosely-knit group having neither dues nor officers. The hunters who attended, together with some of the top sheep guides from the United States and Canada, got together to swap hunting stories, view slides and color films, and talk about the problems of wild-sheep management and protection. The results of the meeting, however, reached far beyond anything its sponsors had expected.

After that meeting, plans were completed to organize a nonprofit Foundation for North American Wild Sheep. Lloyd Zeman, a grand-slam holder from Des Moines and one of the prime movers behind the Foundation, was named president. Bays became first vice president.

The newly formed Foundation was the first sportsman-conservation organization in the country dedicated to the protection and preservation of the continent's four kinds of wild sheep.

"Those of us who have had the privilege of collecting trophy rams want to give something back," Zeman said. "In a small way, we hope to do for sheep what Ducks Unlimited has done for ducks. Maybe that will assure our children and our grandchildren the pleasure of hunting trophy rams in the wild high country of North America."

In the first week of the Foundation's existence, funds totaling more than $12,000 were raised. The money was used to finance the start of an active sheep-conservation program and to establish scholarships and research grants in sheep management.

Annual dues were $25, charter memberships cost $100, and any sportsman interested in sheep hunting was invited to join. Requests for information can be sent to the Foundation, 55 West Ivy, St. Paul, MN. 55117 (612-489-7683). As of August 1979, funds contributed to the Foundation totaled more than $125,000.

One of the first things the new organization decided to press for was the transfer of the National Collection of Heads and Horns from the Bronx Zoo to a new home, where the trophies could be properly cared for and kept on year-round public display. When the collection was on the verge of being broken up and turned over piecemeal—much of it to antihunting groups—the Boone and Crockett Club stepped in. Harold Nesbitt, Director of Hunter Services Division for the National Rifle Association, and Chairman of the Subcommittee of the Boone and Crockett Club that was empowered to seek ownership, initiated plans to acquire the entire collection that included heads and horns from all over the world. At the instigation of Nesbitt, the trophies (designated the "International Collection of Heads and Horns,") were promptly loaned to the National Rifle Association. The North American specimens called the National Collection of Heads and Horns (NCHH), are now on public display at NRA headquarters in Washington.

The remaining trophies in the collection, from Africa, Asia, and the rest of the world, were given to the Safari Club International (SCI), a group of world-renowned trophy hunters, based in Tucson. They were not yet on display when this book went to press, but SCI is presently pushing a drive for funds to build a $2,000,-000 museum, probably at Tucson, that will house this portion of the Collection and any future additions to it.

At the same time, the Boone and Crockett Club was seeking funds to repair and restore the North American heads and enlarge their numbers.

The Chadwick ram speaks today of the challenge of mountain wilderness, and the excitement and suspense of sheep hunting, as eloquently as the day it was shot more than 40 years ago. A great many sportsmen and most sheep hunters rate it the most magnificent of all North American big-game trophies.

It has stood all that time in No. 1 place on the Boone and Crockett record list of Stone sheep. There are very few people who think it will ever be toppled from that ranking.

"There is a chance that some lucky hunter will someday find this old boy's daddy, with a still larger head," Chadwick commented in his own account of killing the ram. It hasn't happened yet, and there is very little chance it ever will. I base that prediction on some authoritative sources. I asked five guides from the United States and Canada, all with long experience in sheep hunt-

267

The Chadwick ram is the only North American sheep ever taken that has horns measuring more than 50 inches along the outside curves. Notice the massive circumferences of bases and the great tip-to-tip spread. This ram is considered by many hunters to be the best big-game trophy ever taken in North America.

ing, how they rate the chances that another hunter will ever take a trophy as good as the Chadwick ram. Here are their replies:

Andy Hagberg, Prince George, British Columbia: "Never. Something extraordinary accounted for that head. The ram's ancestors, food, weather, or all three produced a combination that won't happen again."

Dale Leonard, Sedalia, Colorado: "Probably impossible. That ram is too outstanding and too unusual to ever be matched."

Bill McKenzie, Quesnel, British Columbia: "It could happen, but it sure would astonish me."

Randy Babala, Cadomin, Alberta: "It's possible, but extremely unlikely. A ram that unusual is like a man who's eight feet tall. By now, whatever bloodline he left in that country is diluted out. There's not much chance there will ever be another like him."

Dewey Browning, Rocky Mountain House, Alberta, a sheep guide for 37 years: "As far as I'm concerned, that ram is the greatest North American trophy ever taken by any hunter, and I don't think he will ever be equaled. As hunting pressure gets heavier, there is less chance for a ram to reach peak size. Record-book sheep are getting harder to take. Nobody is ever going to kill another as good as Chadwick's."

28462

28462